BALKAN DEPARTURES

BALKAN DEPARTURES

Travel Writing from Southeastern Europe

Edited by
Wendy Bracewell and Alex Drace-Francis

Berghahn Books
New York • Oxford

Published in 2009 by

Berghahn Books

www.berghahnbooks.com

Library of Congress Cataloging-in-Publication Data

Travel writing from South-Eastern Europe / edited by Wendy
Bracewell and Alex Drace-Francis. -- 1st ed.
    p. cm.
Includes bibliographical references and index.
ISBN 978-1-84545-254-4 (alk. paper)
    1. Travelers' writings, East European--History and criticism. 2. East
Europeans--Travel--Europe--History. 3. Travel writing--History. 4.
Europe--Description and travel. I. Bracewell, Wendy. II. Drace-Francis,
Alex.

PN849.E9T73 2009
809'.935914--dc22
                                    2009006003

British Library Cataloguing in Publication Data

A catalogue record for this book is available from the British Library

Printed in the United States on acid-free paper.

ISBN: 978-1-84545-254-4 (hardback)

Contents

CHAPTER 1

Balkan Travel Writing: Points of Departure

Wendy Bracewell

What is Balkan travel writing? The casual reader, browsing through shelves of travel accounts from the past hundred years or so, might reasonably assume that the phrase refers to travels to the Balkan peninsula. Any number of European and North American travellers published accounts of their 'Balkan' journeys. The precise countries visited may vary – the boundaries of the Balkans are notoriously ill-defined – but the use of the generic label nonetheless implies a sense that the region is a unified and cohesive entity. The travellers' titles and subtitles sum up the characteristics that they associate with the region as a whole: 'Land of Discord'; 'Savage Europe'; 'The Burning Balkans'; 'Between Baedeker and Homer'; 'Wild and Beautiful' as well as 'The Melting Pot'; 'Eternal Epic'; 'Through the Iron-laced Curtain'; 'The Other Europe'; 'Prejudice and Plum Brandy'; 'The Embers of Chaos'.[1] (The titles of travel books suggest that, on the other hand, 'southeastern Europe' has received fewer visitors. The choice of this particular phrase may be no more than elegant variation, but it can also indicate an attempt to avoid the connotations attached to the B-word.)[2]

In recent research on travel writing, the Balkans also most frequently appear as a region travelled *to*.[3] In line with the current fascination with travel writing's role in the workings of power, scholars have read Western travel accounts of the region for the way their authors construct a relationship between their own societies and those they describe – a relationship usually based more on opposition than on similarity or connection. British, American or German travel writing about the Balkans revels in difference and the exotic, and particularly in violence or the primitive – traits that serve (so critics tell us) as a foil to self-congratulatory definitions of the West as modern, progressive and rational. Such representations have promoted a sense of Western cultural superiority at the least, and at worst have justified self-interested political, military or economic policies towards the region. They have helped to set the region apart from 'Europe proper', on the basis of criteria selected by travellers looking more to the norms and interests of their own societies than to the attributes of the lands they travelled through; and they have bolstered the inequalities of political and economic power that hold such perceptions in place. Scholarship has characterized such travel writing as not just about the Balkans, but as 'Balkanist', contributing to a discourse of Balkan difference that is seen as pervasive, persistent and remarkably potent (most recently, Hammond 2007).

However, the Balkans is also a place that has long been travelled *from*. Travellers from the region have offered numerous accounts of their adventures in the West and elsewhere, saying something in the process about themselves and their place in the world. This selection of studies explores the literature of travel in Greek, Romanian, Bulgarian, Serbian and Croatian (and it might well have included several other literary traditions under the Balkan label). These studies approach such writing both on its own terms and in comparison with Western practices and discourses. The authors unravel some of the strategies and rhetorical devices behind images of the Other in both Balkan and Western travel writing, but the emphasis is less on recurring patterns than on specific contexts and interests. The studies show, through a variety of instances, some of the purposes to which these travel accounts could be bent – social critique or reassurance, manifesto or introspection – and they direct our attention to the ways travel writers' attitudes, objects of attention and motives have shifted and changed. Rather than treating travel writing from a European periphery in terms of 'auto-ethnography' or 'returning the gaze', as with Latin American travel writing that engages with the centre's terms, in the language of the metropolis (e.g., Pratt 1992; Beardsall 2000), these essays focus for the most part on vernacular travel writing addressed to a domestic audience. Recognition of the asymmetrical relations between Vienna, Berlin, Paris or London and the states of the region puts the East–West axis at the centre of much of the analysis, but these studies also suggest that the tendency to see self-definition in the region in terms of an all-encompassing East–West polarization may be an optical illusion based on a narrow selection of sources, hinting, for instance, at the relevance of other relationships in other contexts: with Balkan neighbours; or with Russia, the farther East or the Third World. In short, this book constitutes something of a departure from existing scholarship, and one that offers innovative perspectives on both travel writing and the Balkans.

One advantage of grouping these studies together under a single, not entirely arbitrary heading is the stimulus to comparative analysis (something performed to a certain extent in all the studies collected here). This then suggests further avenues for research. Thus, for instance, Maria Kostaridou assesses the travel letters of a sixteenth-century Corfiote, Nikandros Noukios, against the apodemic instructions that defined the conventions of erudite sixteenth-century European travel writing, and against a variety of other contemporary Greek travel texts. Noukios' accounts are distinguished by their 'scope and sophistication', as Kostaridou points out, but also by the language of composition, a formal, archaistic Greek accessible to international readers but also close to the vernacular. Other sixteenth- and seventeenth-century travellers from the region produced similar texts, derived from comparable experiences, in analogous social and intellectual environments, and deployed their travel observations for the same purposes of instruction and self-display; but they composed them in international literary languages, not in their own vernaculars for a domestic audience. This was the case for the escaped slaves who described their experiences for private circulation or for a wider market, whether in Latin, by those held in Ottoman captivity (e.g., Bartolomaeus Georgievits/Đorđević) or in Turkish, by an escaped Habsburg prisoner (Osman Ağa of Temesvar); it was also the case for the embassy translator Benedict Curipeschitz/Kuripešič, who travelled with an imperial embassy to Constantinople in 1530 and wrote in German, and the imperial ambassador and humanist scholar Antonius Verantius/ Vrančić, who described his 1553 journey to Constantinople in Latin; for the seventeenth-century missionary accounts of Ottoman Slavonia in Latin by the Croatian Jesuit Bartolomaeus Cassius/Kašić; for the accounts of Mexico, by another such Jesuit, Ivan Rattkay, who reported in Latin and German; and for the Moldavian Nikolai Spafarii/Nicolae Spathar Milescu, Peter the Great's emissary to China in the 1670s, whose Russian-language travel notes were written for the Russian Foreign Ministry.[4]

But why the paucity of vernacular texts dealing with travel experience before the eighteenth century? It was not that indigenous literary traditions were lacking. Was it simply the case that the institutions that generated accounts of travel and the markets that valued them were for the most part centred outside the peninsula? One notable counter-example is the genre of *proskynetaria*, descriptions of the holy places and monasteries of Palestine and elsewhere, often giving prayers and devotions associated with each place. These gradually began to incorporate travel impressions, though this was incidental to the main purpose of the genre: guides for pilgrims in the holy places, or prompts for a vicarious pilgrimage. In the seventeenth and eighteenth centuries a number of examples were composed in Serbian and Bulgarian as well as Greek (or were translated from Greek originals).[5] Only a few *proskynetaria* were printed before 1700, 'something that clearly shows the lack of special interest in the subject by the reading public of the period' according to Loukia Droulia.[6] But does the lack of texts necessarily indicate a lack of interest? Once the *proskynetaria* began to appear in print, they were very popular, many appearing in multiple editions (the description of Jerusalem, *Opisanie svetago bozhiia grada Ierusalima*, printed by Hristofor Zhefarovich/Žefarović in Vienna, ran to three editions, in 1748, 1778 and 1781; see also Weber 1953). Here we have both an institution – pilgrimage – and a market, as well as a developing tradition of travel narrative. It's suggestive that when vernacular travel observations and first-person narratives do emerge, they often appear on the margins of established genres, as in the *proskynetarion*, or in lists of distances and stopping places on the way to Constantinople, for example, or incorporated into other genres such as saints' lives, not just as itinerary but as experience (Pavić 1970: 305–11; cf. Mullett 2002 for motifs of travel in Byzantine texts). Or else they adapt other forms as a vehicle for a travel narrative: for instance the eclogue, in the case of Petar Hektorović's 1568 Croatian poem on a fishing excursion, *Ribanje i ribarsko prigovaranje* ('Fishing and fishermen's conversation') (see Franičević 1983: 392–393 on this text as epistle–eclogue–travel narrative). Such comparisons pose the question of which is the most important in the early development of the vernacular first-person travel narrative: the experience of travel, an audience, or a model for shaping such texts?

Travel knowledge certainly became more than an export commodity when it could be used in the prosecution of interests at home. Alex Drace-Francis's reading of Dinicu Golescu's deliberate and shaming contrasts with his homeland in his 1826 *Account of my Travels* places the Wallachian boyar in relation to a range of other writers who deployed observations based on travel abroad to make a case for domestic reform. Drace-Francis draws attention to the emergence of a normative model of 'Europe' from the late eighteenth century, in accounts not just by Western travellers but by those from the peninsula as well. One result was the much-cited Balkan habit of locating Europe as somehow elsewhere, betrayed in the customary phrase 'going to Europe' for journeys to the West (Todorova 1997: 43; Jezernik 2004 gives a compendium of travellers' comments on this usage: 29, 236). This suggests the potential for a comparative analysis of the idea of Europe (and its uses) by travellers from outside western Europe's core, but it also raises questions about the role of travel writing itself, as a genre, in producing the sense of difference that separated 'Europe' from 'the

Balkans'. Travel writing is an effective mechanism for organizing difference to generate Otherness. Travellers from Europe's peripheries, as well as those from Europe's metropolitan centres, tended to stress the exceptional or anomalous over the familiar or unexceptional in their accounts of abroad – a tendency inherent in the genre, with its implied promise of supplying readers with novelty (unexpected *familiarity* might supply such novelty, under special conditions, but surely less often). Furthermore, in relaying their travel experiences as a series of impressions (a common strategy), travellers tend to represent difference as a given, rather than explaining it historically. In general, such writings helped to fabricate and sustain a mental distance between 'here' and 'there', 'us' and 'them', rather than bridging or healing it. It's not only travellers from a politically and economically dominant West that find this estranging effect useful. My own essay juxtaposing a selection of English and Yugoslav travel accounts makes this point about the insistence on difference, and its uses: both sets of writers use stereotypes of masculinity and of the Balkans as a resource, deployed to make a whole variety of self-affirming cultural, social or geopolitical distinctions, within their own societies as well as between East and West. Looking at such travel texts makes us ask how far texts and travellers *from* the region, and not only *to* it, were responsible for inventing and perpetuating discourses of difference, including the pejorative Balkanist tropes of backwardness and inferiority.

Vladimir Gvozden, writing about the Serbian poet and travel writer Jovan Dučić, and Dean Duda, analysing texts by the Croatian writers Matoš, Krleža, Batušić and Matković, both place their subjects within the comparative framework of literary modernism, though the questions they pose are different. Gvozden asks how modernism produces travel writing, or at least Dučić's brand of travelogue, with its assumptions about the relationship between a universal culture and cultures understood in particularistic, national terms; while Duda asks how travel writing produces modernism, with respect to both Croatian literature and travel culture. Such an approach raises questions about travel writing's place both in national literary histories and in transnational literary-cultural history. What is travel writing's relation to other literary genres within a single national literature? Does it develop according to the same rhythm or within the same categories as other prose forms? Or is it the case that the genre's marginality and lack of prestige made it a privileged space for experimentation and innovation? And how do these relationships fit with broader literary movements, especially in western European literary culture? As far as modernist travel writing goes, examples surveyed here seem to bear direct comparison with contemporaneous English, American or German developments in the genre (as both Gvozden and Duda demonstrate) – and there are hints that travel texts might even have acted as a vanguard of literary modernism in both Serbian and Croatian literatures. But what of the place of travel writing more generally in both Balkan and European literary histories? A comparative analysis is so far lacking.

Ludmilla Kostova's study of the 'dialectic of self and other' deals with shifts in context and image in Bulgarian travel writing during the forty-odd years of communist rule, while also tracing continuities and disjunctures with respect to prewar patterns of representation. This invites a comparison with travel writing produced elsewhere in the Soviet bloc – in surprising quantity (see, e.g., Balina 1994; Drace-Francis 2004; Bracewell 2006; Gilburd 2006). Or perhaps not so surprising: with their graphic illustrations of the achievements of socialism and the perils of the capitalist world, state-sponsored travel reports served the system well. Yet critics (and socialist-era writers) have also identified travel writing and foreign reportage as a site of resistance to the party-state (see especially Balina 1994 and Kuprel 2004). How effective were these texts, either as propaganda or as dissent? Elsewhere Drace-Francis has argued that travel writing in socialist Romania offered little scope for coded critique or collusion with the reader because of the genre's truth claims (Drace-Francis 2004: 80). In contrast, others have seen in the ostensibly objective presentation of foreign circumstances an apt vehicle for metaphor, parable and allegory, directed to readers whose critical skills, honed by socialism's pervasive double-speak, enabled them to decipher the message beneath the text (e.g., Kuprel 2004: 385, citing Kapuściński). But the two extremes of interpretation need not be seen as the only possibilities. Individuals could arrive at their own conclusions – and their most secret desires – through their readings of travel literature. In doing so, they created 'elsewheres' that did not necessarily correspond to the really existing world, and whose meanings were not determined in any predictable way by the intentions of either authors or censors (see, for example, Yurchak 2006 on the 'Imaginary West' of late socialism). Studies of socialist-era literature have posed the question of reception so pointedly because of the contested relationship between the party-state, the writer and the reader, but an archaeology of reading could offer something to studies of travel writing and power in other contexts as well. How did *Western* readers consume travel accounts about the Balkans, for example? As authoritative guides to political and social realities? As mirror images constitutive of their own 'normal' worlds? As a form of escapism? Critics have shown correspondences between Western travel writers' representations and Great Power interests in the region, but did this in fact translate into the hegemony of Balkanist discourse? Or were the effects of this literature on western reading publics far more diffuse and unstable? (Patrick Patterson has suggested this with reference to the influence of 'Balkanism' in contemporary Austrian and Italian responses to Slovene independence; Patterson 2003.)

These few examples are far from exhausting the possibilities of a comparative approach to travel writing from the region. But can this subject best be described as 'Balkan travel writing'? What do we stand to gain by grouping this specific assortment of texts, languages and cultures together? And what motives lie behind the decision to choose the Balkan label? It is not that these travel accounts share any obvious or easily identifiable qualities that render them 'Balkan', apart from their authors' origins on the peninsula. Reading any more than a few of the travel accounts discussed here undermines any assumptions about the essential homogeneity of the region, or of the travellers' perspectives on the world. Different starting points, in time as well as in space, lead to different journeys and conclusions. Furthermore, the 'Balkanicity' of nearly all of the nations grouped here, except perhaps Bulgaria, has been disputed at one time or another. To take only one example from travel writing studies, Andrew Hammond has chosen to exclude Greece from his survey of British and American travel writing about the Balkans on the grounds that its classical heritage made Western responses to it unique, while Annita Panaretou has advanced a similar argument for distinguishing travel writing by Greeks from the accounts produced by their northern neighbours – in addition citing Greece's position outside the Soviet bloc in the Cold War period (Panaretou 2005; Hammond 2007: 16).

Do these claims hold up? A slightly flippant aphorism asserts that 'the surest sign of Balkan identity is the resistance to Balkan identity' (Ditchev 2002: 244). A more empirical approach would note that a national identity developed in vehement opposition to an Ottoman past, self-definition as a bridge between East and West, and an ambiguous attitude to 'Europe' as both model for modernization and a threat to national specificity, provide a sound basis for comparing Greek perspectives on the world with those of their neighbours. Similar claims could be made in other cases. Each national literature of the region has its own particularities; at the same time, overlapping patterns of culture and historical experience result in commonalities shared to a greater or lesser extent across the wider region. Precisely which of these criteria determine what produces 'Balkan' travel writing and what does not?

Phrasing the problem in this way reduces it to a reprise of debates over the definition of the Balkans more generally.[7] It would certainly be possible, having posited an underlying Balkan historical and cultural unity, to survey travel writing from the region for a shared repertoire of itineraries, vocabularies, or rhetorical figures; and to locate these features in historical context, specifying their pedigree, their social or political significance, and their salience at different times. Thus, to take just one example, Margareta Dumitrescu has identified a salient difference between those Western Romantics who discovered the Orient as an exotic Other, and Romanian travellers of the same period for whom the Orient was Constantinople and the Balkans – an administrative and political reality. Even later, the 'Orient' came freighted with concrete historical resonances that produced characteristic responses from Romanian travellers (Dumitrescu 2003: 11–13; see also Faifer 1993: 75). This response could well be generalized to a much larger group of travellers and writers from across the territories formerly under Ottoman rule, who profess themselves struck by the familiarity of what other Europeans might consider exotic while travelling in the Balkans, Turkey, southern Italy or Spain, and then go on to consider the implications of such a sense of similarity. (The conclusions range from a sense of pollution and shame, to the assertion of the existence of a Mediterranean–Levantine cultural community, to claims of an East–West cosmopolitanism allegedly unavailable to travellers from further West.) Such defining characteristics might be further assessed for their degree of diffusion within the region, or distribution beyond it – thus, for example, accounts of pilgrimages to Paris recounted in terms of 'European' acculturation, though common in nineteenth- and twentieth-century travel writing from the region, were scarcely limited to travellers from the Balkans (Kaspi and Marès 1989). But what end would this exercise in identifying common traits serve, other than an unavoidably tautological confirmation of the region's existence and cohesiveness? (For a similar point see Ballinger 1999; an example of such an exercise, with reference to Central Europe, is the otherwise stimulating manifesto for comparative cultural studies formulated by Tötösy de Zepetnek 2002.)

A different, but possibly more fruitful, point of departure for future research on Balkan travel writing might be to ask not what the Balkans are, nor what is Balkan about any given text, but rather: in what circumstances does the image of the Balkans as such appear in travel writing from the wider region? Concentrating on the discursive construction of the Balkans in this way does not deny the possibility of other ways of understanding the region and its history. Nor does it preclude asking how far travellers' representations correlate with other sources of information, or how far they are falsifiable, but whether such representations refer adequately (or at all) to a separately existing reality is not really the point here. Instead, these questions deal with the emergence, development and above all, the uses of the image of the

Balkans. The ambitions of such an approach fall short of wider-ranging projects of mental mapping which take the Balkan cultural and political fields as their framework, and deal with a variety of different sources – for instance Sorin Antohi's sketch for a study of a Romanian symbolic geography or Diana Mishkova's very suggestive exploration of the origins and meanings of Bulgarian visions of Europe (Antohi 2002; Mishkova 2006). In contrast, looking for the Balkans in travel texts focuses on a narrowly defined lexicon of identity and difference in a single type of text. Attention to the 'Balkan' vocabulary in this way helps avoid anachronism or teleology (not all binary discourses associated with cross-cultural encounters in the area are necessarily 'Balkanist').

And why travel writing? Discourses of Balkanness operate within a whole range of genres: journalism, diplomacy, fiction and others. But how far does the form help shape or fix the meanings attributed to the Balkans? I've argued above that travel writing's conventions help generate and shape perceptions of Otherness. It might also be argued that the genre's tendency to generalize from isolated experiences or events contributes to the evolution of stereotypes, while it confers authority on such generalizations by presenting them as independently derived knowledge grounded in personal observation. On the other hand, the demand for novelty and surprise means travel writing is also licensed to mock or overturn assumptions. This more narrowly defined approach thus focuses some attention on the interplay between historical contingency and convention – the predispositions inherent in travel writing as a genre – in the invention of the Balkans.

How do travellers from the region deploy concepts of the Balkans? Take, for example, the words of a mid twentieth-century Greek traveller, explaining the anger of Zagreb's chief customs officer when confronted with claims to a customs exemption for a painting being sent abroad by the Greek government:

> When I found myself afterwards in the wooded surroundings of the city, and when I saw the nearby hills, and the typical Balkan woodland – pin-oaks and maples; when I saw the shape of the hills, also Balkan, then the customs director's rage seemed predetermined. I found my explanation in the geography of the Balkans, which differs so much from that of Austro-Germany. (Papantoniou 1955; translation by Tania Kantzios)

Zacharia Papantoniou, baffled by the paradoxical contrast between the cleanliness and order of the Zagreb customs depot and the histrionics of its director, seized the concept of the Balkans to explain and to underline the differences he felt between Zagreb's historical legacy and its people, and between his own (non-Balkan) self and his antagonist. Evidence that Greece is not a part of the Balkans? Two years later, however, a second traveller from Greece also republished a selection of travel texts written at about the same time as Papantoniou's. Here there is a very different image of Balkan belonging. The author, Kostas Ouranes, disputed the characterization of Bucharest as 'the most European of the Balkan capitals': this epithet did not say nearly enough – Bucharest was not matched even by Athens, which 'although unique in some ways, still has many deficiencies and thus cannot be considered a "European" megalopolis' (Ouranes 1957; translation by Tania Kantzios). For Ouranes, 'the Balkans' included both Bucharest and Athens, but at the same time the concept had little of the geocultural explanatory power ascribed to it by Papantoniou (Ouranes understands his Bucharest first by comparison to Vienna and then Madrid). Why such differences in perception (and self-perception)? Are they nothing more than the mechanical appropriation or contestation of Western discourses? At this point in our knowledge, it is difficult to say. The analysis of the Balkan trope in travel writing both over time and across the region might at least provide a context in which answers could be sought.

Such an approach would by no means exhaust the subject of 'Balkan travel writing', but it does offer one key to the history of self-perception and self-presentation in the region. Ideas of 'the Balkans' played their own part in local narratives of collective cultural and social identity, articulating a variety of relationships – not only with 'Europe' but also with neighbouring nations, or with domestic Others of various sorts (minorities, or women, for instance). While the West may have 'invented' the Balkans, these articulations of Balkan identity and difference were not *imposed* on the region; they had their own internal logic and functions. These must be analysed in each case. All that can be asserted on the level of generalization is that the meaning of the Balkans is anything but stable and consistent. What follows is no more than a handful of examples, but it indicates some ways in which the idea of 'being Balkan' in travel writing has both created and destabilized essentialist categories of Self and Other.

The emergence and use of the concept of the Balkans outside the peninsula is better known than the processes by which it was adopted within the region it designates. Still, the concept owed as much to the work of local historians, linguists and ethnographers as it did to foreign usage. Some of these scholars also wrote travel accounts: narrative versions of private journeys, conference tours or the scholarly research trips which shaped their analyses (see, e.g., Novaković 1892; Iorga 1904, 1907; Cvijić 1965). Their writings contributed to a widespread conviction that something called the Balkans existed, that it could be defined by criteria that were not just geographical but also cultural and civilizational, and that 'the Balkans' was not just a matter of classification, but also of explanation. The idea that behaviour, as well as food or architecture or linguistic forms, could be understood by locating it as 'Balkan' was something that travel writing would borrow. So was the pleasure of finding one's preconceptions confirmed: there, *that's* Balkan.

In the last quarter of the nineteenth century, the category of 'the Balkans' was inserted into the long-standing opposition between Europe and Asia as an ambiguous third position, neither the one thing, nor the other. These oppositions – and Balkan ambiguities – emerge clearly in descriptions of travel. One of the paradigmatic (anti-) heroes of Balkan Balkanism is in fact a traveller himself, someone whose journeys though Europe reveal his defining qualities: crudity, avarice, suspicion and shamelessness. This is of course Aleko Konstantinov's fictional character Bai Ganyo, who was first developed in sketches, published in book form in 1895 (Konstantinov 1966 [1895]). His surname – Balkanski – is common enough among Bulgarians, but it can also be read as a descriptive epithet and as a statement of Bai Ganyo's exemplary status as *homo balcanicus* (Igov 1990: 104–15; see also on Bai Ganyo, in English, Todorova 1997: 39–42; Kiossev 1995; Daskalov 2001; Neuburger 2006). The famous opening sentence of 'Bai Ganyo Travels through Europe' sets out the civilizational categories Konstantinov uses to locate his hero: 'They helped Bai Ganyo slip the Turkish cloak off his shoulders, he put on a Belgian mantle, and everyone agreed that he was a European from head to toe' (ibid.: 1). Elsewhere in these tales this framework of Turkey and Europe is reworked as the 'Orient' and 'the West' (ibid.: 69–70; 78 ff.). Yet although defined in opposition to one another, these categories cannot be kept entirely separate. Bai Ganyo collapses them. He carries his own world with him wherever he goes on his travels. Even in Vienna's Hotel London, he 'meets with the same Turks, Greeks, Armenians, Serbs and Albanians he was accustomed to see every day'; as a result he is unable to recognize the differences between East and West that matter so much to the educated young Bulgarians who narrate Bai Ganyo's travels (ibid.: 69). But what's more, he reconciles them: the superficiality of Bai Ganyo's Europeanization conceals a deeper congruence between East and West, a shared worship of profit. The sense of the Balkan that Bai Ganyo evokes is something anomalous and disreputable, but it is not necessarily opposed to 'European' values. This instability of classificatory categories is even more marked in Konstantinov's earlier, non-fictional travel account of a journey to the 1893 Chicago World's Fair, where Bai Ganyo first makes his appearance. It's only in retrospect, in the light of the fictional Bai Ganyo Balkanski, that *To Chicago and Back* can be used as an illustration for the image of the 'Balkans' in travel writing: Konstantinov doesn't use the term there at all. However, the instability of the 'East' or Orient that is created in the description of the World's Fair throws the fictional Bai Ganyo's Balkan in-betweenness into sharper relief (Konstantinov 2004). In effect, Konstantinov both sets up, and then undermines, the taken-for-granted categories by which 'the Balkans' will come to be located as different and specific. He does this in an even more radical way in his travel account than in the Bai Ganyo stories: in *To Chicago and Back* Kostantinov shows that 'we Bulgarians' are in many ways the *same* as their despised Turkish and Greek Others, and that the differences that are so important to them – between East and West, the Orient and Europe, Europe and America – are in fact relative and mutable.

Reading Konstantinov is a slightly disorienting experience. Paradoxically, however, later travel writers' tendency to meet and describe Bai Ganyo on their travels helped to fix the meanings of East, West and Balkan in ways that traduced Konstantinov's considerably more ambiguous treatments. Laughing at Bai Ganyo – or any insufficiently 'Europeanized' compatriot – and so differentiating oneself from all that is perceived as unacculturated, embarassing or ugly in the Balkan presence in Europe, has something in common with the strategy of 'nesting Orientalism'. This describes the application of Orientalist distinctions to one's neighbour in an attempt to offload the stigma of difference onto others, thus asserting one's self as non-Oriental and as European, in the eyes of the West as well as in one's own estimation (Bakić-Hayden 1995). Travel writing from the wider region abounds in such self-differentiating strategies. The passage cited above about Zagreb's Balkan character is a convenient example, simultaneously offering an explanation of an incident in terms of civilizational categories and distancing the writer, whose society is by implication 'non-Balkan', from the anomalous behaviour he observes. When applied in this way, the strategy becomes a means of an escape from the Balkans, emancipating whole nations and societies from their worryingly liminal status.

The concept of 'nesting Orientalism' was formulated as a result of attempts to apply the approaches of Edward Said's *Orientalism* within the Balkans (or, more accurately, in post-Titoist Yugoslavia), but this project has been controversial. Much has been made of the differences between Orientalism and its Balkan variant, particularly the presence or absence of a colonial relationship to the West, but also the different relationships to Europe constructed through discourses of Orientalism and Balkanism – an 'imputed opposition' in contrast to an 'imputed ambiguity', to use Todorova's formulation (Todorova 1997: 16). The debate may be powered by the familiar dichotomy between lumpers and splitters (with all the problems and advantages associated with each tendency), but understanding Balkanism as a discourse driven by worries about ambiguity and liminality does highlight the possibility for *self*-critique implied in the notion. This is something that has been largely ignored in discussions of Western representations. The implications are more obvious for travellers from the region. The passage on the 'Balkan Orient' from Jovan Dučić's 1908 'Letter from the Ionian Sea' (Dučić 1969, also cited in Gvozden, this volume, ch. 4) conveys something of this sense – Dučić's Serbs, as well as the Turks, Greeks, Romanians and Bulgarians, are fully part of the Balkan nullity and wretchedness that is the Ottoman legacy. Dučić provides a number of further examples, in which 'Balkanites' are distinguished from one another only by the precise form their vices take:

> All Balkanites who come to Paris resemble one another. The Greek immediately asks how many drachmas the Eiffel Tower cost; the Bulgarian, how many fiacres there are in Paris; the Romanian, how much a prima donna in the Opera would cost; the Serb, which is the best restaurant. (Dučić 1969: 80)

Such differentiations suggest a paradoxical sense of unity, based on a shared abjection. This pessimistic recognition of Balkan commonality is, according to Alexander Kiossev, 'a constantly repeated sign of unsuccessful self-differentiation and self-determination', the mirror image of Western refusal to recognize the individuality (and worth) of each separate Balkan nation. As such, Balkanism is the repository of all that is disgusting, deplorable, Oriental, 'anti-progressive' in the self-perceptions of would-be Europeans: what can you expect from 'Balkan shit' like us? (Kiossev 2002: 180–83). In Balkan discourses of Europe, Oriental opposition and Balkan ambiguity are not mutually exclusive. They can exist side by side: the Balkans can be both utter Other and ambiguous Self (as for instance in the examples by Papantoniou and Ouranes cited above).

Perhaps it's useful, however, to remember the functions of 'nesting' Orientalism when considering derogatory Balkan Balkanism as a psychological mechanism of self-stigmatization. Dučić may have depicted his present-day Balkans as crude, backward, lacking in culture or refinement, but his whole work serves to distinguish Dučić *personally* as the consummate European intellectual, his achievements set into sharper relief by this Balkan background. From this perspective, disparaging the 'Oriental' Balkans can serve as a strategy for aggressive self-differentiation, as well as a self-protective response to stigma. This raises the question of how far the rhetoric of self-representation correlates to changing circumstances and to individual purposes, rather than to a general (and generalized) psychological trauma derived from the Balkans' European location and Oriental legacy. What's needed is an examination of the uses of such Balkanisms in specific contexts, at particular times, by individuals with their own axes to grind.

The variations can be instructive. This is not the place for a detailed survey, but for an example, just glance at the first few decades of the twentieth century, when Western discourses of Balkanism were becoming fixed and hardened, particularly in the wake of the Balkan Wars and the First World War (Todorova 1997: 33–34). The period saw a proliferation of accounts of journeys within the region itself. There seems to be a new interest, in all the countries of the region, in seeing and reporting circumstances in neighbouring territories. Many authors use the picture of the Balkans as a wild and unknown land as a way of justifying their travels. Marijan Alković, a Sarajevo Croat travelling before the First World War, provides a typical example:

> In Croatia they consider the Balkans to be lands where they live even today by the customs of old, crude fables. When Westerners ask 'What is it like down there?' you see on their faces the inquisitive expectation of hearing something that lies entirely beyond the peripheries of Europe – or that you will regale them with the circumstances of the half-educated and naïve inhabitants of Europe's forests. [...] So, in order to compensate at least a little, and if possible to extend my own understanding of the Balkans, I set out ... (Alković 1911: 4–5)

Having laid out their motives in such a way, it's not surprising that such writers make a point of undermining these expectations – again, given that the point of the travel account is to tell the reader something new and unexpected. Alković's account reads as a progress report on Serbian and Bulgarian aspirations to western European standards, interspersed with comparisons to his own, often still more 'Oriental', Sarajevo. Similar moves can also be found in more sceptical travel accounts of Balkan neighbours in the interwar period (for Greek examples, see Velkova 2000). 'Not as black as they're painted' is a frequent conclusion to such accounts of the Balkans through the 1920s and 1930s. Not as 'Other' as they're generally described, either: Alković and other travellers from the contested peripheries of the Balkans are willing to see much of themselves in these countries. But it's not simply the pressures of the travel genre that are at work in this period: in spite of continuing international rivalries, this is also a time when moves were being made towards regional cooperation through the Balkan Conferences and the Balkan Entente (in part as a counterweight to Great Power influence), and when scholarly institutions and periodicals for the study of the region as a whole were being founded, with political as well as academic ends (e.g., *Revue internationale des études balkaniques* [Belgrade, 1934–1938]; Parežanin 1976). In short, this was a period when the

Balkans may have been seen as a hell of ethnic particularism and provincialism; but when intra-Balkan communication was also promoted as a means of escape from this. (One pertinent example, on a popular level, is that of region-wide travel and tourism, promoted and pursued in the 1930s through pan-Balkan automobile rallies and touring clubs [Popova 1999].) Travel writing followed these trends as well as the political and ideological predilections of the writers.

Travellers' reassessments of the degree to which these territories merited their poor reputation, however, didn't necessarily call into question the validity of the categories of East and West, Balkan and European, by which they were usually judged. A different rhetorical move, equally characteristic of travel accounts of this period, is more destabilizing. Here, for example, is the novelist and critic Miroslav Krleža, denouncing the social and spatial divisions of Zagreb in the 1930s: on one hand he points to the luxurious Hotel Esplanade, 'Hot and cold water, French cuisine, roulette, lifts, uniformed bell-boys, "*on parle français*", "Europe", good!' Just metres away, on the other side of the railway underpass: 'Ducks in the standing water, open cesspits, stench, malaria, typhus and seven thousand other diseases like the fate of the fellaheen in the Nile Delta ... All grey, all disgusting, all offensive. All – Balkan, a sorry province'. If this meant to shock by rubbing Balkan shit in the face of a bourgeois society nervously proud of its European credentials, it also turns 'the Balkans' into metaphor, one in a chain of symbolic images. The world on the other side of the tracks is not just Balkan but also Middle Eastern, and later in the same passage, 'the back of beyond, Asia, the most banal province of a backward and wretched peasant country' (Krleža 1937: 124–25). This is the same move that Dean Duda identifies below (Duda, this volume, ch. 5) in Krleža's refusal to say 'where Europe begins and where Asia ends' in his 1926 account of an outing to Moscow: not only have the things they symbolize spread everywhere by now, but as figures of modernity and backwardness they are inextricable. Even more striking is the use of a similar tactic by the Serbian critic Stanislav Vinaver in 1924, in a travel letter from Germany, 'Watch on the Rhine'. After recounting Franco-German polemics over everything from the right way to drink beer to the identity of the Rhineland, he sums up what is happening among the great nations of Europe: 'Look! look! – they have begun, unexpectedly, under the pressure of similar but more monstrous circumstances, to become Balkanites' (Vinaver 1991: 215). Such figurative language worked to detach the Balkans from its immediate geographical referents and converted the term into the marker of a more general condition: a sorry one, true, but one not limited to the people of the region itself, and therefore scarcely evidence of their singularity. If metaphors have their own foreign policy, exerting their power by assimilating the strange to the familiar, collapsing the differences between home and abroad, as Eric Cheyfitz has argued in *The Poetics of Imperialism*, then this power is available not only to imperial translators. By spreading beyond its physical borders, 'Balkan' as metaphor could liberate the region, as well as subjugate it (cf. Bjelić and Savić 2002).

A similar point might be made about the superfluity of meanings attached to the word 'balkanization'. While the term derived its initial connotations of political fragmentation and instability from reference to the Balkan Peninsula, it was introduced not to describe the region itself, but to characterize the divisiveness and fragmentation of the *rest* of Europe in the wake of the First World War (something already pointed out by promoters of Balkan redefinition in the 1930s; *Knjiga o Balkanu* 1936: 1, xii). Moreover, in the following three-quarters of a century, 'balkanization' was gradually extended to a multiplicity of different places and phenomena beyond international relations, as a synonym for decentralization or pluralism of almost any kind (the 'balkanization' of India, of Africa, of Hungarian agriculture, the California school system, the literary canon, the internet, etc., ad infinitum). This may have led to negative back-projection, as the qualities attributed to each of these projects were then associated with the peninsula (what Todorova calls 'interpolation'; 1997: 37). But this was not a consistent process, particularly when 'the Balkans' as a geopolitical concept faded out of common use, superseded by different Cold War divisions of Europe. The Balkan signifier floated free of its original geographical and historical referent, losing much of its stigmatizing power – at least until the Yugoslav wars of the 1990s dragged it back to its starting point, this time reinforced by the additional connotation of ethnic violence.

The breaching of the Berlin Wall and the break-up of Yugoslavia generated two contradictory narratives: that of a reunited Europe and that of the rebirth of the Balkans. These had their echo in travel writing – both to and from the Balkans. Scholarship has emphasized the Western revival of Balkanism as part of the attempt to make sense of what was happening in Yugoslavia – or as part of an effort to keep it at a distance – but wasn't the lexicon of 'Balkan' difference revived even earlier in intra-Yugoslav depictions of internal others? (Bakić-Hayden 1992 captures both the tone and the content.) Subsequently writers and travellers from Yugoslavia would use the same Balkanist imagery, while at the same time castigating Western pundits for their failure to look beyond easy Balkan stereotypes. Slavenka Drakulić's sketches from the beginning of the war provide one example, summing up the accelerating plunge into chaos with the title *Balkan Express* but also expressing resignation at the views of those outside the conflict:

The West tells us, 'You are not Europeans, not even Eastern Europeans. You are the Balkans, mythological, wild, dangerous Balkans. Kill yourselves, if that is your pleasure. We don't understand what is going on there, nor do we have clear political interests to protect.' (Drakulić 1993: 2–3)

No wonder that one response to this critique was to revise Europe's symbolic geographies in ways that erased the Balkans from the map. Statesmen, scholars and travel writers reimagined its component parts, in earnest or ironically, as Southeastern Europe, Central Europe, the Eastern Adriatic, or, for the most troublesome bits, the Western Balkans (but not the Eastern or Southern Balkans). Or as nothing at all. Mileta Prodanović, a Belgrade writer and artist, neatly suggests an ironic erasure of the Balkans in the back-cover blurb for his 2000 travel account, *Oko na putu* ('Eye on the Road'), describing his book as a Mediterranean tour, 'which begins in Venice, descends the Apennines, touches the Maghreb and the spaces of the eastern Mediterranean and, by way of Istanbul, Thrace, the Greek islands, Epirus and Macedonia, reaches as far as Belgrade, a city which is not on the Mediterranean, but might be. At least in as much as it isn't in Central Europe, where it also might be ... but isn't'. In fact, the Balkans features explicitly in his text, but as a blank space on the map, marked by absences and failures, a terra incognita signalled by the kitschy plaster lions guarding profiteers' provincial palaces (*'hic sunt leones'*).

This back-and-forth process of definition and redefinition raises the question whether it is useful to think about Western and Balkan representations of the region separately and independently of one another. Even if the aim is the narrower one of understanding discourses and motifs of 'the Balkans' in indigenous travel writing, can this be done without also acknowledging the view from outside? Clearly this isn't entirely possible: the notion of the Balkans, with its connotations of difference, of a semi-Orient, of an Other to the West, has always been shaped by Western perspectives on the region, though the invention and perpetuation of concepts of the Balkans was never a wholly one-sided affair. The Balkans' Balkans and the West's Balkans may have coincided to a great extent (in part, as Ellie Scopetea has argued, because they are both different aspects of the vision of Europe-as-modernity), but it is still useful to keep in mind 'their different backgrounds, points of departure, and perspectives' (Scopetea 2003: 172). All the more so in travel writing, as already noted with reference to different starting points. But different audiences matter too. 'The Balkans' presented for a Western public, as in Drakulić's text, is not necessarily the same as that discovered in writings for a local audience.

Can we guess where Balkan travel writing might go in the future? The genre itself seems unlikely to fade away, in spite of numerous predictions of its imminent demise, whether this is supposed to come from the retreat of the perceptive traveller in the face of mass-market tourism or from the erasure of the strange and different in an age of accelerating globalization. Nor do 'the Balkans' seem likely to vanish as a result of well-meaning re-mappings. Instead, recent representations promise to reconfigure the Balkans, delivering it to globalized readerships as a brand in the international marketplace, a space of aestheticized difference, simultaneously attractive and repulsive (for such a Balkans in recent film and art exhibitions: Iordanova 2001; Avgita and Steyn 2007). Under such circumstances, it's easy to imagine a new Bai Ganyo Balkanski on the road, an unacculturated and unashamed Zorba for a twenty-first-century Western audience, perturbing and titillating a metropolitan readership with evidence of its own blandness and superficiality, but at the same time reassuring it as to its tolerance of difference. One version of this can be found in Andrei Codrescu's travel writings, which locate the off-beat character of his visions of America in his essential Romanianness (he emigrated to the U.S. in 1966; at other points he also draws on his Jewishness as a source of authority for his perceptions) (Codrescu 1991; 1993; 2001). At its best this is the sort of perspective that animated such classic insider–outsider works as George Mikes's *How to Be an Alien* (1946), which comments simultaneously on English and Hungarian stereotypes. At worst, it can be an exercise in marketing the West's image of the Other – the West's Balkans – back to it, and in the process perpetuating the same clichés.

'The Balkans does not exist without the West'. But even if this is so, it does not mean, as Louisa Avgita concludes, that 'there is no Balkan side of the Balkan story' (Avgita 2007: 219). Not all evocations of the Balkans are, necessarily and primarily, reflections in the mirror of the West. Travel writing from the region also suggests other contexts. An account by two Bulgarian journalists, Georgi Kalendarov and Dilian Vŭlev (2004), provides one recent example, in a seriocomic exploration of migrant life in neighbouring Greece (reached 'most directly', at least before Bulgaria's 2007 entry into the EU, by bus through the former Yugoslav states and by ferry from Italy, where border controls were laxer). While primarily an exposé – the streets of Athens are not paved with gold – the book is also about being Balkan in the Balkans. Its title, 'The Art of Being a Foreigner' or, in an unintended echo of Mikes, 'How to Be an Alien', promises survival tips for the Bulgarian abroad. However, it must also be read as instructions for maintaining a sense of estrangement against a new type of culture shock: the shock of the *familiar* in the face of expectations of difference. (Here travel writing once again fulfils its promise of delivering surprise.) Encounters abroad, not just with Greeks but with other denizens of the peninsula, force Kalendarov and Vŭlev to conclude that 'they are just like us'. But here this familiar travellers' trope is not one more discovery of a universal humanity, but rather the recognition of a very particular, Balkan, commonality. (And one defensive reaction, also amply demonstrated in the text, is the exaggeration of small differences.) The jolt of recognition across Balkan boundaries (on the map, in the head) is scarcely new (for a similar discovery, see Iorga 1929: 4). However in spite of – or because of? – the stereotype of Balkan diversity and fragmentation, the exploration of Balkan commonalities has become something of a recurrent topic in recent writing from the region (e.g., in a travel text, Rădulescu 2000; more generally, Kiossev 2002; for similar issues explored in fiction or in the critical essay, see Muthu 2004; Yannakakis 2004). Not-quite-European is not what is foregrounded as the defining feature of the Balkans here: this is the Balkans' Balkans, with its own points of departure and destinations. EU accession has erased some frontiers – including the barrier to free migration between Greece and Bulgaria – but at the same time it has created new lines on the map, without necessarily revising those that exist in the mind. While there are still such frontiers to cross (and assumptions to overturn), Balkan travel writing seems unlikely to go away.

Wendy Bracewell
London, 2008

Notes

Much of the research gathered together in this volume was carried out in the framework of the AHRC Research Project 'East Looks West: East European Travel Writing on Europe', or presented at seminars and conferences sponsored by the project, in London and in Sofia. Most of the chapters were first published in a special issue of *Journeys: the international journal of travel and travel writing* (2005), edited by Wendy Bracewell and Alex Drace-Francis, but appear here in revised form, while Ludmila Kostova's study and this introduction were written for this volume. Alex and I owe a special debt of thanks to Garry Marvin, co-editor of *Journeys*, for his support and encouragement (not to mention his inimitable brand of hospitality).

1.   A.V. Amfiteatrov, *Strana razdora. Balkanskiia vpechatleniia* (St Peterburg, 1903); Harry De Windt, *Through Savage Europe, being a Narrative of a Journey through the Balkan states and European Russia* (London, 1907); Sándor Hangay, *Az égő Balkánon keresztül* (Budapest, 1918); Albert Koehler, *Sonne über dem Balkan: ein Reisebuch zwischen Baedeker und Homer* (Dresden, 1930); Hakån Mörne, *Vilde vackra Balkan!* (Stockholm, 1935; trans. *The Melting Pot: an Account of Travels in the Balkans*, London, 1937); Václav Fiala, *Věčný epos*

Balkánu (Prague, 1947); M. Philips Price, Through *the Iron-Laced Curtain: a Record of a Journey through the Balkans in 1946* (London, 1949); Robert Bassett, *Balkan Hours: Travels in the Other Europe* (1990); Alec Russell, *Prejudice and Plum Brandy: Tales of a Balkan Stringer* (London, 1993); Dervla Murphy, *Through the Embers of Chaos: Balkan Journeys* (London, 2003). Unless otherwise noted, translations are my own.

2. Compare e.g. Archibald Lyall, *The Balkan Road: an Account of Travels in South-eastern Europe* (London, 1930) and Heinrich Hauser, *Süd-Ost-Europa ist erwacht. Im Auto durch acht Balkanländer* (Berlin, 1938), with Brian Hall, *Stealing from a Deep Place: Travels in South-Eastern Europe* (London, 1988) or Scott Malcolmson, *Empire's edge: Travels in South-Eastern Europe, Turkey and Central Asia* (London, 1994).

3. The most influential analysis has been that by Todorova 1997, but some earlier studies of travel writing on the Balkans had raised similar questions: Golczewski 1981; Bracewell 1988; Pederin 1989; Allcock 1991; Petkov 1997. See also Markovich 2000; Jezernik 2004; Hammond 2007.

4. For Georgević and Vrančić, Birnbaum 1986; for Milescu, Hill-Paulus 1978. See also Osman Ağa Tercüman 1962; Kuripešić 1997; Rattkay 1998; Kašić 1999.

5. For the genre, and printed *proskynetaria* in Greek, see the catalogue of the Gennadius Library, Weber 1953. Kadas 1986 presents ten Greek manuscript examples (with a summary of the accompanying text in English). See also Giurova and Danova 1985 for the preface to an eighteenth-century Bulgarian translation of a Greek *proskynetarion* 'so that it can be read in our tongue. [...] Whoever has this in his house, possesses a great treasure', 303.

6. Droulia 2003: 10 (many thanks to Maria Kostaridou for this reference and the translation).

7. For a survey of earlier debates, focusing on the disciplinary approaches and political assumptions structuring them, see Bracewell and Drace-Francis 1999; for a review in the context of Orientalism, Fleming 2000. More recent contributions are set in a wider context in Petrungaro 2004. The subject is less in need of an update than a new approach.

References

Alković, M. 1911. *Put Beograd-Sofija-Carigrad*. Sarajevo: Tiskara Vogler.

Allcock, J. 1991. 'Constructing the Balkans', in *Black Lambs and Grey Falcons: Women Travellers in the Balkans*, ed. J. Allcock and A. Young. New York: Berghahn Books.

Antohi, S. 2002. 'Romania and the Balkans: From Geocultural Bovarism to Ethnic Ontology', *Tr@nsit-Virtuelles Forum* 21, http://www.iwm.at/t-21txt8.htm. Accessed June 2007.

Avgita, L. 2007. 'The Balkans Does Not Exist', *Third Text* 21:2, 215–21.

Avgita, L. and A. Steyn. 2007. *The Balkans* [special issue], *Third Text* 21:2.

Bakić-Hayden, M. 1992. 'Orientalist Variations on the Theme "Balkans": Symbolic Geography in Recent Yugoslav Cultural Politics', *Slavic Review* 51:1, 1–15.

Bakić-Hayden, M. 1995. 'Nesting Orientalisms: The Case of Former Yugoslavia', *Slavic Review* 54:4, 917–31.

Balina, M. 1994. 'A Prescribed Journey: Russian Travel Literature from the 1960s to the 1980s', *Slavic and East European Journal* 38:2, 261–70.

Ballinger, P. 1999. 'Definitional Dilemmas: Southeastern Europe as "culture area"?', *Balkanologie* 3:2, 73–91.

Beardsall, P.R. 2000. *Europe and Latin America: Returning the Gaze.* Manchester: Manchester University Press.

Birnbaum, M.D. 1986. *Humanists in a Shattered World: Croatian and Hungarian Latinity in the Sixteenth Century.* Columbus, OH: Slavica.

Bjelić, D. and O. Savić. 2002. *Balkan as Metaphor: Between Globalization and Fragmentation.* Cambridge, MA: MIT Press.

Bracewell, W. 1988. 'Opinion-makers: The Balkans in British Popular Literature, 1856–1876', in *Jugoslovensko-Britanski odnosi/Yugoslav-British Relations,* ed. P. Kačavenda. Belgrade: Institut za savremenu istoriju.

Bracewell, W. 2006. 'Adventures in the marketplace: Yugoslav travel writing and tourism in the 1950s–1960s', in *Turizm: The Russian and East European Tourist under Capitalism and Socialism,* ed. A.E. Gorsuch and D.P. Koenker. Ithaca, NY: Cornell University Press.

Bracewell, W. and A. Drace-Francis. 1999. 'Southeastern Europe: History, Concepts, Boundaries', *Balkanologie* 3:2, 47–66.

Cheyfitz, E. 1997. *The Poetics of Imperialism.* Philadelphia: University of Pennsylvania Press.

Codrescu, A. 1991. *The Hole in the Flag: A Romanian Exile's Story of Return and Revolution.* New York: William Morris.

———— 1993. *Road Scholar: Coast to Coast Late in the Century.* New York: Hyperion.

———— 2001. *Ay, Cuba! A Socio-erotic Journey.* New York: Picador.

Cvijić. J. 1965 [1902]. 'Istraživačka putovanja po Balkanskom poluostrvu', in *Autobiografija i drugi spisi.* Belgrade: SKZ (First published in *Zeitschrift der Gesellschaft für Erdkunde,* Berlin).

Daskalov, R. 2001. 'Modern Bulgarian Society and Culture through the Mirror of Bai Ganyo', *Slavic Review* 60:3, 530–49.

Drace-Francis, A. 2004. 'Paradoxes of Occidentalism: On Travel and Travel Writing in Ceauşescu's Romania', in *The Balkans and the West: Constructing the European Other, 1945–2003,* ed. A. Hammond. Aldershot: Ashgate.

Ditchev, I. 2002. 'The Eros of identity', in *Balkan as Metaphor: Between Globalization and Fragmentation,* ed. D. Bjelić and O. Savić. Cambridge, MA: MIT Press.

Drakulić, S. 1993. *Balkan Express: Fragments from the Other Side of War.* New York: W.W. Norton.

Droulia, L. 2003. 'Taxidia, ploia kai periegetes', in *To taxidi apo tous archaious os tous neoterous chronous.* Athens: Ethniko Idrima Ereunon.

Dučić, J. 1969. *Gradovi i himere* (Sabrana djela, vol. 2). Sarajevo: Svjetlost.

Duda, D. 1998. *Priča i putovanje: hrvatski romantičarski putopis kao pripovjedni žanr.* Zagreb: Matica hrvatska.

Dumitrescu, M. 2003. *Viaggiatori romeni in Sicilia.* Palermo: Sellerio.

Faifer, F. 1993. _Semnele lui Hermes: memorialistica de călătorie, pînă la 1900, între real și imaginar._ Bucharest: Minerva.

Fleming, K.E. 2000. 'Orientalism, the Balkans, and Balkan Historiography', _American Historical Review_ 105:4, 1218–33.

Franičević, M. 1983. _Povijest hrvatske renesansne književnosti._ Zagreb: Školska knjiga.

Gilburd, E. 2006. 'Books and Borders: Sergei Obraztsov and Soviet Travels to London in the 1950s', in _Turizm: The Russian and East European Tourist under Capitalism and Socialism,_ ed. A.E. Gorsuch and D.P. Koenker. Ithaca, NY: Cornell University Press.

Giurova, S. and N. Danova, eds. 1985. _Kniga za bŭlgarskite khadzhii._ Sofia: Bŭlgarski pisatel.

Golczewski, M. 1981. _Der Balkan in deutschen und österreichischen Reise- und Erlebnisberichten 1912–1918._ Wiesbaden: Steiner.

Hammond, A. 2007. _The Debated Lands: British and American Representations of the Balkans._ Cardiff: University of Wales Press.

Hill-Paulus, B. 1978. _Nikolaj Gavrilovič Spatharij (1636–1708) und seine Gesandtschaft nach China._ Hamburg: Gesellschaft für Natur- und Völkerkunde Ostasiens.

Igov, S. 1990. _Istoriia na bŭlgarskata literatura, 1878–1944._ Sofia: BAN.

Iordanova, D. 2001. _Cinema of Flames: Balkan Film, Culture and the Media._ London: British Film Institute.

Iorga, N. 1904. _Pe drumuri depărtate._ Bucharest: Minerva.

_____ 1907. _Prin Bulgaria la Constantinopol._ Bucharest: Minerva.

_____ 1929. _Le caractère commun des institutions du sud-est de l'Europe._ Paris: J. Gamber.

Jezernik, B. 2004. _Wild Europe: The Balkans in the Gaze of Western Travellers._ London: Saqi Books.

Kadas, S. 1986. _Proskynetaria ton Hagion Topon: deka hellenika cheirographa 16ou–18ou ai._ Thessalonika: n.p.

Kalendarov, G. and D. Vŭlev. 2004. _Izkustvoto da budesh chuzhdenets._ Plovdiv: Khermes.

Kašić, B. 1999. _Život Bartola Kašića,_ ed. and trans. S. Sršan. Osijek: Matica hrvatska.

Kaspi, A. and A. Marès, eds. 1989. _Le Paris des étrangers depuis un siècle._ Paris: Impr. nationale.

Kiossev, A. 1995. 'The Debate about the Problematic Bulgarian', in _National Character and National Ideology in Interwar Eastern Europe,_ ed. I. Banac and K. Verdery. New Haven, CT: Yale Center for International and Area Studies.

_____ 2002. 'The Dark Intimacy: Maps, Identities, Acts of Identification' in _Balkan as Metaphor: Between Globalization and Fragmentation,_ ed. D. Bjelić and O. Savić. Cambridge, MA: MIT Press.

Knjiga o Balkanu. 1936–37. Belgrade: Balkanski institute, 2 vols.

Konstantinov, A. 1966 [1895]. _Baĭ Gan'o._ Sofia: Bŭlgarski pisatel.

_____ 2004. _To Chicago and Back,_ trans. R. Sturm. Sofia: Bulgarian Bestseller.

Krleža, M. 1957. _Deset krvavih godina_ (Sabrana djela, vol. 14/15). Zagreb: Zora.

Kuprel, D. 2004. 'Literary Reportage: Between and Beyond Art and Fact', in *History of the Literary Cultures of East-central Europe: Junctures and Disjunctures in the 19th and 20th Centuries*, ed. M. Cornis-Pope and J. Neubauer. Amsterdam: John Benjamins.

Kuripešić, B. 1997. *Itinerarium oder Wegrayß Küniglich Mayestät Potschafft gen Constantinopel zu dem Türkischen Keiser Soleyman. Anno 1530*, ed. G. Neweklowsky. Klagenfurt: Wieser.

Markovich, S.G. 2000. *British Perceptions of Serbia and the Balkans, 1903–1906*. Paris: Dialogue.

Mikes, George. 1946. *How to Be an Alien*. London: André Deutsch.

Mishkova, D. 2006. 'In Quest of Balkan Occidentalism', *Tokovi istorije* 1–2, 29–62.

Mullett, M. 2002. 'In Peril on the Sea: Travel Genres and the Unexpected', in *Travel in the Byzantine world*, ed. R. Macrides. Aldershot: Ashgate.

Muthu, M. 2004. *Balcanologie II*. Bucharest: Fundaţia Culturală Libra.

Neuburger, M. 2006. 'To Chicago and Back: Aleko Konstantinov, Rose Oil, and the Smell of Modernity', *Slavic Review* 65:3, 427–45.

Novaković, S. 1892. *S Morave na Vardar 1886, putne beleške*. Belgrade: Kraljevska Državna štamparija.

Osman Ağa Tercüman. 1998. *Prisonnier des infidèles*, trans. F. Hitzel. Arles: Actes Sud.

Ouranes, K. 1957. *Taxidia: apo ton Atlantiko ste Maure Thalassa*. Athens: Hestia.

Panaretou, A. 2005. 'Particularities of Greek Travel Writing in a Balkan and European Context', *Journeys: The International Journal of Travel and Travel Writing* 6:1–2, 117–22.

Papantoniou, Z. 1955. *Taxidia*. Athens: Hestia.

Parežanin, R. 1976. *Za balkansko jedinstvo: Osnivanje, program i rad Balkanskog instituta u Beogradu (1934–1941)*. Munich: Istra.

Patterson, P. 2003. 'On the Edge of Reason: The Boundaries of Balkanism in Slovenian, Austrian, and Italian Discourse', *Slavic Review* 62:1, 110–41.

Pavić, M. 1970. *Istorija srpske književnosti baroknog doba (XVII i XVIII vek)*. Belgrade: Nolit.

Pederin, I. 1989. *Njemački putopisi po Dalmaciji*. Split: Logos.

Petkov, K. 1997. *Infidels, Turks and Women: The South Slavs in the German Mind, ca. 1400–1600*. Frankfurt: Peter Lang.

Petrungaro, S. 2004. 'L'Est europeo o a est dell'Europa', *Novecento* 10, 77–86.

Popova, K., ed. 1999. 'Balkanskiiat turizŭm e zalog za uspekha na mezhdubalkanskato delo', *Balkanistichen forum* 1–3, 190–202.

Pratt, M.L. 1992. *Imperial Eyes: Travel Writing and Transculturation*. London: Routledge.

Prodanović, M. 2000. *Oko na putu*. Belgrade: Beogradski krug.

Rădulescu, S. 2000. 'Travel Diary from the Balkans', extracts trans. in *The Romanian Pilgrim* [*Plural* (2003) 4], ed. A. Fabritius. Bucharest: The Romanian Cultural Institute.

Rattkay, I. 1998. *Izvješća iz Tarahumare*, ed. M. Korade. Zagreb: Artresor.

Scopetea, E. 2003. 'The Balkans and the Notion of the "Crossroads between East and West"', in *Greece and the Balkans: Identities, Perceptions and Cultural Encounters since the Enlightenment*, ed. D. Tziovas. Aldershot: Ashgate.

Todorova, M. 1997. *Imagining the Balkans*. New York: Oxford University Press.

Tötösy de Zepetnek, S., ed. 2002. *Comparative Central European Culture*. Purdue, IL: Purdue University Press.

Velkova, S. 2000. 'The "Slav Neighbour" in the Eyes of Noted Greek Intellectuals from the End of the 19th and the Beginning of the 20th Century', *Études balkaniques* 36:1, 128–38.

Vinaver, S. 1991. *Evropa u vrenju. Putopisi i memoarski spisi*. Novi Sad: Dnevnik.

Weber, S.H. 1953. *Voyages and Travels in Greece, the Near East and Adjacent Regions Made Previous to the Year 1801. Being Part of a Larger Catalogue of Works on Geography, Cartography, Voyages and Travels, in the Gennadius Library in Athens*. Princeton, NJ: American School of Classical Studies at Athens.

Yannakakis, E. 2004. 'Geographical and Ideological Wanderings: Greek Fiction of the 1990s', in *Contemporary Greek Fiction in a United Europe: From Local History to the Global Individual*, ed. P. Mackridge and E. Yannakakis. Oxford: Legenda.

Yurchak, A. 2006. *Everything was Forever, until it was No More: The Last Soviet Generation*. Princeton, NJ: Princeton University Press.

CHAPTER 2

Hodoeporicon, Periegesis, Apodemia: Early Modern Greek Travel Writing on Europe

Maria Kostaridou

In the spring of 1952, the Greek poet George Seferis, then acting as a counsellor at the Greek Embassy in London, gave a brief talk on BBC Radio on 'A Greek in England in 1545' (Seferis 1981).[1] The Greek of the title was Nikandros Noukios, a native of Corfu and resident of Venice, who, in the middle of the sixteenth century, travelled extensively through Europe, eventually crossing the English Channel and reaching the British Isles. Rather unusually, he also left behind a three-volume narrative of his travels, entitled *Apodemiai*.

At the time of Seferis' talk the *Apodemiai* were 'still resting in manuscript form in the Bodleian Library at Oxford, the Ambrosiana in Milan, the Escorial'. Only one part of the work, the book that relates the voyage to England, had been put into print by an 'inquiring philologist at Oxford'. Leafing through this 'rare, slim volume of 1841', Seferis became fascinated by this Corfiote scholar, whose descriptions of England – a land as 'foreign' and 'remote as Thule' – resemble those of 'an explorer who talks to his audience about places whose existence they never even suspected'. Above all, he was captivated by the traveller's nonchalant response to the world that he encountered, by 'the composure of the intellect that wants, above all else, to understand' (Seferis 1981: 101–4).

Seferis' talk, later turned into a short but typically thoughtful and incisive essay, was instrumental in reviving interest in this nearly forgotten 'post-Byzantine Greek of the age of the Renaissance' (ibid.: 108). Half a century later, the *Apodemiai* seem to have found their rightful place in the long history of Greek letters. As the most extensive Greek travel account that has survived from the sixteenth century, it has been hailed as 'probably the most important and most consummate' travel narrative in early Modern Greek letters, 'on a par with the best travel accounts of western European literature' (Angelomatis-Tsougarakis 2000: 161). Even though the only existing edition of the text is considered rather unsatisfactory (Kechagioglou 2001: 715) and a sustained critical analysis of it is still lacking, the *Apodemiai* are generally regarded as 'the first Modern Greek humanist narration of travel impressions' and have been loosely situated within a context of 'apodemic' writing that places emphasis on the educational value of travel and the projection of knowledge gained through personal experience (Kechagioglou 1999: 94). At the same time, the fact that the account is not written in the spoken vernacular of the time but in an 'archaic' and rather 'rigid' language is considered an unfortunate handicap, as it restricts its ostensible didactic appeal to a limited audience of Greek and, possibly, European humanists (ibid.: 96).

While on the whole sound, such a perspective is also misleading. By placing emphasis on a rather generalised notion of education, it is not sufficiently attentive to the ways in which early modern travel functioned both as a path to social advancement as well as a path to the acquisition of knowledge; nor to the ways in which the early modern travel narrative was not simply meant to educate the public at large but was also used as a platform for the display of the traveller writer's learning, experience and authority to a carefully selected audience – the ways, in other words, in which it became a vehicle of self-definition. In this essay I propose to examine some of these issues focusing on their impact upon Noukios' self-presentation as a Greek, a humanist, a traveller and a writer. In the process I will also situate the *Apodemiai* within the context of sixteenth-century Greek travel writing at large, discussing briefly some other accounts from the same period and paying particular attention to the conditions of their production and their intended audience.

Nikandros Noukios

The author of the *Apodemiai* was born in Corfu, probably towards the end of the fifteenth or the beginning of the sixteenth century.[2] According to the records of the island, his name was Andronikos Nountsios and he was member of a Greek burgher family that entered the *Libro d'Oro* of the nobility of the island in 1537 (Giotopoulou-Sisilianou 1978: 75; Layton 1994: 421).[3] During the autumn of the same year, after the siege and sacking of Corfu by Khair ed-Din, known as Barbarossa, Nountsios' father moved his whole family to Venice, seat of one of the oldest and most populous Greek communities in Europe (Geanakoplos 1962: 53–70). Although his family moved back to Corfu as soon as the immediate danger was over, Andronikos decided to stay on in Venice.

The years of Andronikos' sojourn in the city are among the better documented in his life, mainly due to his professional and social activities. From at least 1541 to 1543, he appears as a Reader in the Greek Church of St George as well as an active member of the Greek community and Secretary of the Greek Brotherhood (Layton 1994: 421). During the same years he earned a living as a copyist of Greek manuscripts in the service of Don Diego Hurtado de Mendoza (1503–1575), Spanish Ambassador to Venice and one of the most famous private collectors of Greek codices of his age. By the mid sixteenth century Venice had emerged as the most important centre in the traffic of manuscripts from the Greek lands, now largely under Ottoman rule, to the private collections and libraries of Europe (Giotopoulou-Sisilianou 1978: 27). Many Greek scholars travelled frequently to Greece in order to secure and copy manuscripts for foreign patrons. Among them were Antonios Eparchos and Nicolaos Sophianos, two of Andronikos' compatriots and close friends. Eparchos, himself the owner of a large and immensely valuable library, was one of the better known dealers in manuscripts operating in Venice at the time and had frequent dealings with Mendoza (Giotopoulou-Sisilianou 1978). Sophianos, a gifted and multi-faceted Greek scholar living in Venice at around the same time, also spent long periods in Greece negotiating the purchase of manuscripts (Layton 1994: 461; Knös 1962: 293–94). It is, therefore, likely that Andronikos entered Mendoza's scriptorium through the recommendation of one (or both) of these two close friends (Foucault 1962: 10). Even though it is not known whether he ever travelled back to Greece looking for manuscripts on behalf of Mendoza, Andronikos gained considerable fame as a copyist. Manuscripts in his hand are still in existence in the Mendoza cabinet in the Escorial as well as in numerous other libraries in Europe. The manuscripts are signed as in 'the hand of Andronikos Nouk[k]ios,' Noukios being the more 'archaic' version of his surname that Andronikos adopted in accordance with the humanist trend prevalent throughout Europe at the time (Malina 1968: 53–54; Giotopoulou-Sisilianou 1978: 75).

From 1542 until 1545 Andronikos also worked as an editor and corrector for the Greek press of Damiano di Santa Maria (Layton 1994: 421–23). This was one of the numerous printing houses that had turned

Venice into the most important centre for the production and dissemination of Greek books during the fifteenth and sixteenth centuries, attracting scholars from the whole of the Greek-speaking world and offering employment opportunities to Greek exiles in the city (Geanakoplos 1962: 57). The press of Damiano di Santa Maria, however, occupies a special position within the general history of early printing in Venice, because it was the first to specialise in the production of books specifically directed to a Greek audience (Layton 1994: 337). By 1521, the year when Andreas Kounadis assumed leadership of the press, only one book had appeared in the Greek vernacular and was thus meant for a contemporary Greek audience. The rest of its considerable output was primarily directed to a wider European humanist readership, which had created a market for the publication of the original texts of the classics within the general spirit of the Renaissance. However, the press of Damiano di Santa Maria moved towards the printing of books, both secular and liturgical, that were designed to meet the needs of a growing Greek population in Venice, as well as for export to the wider Greek-speaking world. During his tenure as an editor Andronikos contributed to this output with his own translation and edition of 150 of Aesop's fables, which were published in 1543. This was one of the very first translations of a classical author to appear in the Greek vernacular and had a clear, broad pedagogical aim in mind (Parasoglou 1993: 69–90).

If, with his activities as a copyist of Greek manuscripts and editor in one of the numerous Venetian printing presses, Andronikos follows a path similar to that of many other Greek exiles in the city, his activity during the following two years represents a clear break from this pattern. For it is during 1545 to 1547 that he left Venice behind and travelled extensively, first to Constantinople and later to Europe, accompanying the Fleming Gerard Veltwyck von Ravenstein (Rosenberg 1935) in a succession of diplomatic missions. In the late spring of 1545 Ravenstein, celebrated orator at the University of Louvain and Envoy to the Emperor Charles V, stopped briefly in Venice on his way to Constantinople and took up residence in the Mendoza household. It is probably there that Andronikos met him, introduced himself to him and asked whether he could become a member of his retinue. Ravenstein accepted and took Andronikos with him on his mission to Suleiman. In his own narrative Andronikos gives very little information on this stage of the voyage; however, he appears as a minor personage of the delegation in the *Hodoeporicon Byzantinum*, the account of the journey written by Hugo Favoli and printed at Louvain in 1563 (Foucault 1962: 7; for brief information on the voyage and its itinerary see Yérasimos 1991: 203–4). In his *Apodemiai* Andronikos decided, as he writes, not to dwell on the events of the voyage to Constantinople but to focus instead on the journey to Europe and describe countries and people that are far less known to 'everyone' (Noukios 1962: 41). He describes in vivid detail his voyage through Italy, Switzerland, Germany, Holland and Belgium, the adventurous crossing of the Channel and his residence in Britain, as well as the way back to Italy via France. The first sight of the ocean; the production and excessive consumption of beer in the countries of northern Europe; the wooden houses of the Germans; the bustling trade cities of Amsterdam and Antwerp; the wives of Henry VIII; Erasmus, Luther, and the Anabaptists; his own descent into a Belgian mine and his adventures fighting against the Scots – all combine to turn his narrative into a rare and entertaining record of the journey of a Greek traveller through mid-sixteenth-century Europe. The account is divided into three books, each dealing with a different stage of the voyage and written as a letter addressed to a close friend. It survives in three contemporary manuscripts, none of which is in Andronikos' own hand; and the author is now called Nikandros Noukios (Foucault 1962: 7) – both name and surname have thus been changed to their more 'archaic' versions, signalling yet another progressive step towards Andronikos' self-definition as a European humanist.

Noukios' close association with Eparchos and Sophianos, as well as his own activities as the writer of the *Apodemiai* and the translator of Aesop's fables, place him within a circle of 'non-clerical Greek scholars who, in the first half of the sixteenth century, were instrumental in combining an archaic – in manner and language – humanism with the cultivation of the vernacular' (Kechagioglou 1999: 92). It might be worthwhile pointing out at this stage that 'whereas the gradual demise of Latin as the common language of Europe signalled the rise of "national" vernaculars, the same cannot be said to apply to Greek. Byzantium bequeathed an almost self-evident bilingualism', whose use gradually lead to 'the creation of two worlds: the one consciously present within intellectual life, the other existing without a deeper self-consciousness of its presence' (Toufexis 1999: 319). Different registers of the Greek language, then, are used for different genres, with the vernacular more or less reserved for works of an educational and practical character. Both education and practical use are recognised as integral parts of a travel book, so Noukios' choice of language seems at first to be at odds with two of the primary functions of a travel narrative. This, together with a rather misguided sense that the author necessarily intended his account for publication ('Noukios is still queuing to find his publisher' [Seferis 1981: 102]) have confused matters somewhat. However, the majority of travel narratives from this period were not intended for publication but rather for circulation among the author's friends (Hale 1979: 20). Moreover, one should bear in mind that narratives of the length and sophistication of Noukios' were by no means usual or plentiful: only a small minority of the people who travelled took the trouble to write a record of their voyage. Finally, in a marketplace eager for accounts of far away places, the record of a journey within Europe held little appeal; such narratives were not usually put into print, but distributed within exclusive circles (Hale 1979: 20–21). All the above seem consistent with Noukios' own *Apodemiai*. His choice of language, which limits the audience of the account to a small, educated readership; the presentation of the three books as letters addressed to a close friend; the attendant language of intimacy, which creates an exclusive bond between writer and reader; and the deliberate exclusion of the voyage to the East and focus on the journey to the West – all are powerful indications that Noukios did not wish to educate a general public but rather reach a small, but powerful, readership. Aware of the social advantages of travel, as well as of the demands and conventions of the newly emerging genre of travel writing, Noukios takes to the road and in his travel narrative explores the genre's formal possibilities. Operating within a humanist context that regarded the written record of a journey as a proof of one's accomplishments, he addresses a circle of like-minded individuals, men with further connections and associations in professional, scholarly and humanist circles, who would recognise the author's worth and erudition and help to further his career through references and recommendation. To them, he presents a narrative, which in its scope and sophistication seems unlike any other travel account produced by a Greek traveller of the same period.

Hodoeporicon, Periegesis

Even though there is a fair amount of information about Greek travel during the sixteenth century, Greek travel accounts from the period are not numerous (Angelomatis-Tsougarakis 2000).[4] Nevertheless, the surviving texts reveal a considerable formal and linguistic diversity. Most accounts from the period are written in prose – like the *Hodoeporicon* of Theodosios Zygomalas (1576), the *Hodoeporicon* of Iakovos Miloitis (1588) or Noukios' own *Apodemiai* – but there are also examples in verse, like the *Kopoi kai diatrivi* by the Bishop Arsenios Elassonos, which narrate his voyage to Moscow and Lvov (1590–1593). Information on travellers and their travels can also be found in letters and dedications (the voyages of Eparchos and Sophianos and members of their circle, for example); works on geography, like the *Del sito, e lodi della città di Napoli*, written in Italian by Ioannis Tarchaniotis and published in Naples in 1566 or the *Geography* of Nicolaos Sophianos (Rome, 1552); as well as in autobiographical tracts and reminiscences, like those of Arsenios

Elassonos (n.d.) that expand upon and supplement his *Kopoi*. A separate but immensely interesting category comprises oral reports by returning travellers which are taken down by someone else: the narrative of Ioannis Focas, a Greek captain in the service of the Spanish navy, who related his adventures to Mr Locke, English factor in the Levant, is a notable example here. Focas' report was published by Locke after the traveller's death and soon found its way to the monumental collection of seventeenth-century travel, Purchas's *Pilgrimes* (London, 1613–26). To these we can add the continuous production of *itineraria* and *peregrinationes* to the Holy Lands as well as the production of portolans and *isolaria*, maps of the coast and the islands of the Archipelago. Even though these were manuals intended for use by mariners, they can be included within the genre of travel writing because of their author's claim to experiential authenticity (Chatzipanagioti 1993: 461). In linguistic terms, the aforementioned accounts range from the *logia* or learned language of Zygomalas to the demotic of Miloitis, to the Italian of Tarchaniotis and the English of Focas via Locke.

Only a small proportion of these narratives were put into print during the sixteenth century; most, like the *Apodemiai*, were discovered in manuscript form in various European libraries during the nineteenth century. In their majority the surviving accounts were written at the behest of European humanists who asked Greek scholars and other travellers for first-hand reports of the Greek lands (Angelomatis-Tsougarakis 2000: 163–64). One such humanist was Stephan Gerlach, the recipient of the *Hodoeporicon* of Theodosios Zygomalas (Legrand 1889). Zygomalas had travelled to Asia Minor and the Aegean islands collecting dues on behalf of the Patriarchate. In his impressions he does not only offer geographical descriptions of the places he visited but also notes with sadness the poor living conditions of his enslaved countrymen. His account was copied for Martinus Crusius, Professor of Ethics, Latin and Greek at the University of Tübingen (Angelomatis-Tsougarakis 2000: 163). Crusius was an assiduous collector of reports from Greek travellers as well as of Greek manuscripts, some of which came to him from Mendoza via Eparchos. The existence of Zygomalas' account in more than one copy highlights another important aspect of the production of the early modern Greek travel narrative, namely its use in the teaching and learning of the Greek language in the various humanist centres of Europe. Crusius, always willing to receive and help Greek travellers who came to him with various kinds of petitions, usually asked for a report of their travels in exchange. Some were more obliging than others – in a letter to his friend Maximus Margunius, Crusius complains that sometimes it was excessively difficult to make those Greeks commit themselves to paper (Zerlentes 1922: 8) – but a great number of reports written at his request are still in existence at Tübingen Library. The reports of Andreas Argyros, who travelled to Santorini and Alexandria; Ioannis Tholoites' voyage to Thessalonica, and Symeon Kavassilas' voyage to Athens and Mount Athos were also written for Crusius (Angelomatis-Tsougarakis 2000: 164).

Probably the most intriguing of these early narratives is the *Hodoeporicon* by the Patmian Iakovos Miloitis. A clearly intelligent man, Miloitis travelled extensively acting as an intermediary between the Patriarch Ieremias II and leading German humanists (Karmiris 1937: 6). He visited Crusius in December 1587 (Legrand 1906: 304), read and summarised at least four books in the Greek vernacular for him (Moenning 1997: 69) and in 1588 set down a brief summary of his peregrinations following Crusius' request (Papageorgiou 1882: 633; for brief information and itinerary see Yérasimos 1991: 366–67). His account, together with the *Apodemiai* and the slightly earlier *Periegesis* by Kananos Laskaris (late fifteenth century), is one of only three surviving Modern Greek accounts in prose from this period that partly or wholly narrate voyages to Europe (Panaretou 1995: 46; Kechagioglou 1999: 67). Writing in an unrefined but vibrant demotic, consistently leaving us in the dark as to the reasons for his continuous journeys, seemingly unsystematic and frequently confusing, Miloitis nevertheless shows considerable awareness of the conventions and traditions appropriate to writing on travel. His account emerges as a fascinating hybrid, an amalgamation of styles and devices familiar from pilgrimages and romances, portolans and *isolaria*, travel diaries and scientific discourse, eyewitness testimony and anecdotal hearsay.

Miloitis begins his *Hodoeporicon* with the first-person narration familiar from the travel accounts of the period, here taking on the added gravity of a personal testimony: 'I, Iakovos Miloitis, born on the island of Patmos, left my own country behind and went at first to Puglia, while I was young, 20 years old' (Papageorgiou 1882: 634). From then on, the narrative voice frequently switches from the first-person singular, indicating the traveller writer who has performed the voyage, to the first person plural, signifying a route that travellers habitually take, as in the case of a voyage from Constantinople to Thessalonica by boat (ibid.: 638) or from Crete to Venice:

> Gulf of Venice: We set off from the island of Crete, and first we find the island of *Diakynthos*, Zante in Italian, then Cephallonia, then Corfu. From Corfu to Otranto, 80 miles; we do not travel on the side of Otranto by boat, but from Corfu we follow the right-hand side of the land and travel to Ragusa. Ragusa is *Principos*, Roman in faith and paying tribute to the Turk, and has a Slavic language. From Ragusa we find an island with the name of Korcula and this belongs to the Venetian, then the island of Lesena, then the town of Zara; we travel to Istria and Parenzo; and from Parenzo to

Rovinio; and from Parenzo and Rovinio we travel to Venice; one hundred miles, 100 Italian, from Rovinio to Venice. (ibid.: 638–39)

The overall 'style and intention' of Miloitis' narrative has been compared to that of a portolan (Kechagioglou 1999: 67), and in cases like the above the comparison seems almost justified. The emerging sense of landscape, however, and the traveller's place within it, are radically different to that of a portolan and this difference is largely a matter of first-hand experience. In a sixteenth century portolan, for example, the description of a similar voyage in the Adriatic gulf takes in the dark colour and round shape of the mountains along the Albanian coast and the red cliffs below (Anonymous 1995: 241); a tiny white island with a small castle on the top (ibid.: 240); and a 'huge fig tree by the side of a beautiful cistern' (ibid.: 241) that signals a good port for calming the night. Landscape turns into a series of 'signs' (ibid.) for the benefit of the traveller, creating a sense of a timeless and immutable nature; and the narrative voice, directly addressing the traveller ('as soon as you put out, look for the ruins' [ibid.: 240]; 'from there you find a long island: leave it to your left' [ibid.: 241]) frequently emerges to soothe and reassure: 'don't be frightened', 'don't be at all afraid' (ibid.: 240). Miloitis' landscape, on the other hand, is filled with information more familiar from the reports of merchants and pilgrims: scriptural episodes (Beirut: 'where the great Martyr of Christ, George, killed with his spear the dragon in the lake' [Papageorgiou 1882: 635]), religious relics (Bari: 'where there is the relic of Saint Nicholas, safe and whole' [ibid.: 634]), birthplaces of religious leaders (Veroia: 'the hometown of the Patriarch of Alexandria, Mister Sylvester' [ibid.: 638]), sites of pilgrimage (Mount Sinai: 'the pilgrims travel in those Holy lands in caravans led by camels ... a *caravan* means many people [travelling] together, up to four and five hundred and even a thousand together because of the fear of bandits' [ibid.: 635–36]).

This intriguing detail, the explanation of the meaning of the word 'caravan', presumably directed to the narrative's intended recipient, can lead us to see Miloitis' *Hodoeporicon* in a different light. Rather than think of it as the haphazard and unsystematic recitation of an actual journey – the narration of an itinerary which becomes too confusing and improbable to follow after a while (Yérasimos 1991: 367) – we can see it as actively involved in the process of *reading* and *interpreting*, as well as of writing. There is enough evidence in the account to suggest that Miloitis is, indeed, reading a map, his eye moving across its surface, briefly highlighting islands and cities, occasionally recording whatever information he thinks worthwhile. This would be consistent with common practice of the time, when maps were used as a visual aid when writing (Hale 1979: 15). It is also known that Crusius asked Greek visitors for help with reading works of geography: in 1587, for example, he enlisted the help of Ioannes Dondes from Crete, who read and explained the portolan of Demetrios Tagias that Crusius had in his possession (Makrymichalos 1963: 212). Combining the pictorial representation of the landscape with explanatory texts of varying length, both portolans and *isolaria* of the time follow almost standardised divisions of large geographical areas into smaller, self-contained units: 'the Archipelago', 'the Cyclades', 'the Gulf of Venice', 'Peloponesus, or the Morea' – divisions which correspond exactly to whole sections of Miloitis' account. Seeing Miloitis' narrative in this light would certainly help explain the almost completely impersonal tone of large parts of it, the lack of autobiographical detail interwoven within the recitation of the journey. On the whole, it is surprising how much information and commentary in Miloitis' account emerges as entirely second-hand and how little self-conscious 'national' feeling permeates the narrative. Writing for the benefit of the continental humanist who is eager for information on Greece, Miloitis devotes far more space to the Mediterranean and the Near East than his voyage to Europe. Myth, history and legend emerge as powerful factors in his perception of Greece, as witnessed by his short survey of the Peloponnese or Morea: 'Near Monemvassia there is an island with the name of Cythera, and it belongs to the Venetian now. This is the island in which Helen of Menelaus was born and the son of Priam stole her and brought her to Troy and for that reason, of Helen of Menelaus, the war of Troy happened and Troy was lost' (Papageorgiou 1882: 638). His description of the Greek landscape is permeated with a sense of the past and is dotted with towns, villages and settlements that have a long history of former importance but are now no more than ruins: 'On the road from the monastery on the way to Corinth we find an old town, with the name of Megara; but it is now in ruins; it is only a village'; 'on the side of Epachtos towards the sea used to be the city of Corinth in older times; but now it is in ruins and a small town' (ibid.: 641). Yet, far from being the expression of an early 'national' consciousness, this vision of Greece in almost total decay seems to reiterate an opinion widespread among European humanist circles up until the end of the sixteenth century (Tolias 2005: 18). As for the connection of Cythera with the Trojan war, it is a staple of almost every pilgrim's account from the previous centuries. Past glory and contemporary suffering, however, are combined at one striking section of the narrative, where they also become intimately connected with the traveller himself. This is Miloitis' description of his entry into Constantinople, symbol of former glory and current enslavement: 'And in 1584, I, Iakovos Miloitis, entered into the City of Constantine, on a Tuesday, the first day of the month of September; and on the tenth day of the same month, on a Thursday, I was put into prison for my many sins; and stayed there for ten and three months. And after this, thanks be to the Lord, I was freed from prison due to my wife and children. And from Constantinople I travelled to Wallachia, and from Wallachia to Russia ...' (Papageorgiou 1882: 639). In the context of Miloitis' breathless account, which at times is no more than a recitation of places along a certain route, the traveller's entry into this most symbolic of cities is rendered with outright solemnity and reverence: this is the only time a date is recorded in Miloitis' account, marking it as the most important event in the whole of his journey. Significantly, this is also a rare instance in which the authorial 'I' emerges clearly at the surface of the account. Miloitis does not normally record his own experiences during his travels, unless they are associated with an adversity, a mishap: like the description of his approach to Frankfurt (where 'I was robbed blind by bandits' [ibid.: 639]) or that of his imprisonment, which obliquely mirrors that of the rest of his nation.

Written almost a century before the account of Miloitis, the *Periegesis* by Kananos Laskaris (Lampros 1881: 708) shows a far greater interest in the systematic recording of scientific phenomena and geopolitical information. In his brief narrative of his travels to the northernmost parts of Europe, Laskaris (ibid.: 706–7) mentions the extraordinary length of a day that lasts for a whole month ('from the twenty fourth of the month of June till the twenty fifth of July all is day and there is no night'), as well as another, this time in Iceland ('according to the wise Ptolemy this is, methinks, Thule'), which lasts for six ('here I found a day of six months, from the beginning of spring till the turning of the autumn'). He carefully distinguishes between the various political authorities that govern over the whole, broad geographical area (ibid.: 706); and briefly mentions a tribe, originally from the Peloponnese, who live scattered in villages in northern Europe and still speak their own language (ibid.: 707). He is also impressed by the natives of Iceland, who 'are men valiant and strong and their food is fish, their bread is fish and their drink is water' (ibid.). Unlike Miloitis', Laskaris' authorial 'I', which introduces the narrative, remains strong throughout and clearly serves as a validation and verification of the narrated facts.

Apodemiai

Unlike Miloitis' 'Hodoeporicon' [itinerary] and Laskaris' 'Periegesis' [geographical description], Noukios' account is an 'Apodemia'.[5] It is most probably this title, similar to those of a cluster of books on travel dating from the second half of the sixteenth century, that leads Kechagioglou to suggest that:

[T]he *Apodemiai* are the first example in Modern Greek letters of the humanist proliferation of 'apodemic' writing, which, during the sixteenth century, goes hand in hand with a theoretical problematic and methodising of the voyage-peregrination (value of the journey, object of observation, recording of information) that places emphasis on the educational value of the journey and the projection of knowledge gained through first-hand experience. (1999: 94)

Locating the account within an 'apodemic' context along these lines, however, is slightly misleading. Even though in his narrative Noukios shows an up-to-date knowledge of the theoretical developments and conventions of travel writing, his is not an 'apodemic' text – at least not as these are defined by the foremost theoretician of this writing, Justin Stagl. In his bibliography of 'Apodemic literature', Stagl (1983) identifies a number of texts, which begin to be published in the second half of the sixteenth century (to disappear completely by the middle of the nineteenth) and which constitute a separate but related genre to travel writing. Their distinguishing characteristic is their methodological nature, since they are primarily concerned with a philosophy of travel (what Stagl defines as the 'Verbesserung der Reisepraxis' and the 'Kunstlehrern des richtigen Reisens' [1983: 9]). Records of actual journeys are also sometimes offered, but mostly as a blueprint for the instruction of future travellers. As Joan-Pau Rubiés has observed, these texts constitute 'a sophisticated discourse on travel as an activity and the traveller as a human type' (Rubiés 1996: 141), a kind of 'meta-cultural discourse' (ibid.: 141) through which 'a new intellectual elite sought to teach Europeans how to see the world' (ibid.: 140). The relationship between such texts and the *Apodemiai* is not a straightforward one. Most of these writings postdate Noukios' own; and the founding theoreticians of the genre (Zwinger, Pyrckmair and Turler) were intellectuals from middle and northern Europe with strong Protestant leanings. However, they all had strong connections to Venice, as they had all visited the University of Padua. In their attempt to provide a theory of the art of travel, they synthesise, systematise and make available in print for the first time certain ideas, notions and beliefs that were already circulating in Venice during the first half of the sixteenth century.[6] Venice had been extremely important in the development of travel writing as early as the Middle Ages (Rubiés 1996: 148–50). As a citizen and resident of the Republic, Noukios was well placed to be informed both of the theoretical developments in travel writing as well as of the general ideas on travel and travellers. Not strictly an apodemic text, therefore, the *Apodemiai* can be seen as simultaneously a nod to European humanism – a signal that the author is fully aware of this emerging concept – while at the same time retaining and developing the strong notion of expatriation, which is inherent in this Greek word, but largely absent from theoretical apodemic writings. The sense of being away on one's travels is now inseparable from that of being far away from home; and to the considerable typology of the sixteenth-century traveller (Sherman 2002) – the scholar and the merchant, the pilgrim and the errand knight, the ambassador and the explorer – Noukios adds another, Greek in hue and in resonance, that of the exile.

One of the most influential of the early apodemic texts was *The Traveiler*, by Jerome Turler, first published as *De Peregrinatione* in 1574. Turler's book, which went through numerous editions in Europe, was translated into English and published in London in 1575. Here is Turler's definition of travel, which I quote from a facsimile of that early English edition:

> Traveill is nothing else but a paine taking to see and searche forrein lands, not to be taken in hande by all sorts of persons or unadvisedly, but such as are meete thereto, eyther to the ende that they may attayne to such artes and knowledge as they are desirous to learne or exercise: or else to see, learne and diligently to marke such things in strange countries, as they shall have neede to use in common trade of lyfe, wherby they may profit themselves, their friends, and countries if neede require. (Turler 1951: 5)

The definition that Turler gives here, and that becomes a *locus classicus* of the art of travel, revolves around three crucial points: the purposes and profits of travel, the proper way of conducting a journey and the people who are able to perform it. For not all travel is profitable and not everyone is fit to travel. According to the early theoreticians of the genre, there was a crucial distinction to be made between useful and aimless travel, between *peregrinari* and *vagari* (Stagl 1990: 316). The traveller was not to pass his time in idle wanderings; he should be well read and prepared for the new country and, while abroad, diligently record his impressions of the voyage. The experience of the traveller, therefore, was to be set down in writing, as memory was not to be entirely trusted (Stagl 1990: 320). Moreover, all information was to be presented in a narrative upon the traveller's return, for the benefit of his friends and, possibly, his country. Aware of this emerging philosophy of the *ars apodemica*, throughout his narrative Noukios presents himself as an ideal traveller: he leaves Venice behind because he is desirous to learn of people and places he has not seen before (1962: 39); he puts pen to paper for the benefit of his friends, men much travelled and desirous of further learning (1841: 2; 1962: 39, 81); he talks of things that were seen, heard or experienced by himself (1962: 39, 41) but further frames his first-hand experience with anecdotes on political and religious leaders in common with the widespread practice of the time (Hale 1979: 27–28, 37); he supplements his observations with knowledge garnered from historians and chroniclers (Cramer 1841; Foucault 1962; Malina 1968); finally, he is careful to show that he has not spent his time in idleness but seeking out and recording all the information that he could find about the country in which he travels.

His description of himself at the beginning of his stay in London, for example, is typical of such an attitude: 'in order that I might not seem to have wasted the opportunity inconsiderably and idly', he writes, 'it appeared good to me to investigate the peculiarities of the island, and to ascertain, as far as lay in my power, the things appertaining to it' (Noukios 1841: 6). The resulting account is a well-structured narrative, clearly influenced by the Venetian *relazione*. Following the advice that was first given to the diplomats in the service of the Republic (Brown 1864: xli–xliv; Williams 1937: 73–74; Hale 1979: 36–38) and which became a blueprint for later 'directions to travellers' and 'letters of advice', which proliferated during the second part of the sixteenth century, Noukios offers an eye-witness account of the city of London, its principal buildings, the manners and customs of its inhabitants ('Almost all, indeed, except the nobles … pursue mercantile concerns … . And to this, they are wonderfully addicted' [1841: 9–10]; 'they resemble the French more than others, and for the most part use their language' [1841: 14]), the form of their government and the relationship to their sovereign ('towards their King they are wonderfully well affected' [1841: 16]); a more general discussion of the whole of the British Isles, its geographical and political divisions, its climate and main produce; and lengthy historical/anecdotal digressions on the character and wives of Henry VIII as well as the behaviour of the nuns and monks before the Dissolution of the Monasteries. These are framed by the chronological unfolding of the events of the journey combined with the narration of the author's own adventures (the crossing of the Channel during a storm as well as his participation in Henry VIII's war against the Scots in the company of Thomas of Argos). As is also the case with the first and third books of the *Apodemiai* (Noukios 1962: 76, 142, 147), writing takes place during a break from travelling – but the formal properties of each book are rather different. The *Apodemiai* have been called 'the travel notebook of a tourist' (Legrand, quoted in Foucault 1962: 18): the first book, with its brief entries that chart the progression of the events of the journey in a strict chronological manner, certainly borrows elements from the diary convention; moreover, Noukios' final summary of the main points of the journey, where he also notes the distances he travelled for the benefit of future voyagers (1962: 7–80) and inserts an appendix on the production of beer (ibid.: 80–81), also helps to present the preceding narrative as a diary. Noukios himself refers to his work as a 'history' (ibid.: 174): both the narration of his own adventures and the more general historical information that he offers in his account conform to the concept of *'peregrinationis historia'* current at the time. A seventeenth-century librarian called the *Apodemiai* a 'universal history of its time' (quoted in Kechagioglou 1999: 95) – the description of the events that led to the Continental wars of the sixteenth century in the third book of his travels, for example, bear this characterization out – and all attest both to the fluidity of the genre at this early stage and to Noukios' own handling of it.

Turler's definition of the ideal traveller, which I quoted above, also takes in the distinction between people who are fit to travel and those that are not. Turler devotes the second chapter of his book to this issue and writes that travel is neither for the very old nor for the very young; not for women (the example of Medea, he writes, aptly illustrates this point: when the comical and tragic poets 'bringe in any far traveiling woman, for the most part they feine her to be incontinent' [Turler 1951: 9]); for the infirm; or for 'frantique and furious persons' (ibid.: 9). Early on in his own account, Noukios makes an intriguing reference to himself in this respect. Upon meeting Veltwyck in Venice, he writes, he introduced himself to Charles' envoy as 'not useless about being on the road' (Noukios 1962: 39). There are various ways in which this word, 'useless', could be read here. It could be an indication that Noukios was aware of this attitude described above, that in order to travel one should be of a certain age, fit in body and of a sound mind. It could also be an allusion to a previous experience of travel, a certain familiarity with the hardships, the 'paine' of being on the move. Over and above that, however, I would like to dwell a while on this notion of 'use' and examine it within the context of sixteenth-century European travel, the people who travelled and their reasons for doing so.

Even though by the mid sixteenth century curiosity and education had already become recognized as legitimate reasons for travelling to Europe, embarking on a voyage was not always straightforward. A good network of roads and certain comforts for the traveller existed, but travel could still be a lengthy and costly undertaking. People desirous to see new places, therefore, had to wait for the right opportunity before travelling. Noukios himself suggests as much at the beginning of his narrative, where he talks of the opportunity that presented itself in the person of Veltwyck (1962: 39). Joining the retinue of an envoy or an ambassador was a usual practice at the time (Mączak 1995: 121). However, our knowledge of the dynamics and conditions of early modern European travel also suggests that these entourages, which normally numbered a great and diverse amount of people, were also governed by a strict hierarchical structure, where each member had a clearly defined task to perform (Mączak 1995: 121). The one possible exception were the gentlemen, who had started travelling for the sake of furthering their education, learning foreign languages, familiarizing themselves with the courts of Europe and generally polishing their manners in preparation for a career in diplomacy or politics back home (Mączak 1995: 122). Judging from Noukios' own presentation of his condition and position in Venice ('living in poverty'; 'beset by misfortunes' [1962: 39]), it seems unlikely that he joined Veltwyck as one of the gentlemen. It is, however, possible that he offered his services precisely as a writer, a secular clerk employed in order to keep a record of the journey. Such practice was not unusual; very important expeditions sometimes included more than one chronicler in their numbers (Mączak 1995: 123–24); and in the same way that Favoli was the chronicler of the journey to the East, so Noukios could now take it upon himself to compile a record of the voyage to the West. Travelling in a diplomat's retinue was a good way of making and cementing friendships (Mączak 1995: 123) and thus entering into a privileged group that would otherwise be outside the reach of the common traveller. Noukios' first description of the Flemish Envoy is important in this respect, as it impacts upon his own presentation. Veltwyck is described not only as a competent diplomat, but also as a consummate scholar, proficient in Latin, Greek and Hebrew, a language in which he composed many learned treatises. Through his humanist education and decorous behaviour, he is like 'us', writes Noukios (1962: 39), thus creating a strong relationship between the envoy, his companion and the account's recipient, making them all belong to a wider, European humanist community.

It was in Veltwyck's company that Noukios was entertained by members of the Gonzaga household (1962: 44), the Cardinals at Trent (ibid.: 45) and Maria, the Emperor's sister (ibid.: 61). All these are briefly mentioned in the first book of his travels, which charts his progression through a series of European cities on the way to the northern coast of France, in a manner reminiscent of a diary. Unlike other diarists of the time, however, Noukios does not seem to be interested in the minutiae of life on the road: meals, expenses, inns, the small details that make diaries such a fascinating record of sixteenth-century travel are largely absent from his narrative. What he shares with other contemporary travel writers is a predominately urban perspective and a great interest in rivers (Hale 1979: 15). Their course and confluence, the places where they rise and fall, the countries that they pass through, the walled cities that they surround, all are continuously – almost obsessively – recorded in the first book.

The overwhelming presence of rivers in these early travel narratives has an intriguing explanation. According to J.R. Hale (1979: 15), rivers, rather than roads, figured prominently on maps of the period; this in turn becomes a clear indication that maps were used both while travelling and as a visual aid when writing. A further indication is provided by the readiness with which travellers seem to recognize that they have crossed a geographical border (Hale 1979:15). Far from giving a straightforward account of the crossing of a border, however, Noukios seems acutely aware of the difficulty of realizing that one is now in a different place. In the course of his description of the first crossing of a border, from Italy to Switzerland, Noukios at first remarks that the inhabitants of this mountainous area are of the German nation and yet in language, food and customs they are not at all dissimilar to the Italians (Noukios 1962: 46). Once he has crossed the Alps and meets the Swiss, he makes a crucial distinction that centres upon their public attitude towards women: they behave with 'great simplicity' towards the women of their nation, and kiss them openly on the mouth – something that does not seem inappropriate or shameful to them (Noukios 1962: 47). This relationship between the sexes, and the different position of women he encounters, is a subject he will return to time and again throughout the *Apodemiai*; together with religion it becomes one of the most important markers of difference. In his final summary of the contents of the first book, for example, he mentions that the Germans share this attitude with the Swiss (1962: 78); in his account of the French, he mentions that they resemble the Germans in this respect, as well as the British (1962: 147). The women in London are so emancipated that they manage their own stalls in the markets, just like the men:

> and one may see in the markets and streets of the city married women and damsels employed in the arts, and barterings, and affairs of trade, undisguisedly. But they display great simplicity and absence of jealousy in their usages towards females. For not only do those who are of the same family and household kiss them on the mouth with salutations and embraces, but even those too who have never seen them. And to themselves this appears by no means indecent. (Noukios 1841: 10)

This notion of 'simplicity' intensifies the further west that Noukios travels, reaching an apex during his account of Ireland, the westernmost part of Europe that he describes. In the second book of the *Apodemiai*, he includes a brief description of the island and its inhabitants, mentioning also their relationship to the English (Noukios 1841: 22–25). It is clear that Noukios did not visit Ireland himself, but as a conscientious traveller he has asked others for information, which he duly records in his account:

> And respecting the island itself, they related to me certain strange and marvellous tales. They fabulously tell that Hades and the gates of Hades are there, imagining that they hear the groans of men undergoing

punishment; and they add, moreover, that various spectres and adverse powers are seen; and other things equally nonsensical, which I have omitted as fabulous and trifling. Such things then as appeared to me to be true, and susceptible of sober consideration, these I relate. (ibid.: 23)

The traveller's responsibility to distinguish truth from falsehood, which is alluded to here, does not stop Noukios from recording some of the miracles and tales associated with this land. Like Herodotus, he notes the marvellous (Greenblatt 1992: 123), which is now located to the West rather than the East, but still 'at the borders of the map, the farthest reach of the journey' (Campbell 1988: 50); and almost immediately he pushes it aside, to concentrate on things that are 'susceptible of sober consideration' and appear to be 'true.' Here then, is the 'truth' about the inhabitants of this island. For one thing:

> [They] do not pay so much attention to civil polity. As many indeed, as live in cities and walled towns have something of human polity and administration. But such, on the other hand, as live in forests and bogs are entirely wild and savage; and there remains only the human form, whereby they may be distinguished to be men. [...] And to their own females they conduct themselves with too great simplicity, inasmuch as sometimes they have sexual intercourse with them in public; neither does this appear to themselves shameful. (Noukios 1841: 23–25)

This mention of the wild and savage Irish, who are presented as living outside human polity, rejecting political institutions (rather than opposing English domination) and openly exhibiting such beast-like behaviour, comes as a shock in Noukios' otherwise measured and collected narrative. It is an instance, however, of the ways a dominant ideology, in this case the discourse on the uncivilized Irish that was so crucial to Tudor colonial propaganda, inscribes itself in a travel text and serves its purpose.

In contrast to the women that Noukios meets throughout his travels, women who are openly desired, kissed and embraced by the men of their own nation, the woman that dominates his thoughts remains firmly out of reach. This is 'Noukia', the author's beloved, the mere thought of whom 'tears and enflames' his heart and whose love violently 'rules and controls' him (Noukios 1841: xxi). Noukia, it seems, has also played a part in turning him into a traveller: if the desire to get away from all of his life's misfortunes is one of the main reasons that Noukios gives for travelling (1962: 39), then it was 'love for her [that] was the cause of my misfortunes' (Noukios 1841: xxi). This mention of Noukia, and her role in sending the traveller abroad, is also accompanied by a sudden burst of intimacy between the author and the reader of the account, expressed in the end of the first book of the *Apodemiai*. It is an intimacy which is also carried over to the proem of the second book: now both writer and reader are seen as sufferers, this time not from love for a woman but from 'a life spent abroad.' Like Andronikos, Cornelius (the recipient of the second book) has also 'endured and suffered much' (Noukios 1841: 2). He has 'lived much in foreign climes and undergone very many peregrinations' (ibid.); and, like the author, he 'ancestorially hath been fated, if any such a thing is, a life spent abroad.' (ibid.)

I would like to suggest that this notion of expatriation, which is defined not simply with reference to the present and the personal but rather to the past and the collective; which is ordained by fate; which is further framed by mention of a female beloved that becomes the source of the traveller's adventures; and which is, finally, counterbalanced by the presence of all these other women, desired by members of their own nation but firmly resisted by the traveller, resembles a schema familiar not so much from travel accounts of the period but from the Greek folk song of expatriation and exile.

Nowhere is the theme of exile more apparent than in a remarkable section, which occurs towards the end of the third book (Noukios 1962: 166–74). Once more, he is not travelling but writing, this time offering a historical account of the events that led to the wars devastating the Continent. Noukios interrupts his 'history' (ibid.: 174) and goes back in time, focusing on the event that originally sent him on his travels, the destruction of his homeland by Barbarossa's army. Even though he finds himself 'abroad', he writes, it is with 'tears' in his eyes that he remembers the misfortunes of his 'dear homeland' (ibid.: 167). The justification for this 'digression' (ibid.: 174) now follows the same linguistic formula that introduced his travels: in both cases he writes about something he has witnessed with his own eyes (ibid.: 167) and is thus worthy to commit to writing (ibid.: 39, 167). This time he records it not simply for the benefit of an interested friend, but also as a tribute to the homeland that has raised him (ibid.: 174). It is also rather significant that at this stage another marvel is recorded in the narrative: this is the vision of a 'huge dragon', followed by a multitude of smaller ones, that was seen flying above the island of Corfu (ibid.: 173). The vision, Noukios writes, was a sign: the dragon is the Turkish ruler, the smaller dragons his associates; moving from the West on their journey to the East, they found Corfu on their way and set about to destroy everything in their wake (ibid.: 173). Once more, then, the marvellous occurs 'at the furthest reach of the journey' (Campbell 1988: 53) – in this case, its very beginning. Only this time it is not brushed aside but both recorded and explained: or composed in narrative by 'the intellect that wants, above all else, to understand' (Seferis 1981: 104).

Notes

1. Unless otherwise stated, all translations from the Greek originals throughout this article are mine.
2. Most of the biographical information on Noukios in this section is drawn from the following studies: Giotopoulou-Sisilianou 1978; Layton 1994; Kechagioglou 1999. I regret that I have been unable to consult the unpublished doctoral thesis of M.P. Panayioyopoulou (1990).
3. An official book, used mainly in Italy but also in the Ionian islands during the period of Venetian rule, where the names of the most prominent families were noted in gold, thus serving as an official designator of the nobility.
4. For information on the production and general content of the sixteenth-century Greek travel account, I follow Angelomatis-Tsougarakis 2000 and Panaretou, Introduction to eadem, ed. 1995. Angelomatis-Tsougarakis provides full bibliographical references to all the accounts mentioned in this section; extracts of some of the narratives can be found in the first volume of Panaretou's anthology.
5. It is not clear whether the titles are the authors' own, or have been given to the accounts by later scholars. However, in all three cases, the titles correspond to words used by the authors themselves to define their travels.
6. In this respect, therefore, the quotation from sources which post-date the *Apodemiai* seems justified.

References

Angelomatis-Tsougarakis, E. 2000. 'Ellinika perigiitika keimena (16os–19os ai.)', *Messaionika kai nea ellinika* 6, 155–80.

Anonymous. 1995. 'Portolan' (extracts), in *Anthologia ellinikis taxidiotikis logotechnias*, ed. A. Panaretou. Athens: Epikairotita.

Brown, R. 1864. *Calendar of State Papers and Manuscripts, Relating to English Affairs Existing in the Archives and Collections of Venice, and in Other Libraries of Northern Italy*. London: Longman, Green, Longman, Roberts and Green.

Campbell, M. 1988. *The Witness and the Other World: Exotic European Travel Writing, 400–1600*. Ithaca, NY: Cornell University Press.

Chatzipanagioti, I. 1993. 'Towards a Typology of the Travel Literature of the 18th Century', in *On Travel Literature and Related Subjects: References and Approaches*, ed. L. Droulia. Athens: Institute of Neohellenic Research.

Cramer, J.A. 1841. *The Second Book of the Travels of Nicander Nucius of Corcyra, edited from the original Greek ms. in the Bodleian library, with an English translation by the Rev. J.A. Cramer*. London: The Camden Society/J.B. Nichols and Son.

Foucault, J.-A. de. 1962. Editor's Introduction, in N. Noukios, *Apodemiai*, ed. J.-A. de Foucault. Paris: Les Belles Lettres.

Geanakoplos, D.J. 1962. *Greek Scholars in Venice. Studies in the Dissemination of Greek Learning from Byzantium to Western Europe*. Cambridge, MA: Harvard University Press.

Giotopoulou-Sisilianou, E. 1978. *Antonios o Eparchos: Enas kerkyraios oumanistis tou 16ou aiona*. Athens: [s.n.].

Greenblatt, S. 1992. *Marvellous Possessions: The Wonder of the New World*. Chicago: University of Chicago Press.

Hale, J.R. 1979. 'Introduction', in *The Travel Journal of Antonio de Beatis: Germany, Switzerland, the Low Countries, France and Italy, 1517–1518*, trans. J. Hale and J. Lindon. London: Hakluyt Society.

Kallinikos, P. 1970. 'O Nikandros Noukios sti Vretannia', *Deltion Anagnostikis Etairias Kerkyras* 7, 35–42.

Karmiris, I. 1937. *Epistolai tou Iakovou Parkethymi kai tou Theodosiou Zygomala*. Offprint from '*Ekklisia*', Athens.

Kechagioglou, G. 1999. 'Introduction', in *I palaioteri pezografia mas. Apo tis arches tis os ton proto pangosmio polemo*, ed. N. Vagenas, Y. Dallas and K. Stergiopoulos. Athens: Sokolis.

———— 2001. 'Andronikos (Nikandros) Noukios', in *Pezografiki anthologia: Graptos neoellinikos logos*, ed. G. Kechagioglou. Thessaloniki: APTH.

Knös, B. 1962. *L'histoire de la littérature néo-grecque. La période jusqu'en 1821*. Stockholm: Almqvist and Wiksell.

Lampros, S.P. 1881. 'Kananos Laskaris kai Vassileios Vatatzis, dio ellines periegitai tou 15ou kai 18ou aionos', *Parnassos* 5, 705–19.

Layton, E. 1994. *The Sixteenth Century Greek Book in Italy: Printers and Publishers for the Greek World*. Venice: Library of the Hellenic Institute of Byzantine and Post-Byzantine Studies.

Legrand, E. 1889. *Notice biographique sur Jean et Théodose Zygomalas*. Paris: Ernest Leroux.

———— 1906. *Bibliographie Hellénique, ou description raisonée des ouvrages publiés en grec par des grecs au XVe et XVIe siècles*, vol. 4. Paris: Ernest Leroux.

Mączak, A. 1995. *Travel in Early Modern Europe*, trans. U. Philips. Cambridge: Polity Press.

Makrymichalos, S.I. 1963. 'Ellinikoi Portolanoi tou 16ou, 17ou kai 18ou aiona', *O Eranistis* 1, 128–55 and 211–21.

Malina, A. 1968. 'Nikandros Nukios, *Apodemiai* Buch I. Bericht über seine Reise durch Deutschland in den Jahren 1545–1546', in *O Ellinismos eis to Exoterikon. Über Beziehungen des Griechentums zum Ausland in der neueren Zeit*, ed. J. Irmscher and M. Mineemi, Berliner Byzantinistische Arbeiten 40. Berlin: Akademie.

Michaelides, D.K. 1970. 'Vivliographiko Simioma gia ton Nikandro Noukio', *O Eranistis* 8, 220–22.

Moenning, U. 1997. 'On Martinus Crusius's Collection of Greek Vernacular and Religious Books', *Byzantine and Modern Greek Studies* 21, 40–78.

Noukios, N. 1841. *The Second Book of the Travels of Nicander Nucius of Corcyra, edited from the original Greek ms. in the Bodleian library, with an English translation by the Rev. J.A. Cramer*. London: The Camden Society/J.B. Nichols and Son.

―――― 1962. *Apodemiai*, ed. J.-A. de Foucault. Paris: Les Belles Lettres.

Panayioyopoulou, M.P. 1990. *Andronikou (Nikandrou) Noukiou "Tragodia eis tin Autexousiou anairesin"*. PhD thesis, University of Crete.

Panaretou, A., ed. 1995. *Anthologia ellinikis taxidiotikis logotechnias*. Athens: Epikairotita.

Papageorgiou, S.K. 1882. 'Hodoeiporicon Iakovou Miloiti', *Parnassos* 6, 632–42.

Parasoglou, G.M. 1993. 'Introduction', in *Andronikos Noukios, Georgios Aitolos: Aisopou mythoi*, ed. G.M. Parasoglou. Athens: Hestia.

Rosenberg, M. 1935. *Gerhard Veltwyck: Orientalist, Theolog und Staatsmann*. Göttingen: [s.n.].

Rubiés, J.-P. 1996. 'Instructions for Travellers: Teaching the Eye to See', *History and Anthropology* 9, 139–90.

Sathas, K.N. 1870. *Viografikon Schediasma peri tou Patriarchou Ieremiou B (1572–1594)*. Athens: Typografeion A. Ktena and S. Oikonomou.

Saunier, G. 1983. 'Introduction', in *To dimotiko tragoudi tis Xenitias*, ed. G. Saunier. Athens: Ermis.

Seferis, G. 1981. 'Enas ellinas stin Anglia tou 1545', in idem, *Dokimes*. Athens: Ikaros, 101–11.

Sherman, W. 2002. 'Stirrings and Searchings (1500–1720)', in *The Cambridge Companion to Travel Writing*, ed. P. Hulme and T. Youngs. Cambridge: Cambridge University Press.

Stagl, J. 1983. *Apodemiken. Eine räsonierte Bibliographie der reisetheoretischen Literatur des 16., 17. und 18. Jahrhunderts*. Paderborn: Ferdinand Schoeningh.

―――― 1990. 'The Methodising of Travel in the Sixteenth Century', *History and Anthropology* 4, 303–38.

Tolias, G. 2005. 'Gia mia orati archaiotita: Methodologia, chresis kai leitourgies tou charti tis Elladas tou Nikolaou Sophianou', *O Eranistis* 25, 9–49.

Toufexis, P. 1999. '"Apo tis dimotikis eis ton Ellinon meteglotissa ... " Apo tin allilografia tou Martinus Crusius me Ellines logious tou 16ou aiona', in *O Ellenikos Kosmos anamessa stin Anatoli kai ti Dysi, 1453–1891*, ed. A. Argyriou, K.A. Dimadis and A.D. Lazaridou. Athens: Hellenika Grammata.

Turler, J. 1951. *The Traveiler (1575) by Jerome Turler*. Gainsville, FL: Scholars' Facsimiles and Reprints.

Williams, C. 1937. *Thomas Platter's Travels in England, 1599*. London: Jonathan Cape.

Yérasimos, S. 1991. *Les voyageurs dans l'Empire Ottoman: XIV–XVI siècles. Bibliographie, itinéraires et inventaire des lieux habités*. Ankara: Imprimerie de la Société Turque d'Histoire.

Zampelios, S. 1859. *Kathidrysis Patriarcheiou en Rossia*. Athens: [s.n.].

Zerlentes, P. 1922. *Simeiomata peri ton Ellinon ek tou Martinou Krousiou souivikon chronikon*. Athens: G. I. Vassileiou.

CHAPTER 3

Dinicu Golescu's *Account of My Travels* (1826): Eurotopia as Manifesto

Alex Drace-Francis

If you get off the train at Bucharest's *Gara de Nord* and walk out of the front entrance, you will see (across the busy traffic) a park, flanked on the right-hand side by Dinicu Golescu Boulevard. Some distance down this road there is a statue of Dinicu Golescu. Dinicu owned most of the land on which the park, the statue and the boulevard are situated. In 1826, he did something none of his fellow-countrymen had ever done before: he published an account of his travels.

The structure of the book appears simple. After insisting in his preface on the popularity and utility of travel accounts in Europe and bemoaning their absence in his home country, Golescu describes his journey and places visited in Transylvania, Hungary, Austria, northern Italy, Bavaria and Switzerland. He usually writes about the things he sees in extremely positive tones. However, he also regularly breaks off at the end of a descriptive passage in order to criticize the absence or deficiency of such institutions at home. The text ends with a plea for a general reform of domestic institutions in a 'European' direction.

Golescu's book is very well known in Romania today. Although they sometimes questioned its literary value, all major twentieth-century Romanian critics stressed its significance:

- 'The whole of the nineteenth century is in this book' (Eliade 1905: 214).
- 'The book had four editions in less than a century' (Haneş 1934: 73).

- 'The transfiguration of this boyar symbolizes our whole revival' (G. Călinescu 1988: 91).
- 'The most powerful testimony to the crisis of consciousness presented by Romanian culture in its modern times' (Popovici 1945: 83).
- 'Dinicu Golescu's itinerary symbolized our journey through the European world to re-establish the true foundations of our modern social life' (Bucur 1971: 11).
- 'The most powerful expression of the critical spirit applied to Romanian society in the 1820s' (Cornea 1972: 220).
- 'Dinicu Golescu's travel journal had a great influence on the Romanian intelligentsia' (Antohi 1985: 90).
- 'Dinicu Golescu underwent a significant crisis of consciousness on encountering the civilization of the West, being forced to acknowledge that we were "behind all the other nations" and that "the world's ridicule" weighed heavily on our people' (Zub 1986: 77).
- 'The oscillating interpretation of Dinicu Golescu between East and West remains significant at a moment in our history at which the confrontation between two worlds finds its most apt symbol in *Account of My Travels*' (Manolescu 1990: 157).

Modern Romanian travellers have cited Golescu as an antecedent (e.g., Pas 1965; Constantin 1973; Marino 1976; Blandiana 1978); cultural commentators refer to his experiences as possible models for interpreting 'ours', without the need for further explanation (e.g., Pleşu 1996: 227). A clear cultural meaning is attached to his personality: he was the man who *realized* that European culture was better, and he managed to convey this message of change, despite his relative age and the considerable difficulties he had in expressing himself.

Romanians have presented Golescu's book and ideas in French, German, and Italian; the whole text has appeared in German and Hungarian translations. To the English-speaking world he is hardly known at all, and material is much harder to come by: a subchapter of an older literary history (G. Călinescu 1988: 91–94); a one-page extract in a collection of texts on social conditions in the nineteenth-century Balkans (Warriner 1965: 144–45); a slightly more extensive extract in a sourcebook on collective identity in central and southeastern Europe (D. Golescu 2006). Finally, Mircea Anghelescu, the leading scholar of Golescu's work, has published a short but very useful article in English (Anghelescu 1991), which summarizes the main conclusions which he presented at greater length in Romanian in the introduction and notes to his critical edition of Golescu's writings (Anghelescu 1990). My understanding of Golescu's travel, writings, experience and ethics owes much to Anghelescu's scholarship. Here, as well as offering one or two small factual additions, I try to shed further light on the more particular framework of how Golescu used both publishing strategies and rhetoric about Europe to further certain political interests in 1820s Wallachia. To do this, I begin with a short account of Golescu's life in the general context of the social and intellectual transformations taking place in Wallachia at the end of the eighteenth and beginning of the nineteenth centuries. I then focus in detail on the period 1821–1826; tracing Golescu's geographical, political and editorial steps will, I hope, enable me to convey what it meant for a Wallachian boyar to travel West at this precise time, to write about his experiences and also to try to influence contemporary opinion through publication.[1] Finally, I interpret the content of the book: primarily against the political background, but also in the light of certain aspects of the book's rhetorical structure, which I seek to situate in the nineteenth-century Romanian literary tradition. I want, then, not only to find out where Golescu went, and what he wrote; I also want to consider how he wrote; why he published his account; why he did so when he did; and what effect his book had on contemporaries. It's a story as much about the uses of travel writing as about the discovery of Europe.

Account of a Traveller

Dinicu Golescu ('Dinicu' is an informal diminutive of Constantin) was born in 1777 into one of the most distinguished noble families of Wallachia, which was then a tributary province on the Ottoman Empire's northern frontier: it was ruled by princes appointed from the Greek or Greek-speaking Orthodox elite of Istanbul, but the nobility remained largely Romanian. The family had been active in Wallachian politics for over a hundred years: Dinicu's great-grandfather Radu had in the early eighteenth century attempted to bring the province under Austrian rule, and pleaded with the Emperor that should this plan fail, the Porte might at least be persuaded to let Wallachia be ruled by 'a true Wallachian' and not a Greek (Abramos, Golescu and Ştirbei 1718: 208). But by the end of the century, a relatively harmonious symbiotic relationship had grown up between Romanian and Greek elites, and Dinicu and his older brother George ('Iordache') received a good education in Greek at the school in Bucharest. Iordache in particular had links with liberal and enlightened Greek patriots in the Principalities, and is mentioned in a document of 1797 as being party to a revolutionary plot alongside the famous Greek patriot Rigas Fereos (Elian 2003: 296–97). For his part, Dinicu married a Greek woman, Zoe Farfara (1792–1879) renowned for her spirit and beauty, and testified in his *Account* that he felt more comfortable writing in that language.

The public culture of Wallachia was thus dominated by a small Greek-speaking elite who dabbled in secular literature and whose works circulated mainly in manuscript; the few that appeared in book form did so largely on the presses of the Greek merchant communities in Vienna and Venice. Iordache Golescu, for instance, published an atlas at Vienna in 1800 (*BRV* 2: 420–21). However, the princes did not neglect Romanian and it was under their rule that Romanian replaced Slavonic as the language of liturgy and prayer in the country's (overwhelmingly Orthodox) churches; Romanian also remained the language of administration, and, while absorbing a large number of Greek and Turkish loan words, developed considerably as an instrument of bureaucratic communication in the period.

Numerous contemporary Western observers referred to the changing culture of Wallachia in terms of its Europeanness. The philosopher Jeremy Bentham passed through Bucharest in 1786 on his way to visit his brother in Russia and noticed a couple of 'Europeanized' boyars, although he considered the majority of the inhabitants to be 'vegetables' (Bentham 1971: 438); four years later a French count who had fled the Revolution described the nobility 'mixing European grace with that Asiatic negligence which has something noble and tender about it' (Salaberry 1799: 115–16). A Scotsman, William Macmichael, found 'the combination of Oriental and European manners and costume' to be 'irresistibly ludicrous. The boyar looks like a grave Mahometan; but speak to him, and instead of the pompous and magnificent sounds of the Turkish idiom, he will address you in tolerable French, and talk of novels, faro, and whist' (Macmichael 1819: 83). Many other British and European travellers echoed their comments (Djuvara 1989). Such characterizations were not especially specific to Bucharest: similar comparative terms had been used by the Comte de Ségur and the Prince de Ligne about eighteenth-century Russia (Wolff 1994: 22).

Occasional echoes of this language can be found in Greek and Romanian documents from the late eighteenth century onwards (e.g. Camariano-Cioran 1974: 80–81, 222, 330, 578). Reservations were also formulated, such as those of the monk Gregory of Râmnic writing in 1798:

> [T]he Rumanian land [...] is located in a select part of Europe, has a
> healthy and fine air, and neighbours upon peoples who pride themselves
> on and rejoice in the philosophical sciences, all these being easy means to
> bring up the sons of this our own Fatherland to the high standards of the
> other Europeans in many sciences. But even so, the Romanian inhabitants
> of this God-protected land did not often spend time in those [countries].
> They, since receiving the light of Orthodoxy, have busied themselves
> rather with the establishment of the faith in their own land [...] they have
> so little dependence upon, or need for, superficial intelligence, in order to

attain the qualities attributed by geographers to Europe; but are always supported by the undefeated arm of Holy care. (Preface to *Triod*, in BRV 3: 406–7)

But at least a dozen writers in the decade before Golescu's travels were published made reference to the intellectual, social and economic benefits of 'enlightened Europe' (Duţu 1967, 1980; Georgescu 1971: 40–43; Marino 1981).

One significant aspect of the Romanian idea of Europe, missing from the otherwise excellent accounts given by the Romanian scholars I have just cited, is the place of Russia. But it is quite clear that in this period, 'Europe' meant as much Russia (which in 1826 established a protectorate lasting until the Crimean War) as contact with Britain or France. Supposedly the very first favourable evocation of 'European' civilization in modern Romanian culture, in Metropolitan of Moldavia Gavriil Callimachi's 1773 preface to his translation of Empress Catherine the Great's *Nakaz* ('Instruction'), only referred to the Academies of Europe to note their astonishment at the achievements of the Russian army (*BRV* 2: 202).[2] Twenty years later, the boyar historian Ienăchiţă Văcărescu described the next Russian occupation of Wallachia as bringing Europe to that province (along with the slightly disappointing news, given that he held princely ambitions, that 'in Europe they don't make absolute princes' [Văcărescu 1982: 261]). Eufrosin Poteca, a monk who took some students to France and Italy under the patronage of the Metropolitan of Wallachia in 1820 affirmed that: 'Peter the Great was the glory of Europe, to be praised for his goodness' whereas 'Napoleon, the scourge of Europe, is to be praised for his wickedness' (Bianu 1888: 423). In 1825 the poet Barbu Mumuleanu, in a fairly clear reference to Russia, argued that Romanians should imitate 'not just western Europeans, but also easterners' (Preface to *Caracteruri* ('Characters'), in *BRV* 3: 466). And when a Russian army again invaded the Principalities in 1828, their Minister Plenipotentiary General Pavel Kiselev presented the result as bringing these provinces into 'the great European family' (Hurmuzaki Supl. 1, iv: 359). As we shall see, Golescu was very much party to this Russian connection.

Revolt

In March 1821 a rather disorganized group of insurgents under the leadership of Alexander Ypsilantis, son and grandson of Phanariot princes of Wallachia, invaded the Principalities from Russia, claiming that power's support and asserting that 'Long ago the people of Europe invited us to imitation' (Proclamation, translated in Clogg 1976: 201).

The ostensible aim was the establishment of an autonomous Christian state from some or other of the European possessions of the Ottoman Empire. Although in the medium term this movement was successful, leading to the establishment of an independent Greece by 1830, the short-term effects in Wallachia were fairly disastrous. Claims to have the support of Russia were disavowed by Tsar Alexander I; Romanian insurgents in Oltenia (western, or 'Little' Wallachia) who had initially engaged to collaborate with the Greeks turned against the movement and, under the leadership of Tudor Vladimirescu, resisted Ypsilantis 'in the name of the people'. Tudor was killed and Ypsilantis fled to Austria; an Ottoman army eventually occupied both Moldavia and Wallachia. Golescu was heavily involved in these events, apparently acting as an intermediary between the Greek and Romanian elites and the insurgent peasantry (Tudor had occupied his house in Bucharest). His band of Gypsy musicians, playing at the head of the Greek army, were among the few survivors of the Ottoman onslaught at the battle of Drăgăşani which put an end to the sorry revolt (*Documente 1821* 5: 318, 436).

Golescu fled to Kronstadt in Habsburg Transylvania (today's Braşov, Romania). This was the traditional place of refuge of the Wallachian elite in times of instability. Here a series of political groupings formed: some under the influence of the Russian consul, an excitable Greek named Pinis; some inclined to seek support from Austria; a few remaining independent.[3] In April 1822, a group was summoned to Silistra on the Danube to negotiate with the Ottoman authorities; from there they proceeded to Istanbul, where one of their number, Grigore Ghica, was appointed Prince. This provoked outbursts of criticism from the Kronstadt group, including Dinicu and especially his brother Iordache, who wrote a series of excoriating satires on Ghica and his associates (I. Golescu 1990; cf. Hurmuzaki 16: 1051–92; *Revoluţia* 1: 466–70; and IAkovenko 1834, Letter 27). Dinicu's signature is to be found on a memorandum addressed to the Tsar from August 1822 and on a letter addressed to Ghica in November of the same year, politely refusing a request to come home, pleading lack of funds (Vîrtosu 1932: 141, 167–72; *Documente 1821* 3: 130–33, and 5: 347; IAkovenko 1834, Letter 31). But he clearly remained of the 'Russian' party, and indeed travelled to that country from Kronstadt in February 1823, according to a note by the Prussian consul (Hurmuzaki, 10: 211).

The French consul noted in May 1825 that a boyar called Golescu went down on his knees to beg with the prince to be allowed to send his two sons to the Institut Lemoine in Paris, and was given a passport only as far as the Austrian border (Hurmuzaki, 17: 17–18). This could be Dinicu, but could equally well refer to Iordache, whose presence in Bucharest is attested in this period and whose sons did indeed receive a Parisian education. Meanwhile, Dinicu says in his book that he travelled from Braşov, not Bucharest; he and the other exiled boyars were awaiting the accreditation of the Russian consul Minciaky by the Porte before returning, which had still not happened by June 1825 (Hurmuzaki, 10: 272–73; I. Golescu 1990: 56; *Acte şi fragmente* 2: 706–13). His will, from November 1825, does not give a place of composition (D. Golescu 1990: 349–51). Around this time, alongside a group of known Russophiles, he signed a letter of condolence to Tsar Nicholas I on the death of the latter's brother and predecessor, Alexander I (Hurmuzaki 10: 599). In early 1826, he announced the establishment of a school on his estate at Goleşti, and invited prospective pupils to present themselves by May. He appears to have been in Pest in May, and in Braşov in August 1826 (Anghelescu 1990: xxx). In June, according to a report by the Russian emissary Liprandi, he was involved in a plot to rouse the frontier soldiers of Oltenia against Ghica (*Documente 1821* 3: 354, and 5: 358–59; cf. IAkovenko 1834, Letter 51; Hurmuzaki, 10: 361–64; Vîrtosu 1932: 222–30; Georgescu 1962, 210–18).

Dinicu's book itself offers only sparse details about the precise timing of his travels.[4] As the title states, he was on the road in 1824, 1825, and 1826. The narrative is divided into sections: the first and longest treats places in Transylvania, Hungary, Austria and Habsburg Italy. A second, much shorter section notes three separate routes to Pest, and mentions trips to Mehadia in the Banat of Temesvar, and to the Székely region of eastern Transylvania. However, he refers to being in Pressburg (today's Bratislava, Slovakia) in September 1825 (17), and in Mehadia in 1824 (103), which means he is not recounting his travels in the order in which he undertook them. The third section describes how 'in the year 1826 I travelled again from Braşov to Bavaria and Switzerland' (85). In this last section, he mentions being on the way back home from Vienna on 20th November. Anghelescu (1990: xxx) suggests that Golescu undertook this last journey *after* having submitted his account of the first two to the censor, whose stamp of approval is dated September 1826. As the account of the third journey is relatively short, this is not impossible.

Nor has the question of *why* he went West been fully answered. The standard literary histories (G. Călinescu 1988) write that he went in 1824 to place his sons in educational establishments in Geneva and Munich, but Golescu himself ascribed only his 1826 journey to this motive. Others are 'certain' that his trip to Italy had a conspiratorial purpose involving links to Italian secret societies (Stan 1977; Lăsconi 1998). This possibility is not to be excluded, but cannot be documented either. In Geneva and Munich, Greek emigrés and students, and local Philhellenes prepared to support young Wallachians, have been identified (Pippidi 1980: 295–314; Kotsowilis 1993). In Italy, similar groups existed in Pisa, where some Romanians were also studying (Marcu 1930), but Golescu did not visit this city.

This was a time of exceptional political tension in the Principalities and indeed throughout the Near East. In March 1826 Russia presented the Porte with an ultimatum to withdraw their troops from the Principalities, or face war; a position which was accepted only in May. In November the Treaty of Akkerman confirmed Russia's mandate to act as protector of the rights of the Christian inhabitants of the Principalities, and required that the prince be elected with the consent of the boyars rather than at the whim of the Porte. As this was not the case for Ghica, he was reluctant to make the provisions of the treaty known (Georgescu 1962: 229–30). It was Golescu who had the treaty published, together with extracts from previous treaties upholding Wallachian rights, a fact which was remarked upon in Bucharest and elsewhere, as we know from a minor boyar's diary which has been preserved (Andronescu 1947: 51; Anghelescu 1990: 429–31 notes other echoes). The Russian ambassador-in-waiting to the Porte finally left to take up his post in Constantinople at the end of 1826: passing through Bucharest, he was showered with complaints and protests from the boyars, which he nevertheless chose not to take further (Hurmuzaki 10: 385–409; Georgescu 1962, 49–54).

Reconstructing Golescu's activity in the last three years of his life is no easier than for earlier periods. In 1827 he apparently set up a literary society, which met in his house in Bucharest, and sponsored a Romanian-language newspaper which appeared for a few numbers in Leipzig (Cristea 1967). Also in 1827, Golescu published another work at Buda, his translation of the *Elements of Moral Philosophy* of the Greek scholar Neophytos Vamvas, later Professor of Philosophy at the University of Athens. In May the following year the Principalities were occupied by the Russian army, and a military quarantine set up: a couple of letters have survived from Golescu to Professor Thiersch in Munich informing the latter that 'unforeseen circumstances' have prevented him from travelling to Germany that year (Anghelescu 1990: 362–64). At the end of the year he managed to get Russian support for the publication of a journal in Romanian in Bucharest, *Curierul rumânesc* ('The Romanian messenger'). The first number appeared in April 1829: the journal lasted twenty years and made a decisive contribution to the permanent establishment of a public literary culture in Romania. Golescu's travel book is mentioned in the first issue.

The following year, it was noted that Golescu had compiled a statistical map of Wallachia, including:

> all the counties and their demarcations, the towns, districts and ports both in the uplands and on the Danube, the quarantines, the livestock exchange markets, the paths, the sub-lieutenancies, the villages, families, priests, deacons, boyars, sons of boyars, company men, pandour soldiers,

foreigners, gypsies, Armenians, and Jews, monasteries, metochs, domestic and dedicated sketes, lakes, fisheries, sawmills, wine presses, rivers, streams, brooks, fairs, weekly markets, minerals and the productions of each county. (*BAPR* 1: 567)

This is probably the same as the 'Russian statistical map' produced in 1835 (Giurescu 1957). Ironically for one who had awaited the arrival of the Russians with such high hopes, Golescu was killed by something unexpected they brought to the Principalities: cholera. On 5th November 1830, his death was announced in the newspaper he had helped establish. His brother Iordache was appointed Grand Logothete [Chancellor] of Wallachia in his stead (*BAPR* 1: 567, 1170).

A Traveller's Fortunes

The idea of the whole of Romania's modernization being caused by a travel text can of course only be read symbolically. If we wanted to take it literally, we would have to propose and accept something like the following scenario:

- Golescu travels, and is astonished by the West;
- he consigns his impressions to writing;
- he publishes his book;
- people read it and become aware of their country's shortcomings;
- as a result, they implement modernizing policies;
- then they suffer identity traumas on account of the rupture between the old world which represented their traditional culture and the new world they are trying to join.

Even if we were prepared to admit this very schematic view of the relationship between travel, writing, reading and action, it would be pretty much unhistorical in Golescu's case because of a small fact, overlooked in most histories of Romanian literature and culture: few people appear to have read Golescu's book at all in the seventy or eighty years since it was published. Between 1826 and the critical rehabilitation undertaken by Pompiliu Eliade in 1905, there are barely a dozen references to Golescu's *Account* (Anghelescu 1990: xl–xli, 355–57). A second edition did not appear until 1910: this was prepared by the bibliographer Nerva Hodoş, who had married an indirect descendent of Dinicu's, and by his own account, had great difficulty persuading a publisher to accept the project (Hodoş 1910: lx–lxi). Only one author of a nineteenth-century Romanian travel text actually seems to have had a detailed knowledge of Golescu's work.[5]

If this were not enough, one can draw attention to the fact that a tendency to consider oneself inferior in relation to neighbouring countries, and a desire to reform, were not particularly new elements in Romanian culture. Numerous statements from Romanian chroniclers of the early eighteenth century evinced a strong consciousness of inferiority to Western (or at least 'neighbouring') countries (Marino 2001; Martin 2002: 20–24). In 1818, eight years before Golescu's book was published, the teacher George Lazăr declared at the opening of the Romanian school in Bucharest that the Romanian language and their people had been left 'weaker, lower down and more ridiculed than all the other languages and people on the face of the earth' (Bogdan-Duică and Popa-Lisseanu 1924: 20). The idea that Golescu's text substantially influenced subsequent generations cannot be sustained. Most scholars simply affirm it as part of the received wisdom: others actually mispresent the evidence to buttress this claim.[6] Despite generations of historians insisting on the complexity of processes of change, it is always seductive to have them represented by an individual actor, with a good story to tell. The idea of a journey, a text and an œuvre of historical achievement have become inextricably interwoven (cf. Grivel 1994: 256–57).

An Alternative Route

Part of the problem may lie with the assumption that a travel account – and in Golescu's case, we have little other documentation about him from his own pen – provides sincere and unbarred access to the itinerary of its author's life and mind. But although predicated upon the idea of an exceptional experience, its purpose is not necessarily to record and convey emotional states. As numerous scholars have noted, travel writing may often function as a pretext for ethical or aesthetic digression, and has affinities with the sermon, the essay and the romance as well as the log book (Fussell 1980: 202–15; Hall 1989; Nemoianu 1992). Critics have also compared Golescu's text to the fable, and commented on the way in which its author prefers the exaltation of an exemplary ideal to the banalities of a general narration (Iorgulescu 1979: 20; Ioncioaia 1996: 416, 427). Another has observed that introductions to Romanian books in this period 'do not discuss the content of the writings, but, at a general level, eulogize the moral consequences of reading them' (Hanța 1985: 254).

In his preface, then, Golescu does not tell us why he travelled, or when, but rather concentrates on why he has taken account of what he has seen, and why he is giving an account of it to his people.

[Europe] makes her nations happy through the communication of goodness gathered through the travels made by some nations in the lands of others, and through publishing them in books.

Europe is full, as of other things, so of such books. There is no corner of the Earth so overlooked, no country, no city, no village unknown to a single European, so long as he knows how to read. But we, in order to know our country well, have to obtain this knowledge by reading some book written by a European. There are a great number of histories of the Romanian Land in Europe, written in her languages, and in the Romanian language, but still by foreigners; while there is no mention of one made by a native of this land. [...] When many of the noble youth of our Fatherland, after having completed a course of studies in enlightened Europe, have returned to the Fatherland, we can obtain from them many translations of books into the national language, as a means towards enlightenment, ornament, and the good organization of our Fatherland. It is time for us to wake up, like good landlords who when they go out of their houses acquire things for themselves but also for their fellow householders; so we, gathering good things either by reading good and useful books, or by travelling, or by encounters and gatherings with men from the enlightened nations, should share them with our compatriots and plant them in our land, in the hope of a hundredfold yield, and that we too may obtain from our descendants the gratitude heard by those of our fathers and grandfathers who left to us a good thing either discovered by themselves or taken from others. (4)

The relationship between travel, social communication, and patriotic improvement is stressed; more particularly, that between travel *books* and the public good. Travelling is, it turns out, really no different from reading: they are both mere means for the attainment of improving knowledge. But although Golescu criticizes his people for having neglected this genre of writing, he situates his own text within an already existing native tradition of literary culture, which he links back in time to the fifteenth-century Prince Vlad the Impaler and ultimately to Cyril and Methodius, 'the creators of the Romanian word' (4) – for, unlike some of his Romanian contemporaries, Golescu saw nothing unnatural in the use of the traditional Cyrillic alphabet. Moreover, despite his insistence on the European travel writing tradition, he cites no specific works that he used as a model. The first Romanian travel text thereby becomes *both* a borrowing from Europe *and* a continuation of an identifiable preexisting cultural tradition (as Duţu 1972: 231 showed).

The focus of Golescu's text oscillates throughout between two principal objects. There are descriptions of places, ostensibly in the order in which the author has travelled through them, with not infrequent notes on routes, distances, means and conditions of travel, etc. Interspersed with these, there are what Golescu calls 'separate discourses' (*cuvântări deosebite*), in which he praises some institution or practice encountered abroad, often going on to criticize its Wallachian equivalent. By summarizing briefly the content of these 'discourses' or homilies, I hope both to give an idea of the kinds of things that caught Golescu's attention, and to enable an understanding of their rhetorical function within the economy of his text as a whole:

- the gratifying manifestations of mutual honour and love between sovereign and people at the coronation of Francis II at Pressburg (18–19);
- the sights of Vienna, architectural, aesthetic, civil: their superiority to home (21);
- the city's internal messenger service, its superiority to domestic arrangements: 'how useful this intra-urban post would be in our country, so those who come awaiting replies need tremble no longer in doors and hallways, or come twenty times after a single piece of business; despatchees would no longer have to be told "come tomorrow at such-and-such a time" and, on coming, find that the boyar had left long ago (reproach me not, Brother Reader, where you find the truth, but hold your tongue until you find a false representation or some custom which is also followed in other parts of the enlightened world, and whose practice in our country is therefore nothing outlandish - and then, and only then, may you reproach me)' (24–25);
- Vienna's philanthropic institutions (26–27);
- its hospitals (27–28);
- its schools (28);
- how the above should be entrusted to the state, not the church, or at least to a church working for the Fatherland (30–33);
- how the monarch nods to the people; its difference from the custom at home (34);
- how the Viennese women don't make abusive use of luxury – their dress is relatively similar to that of lower people, unlike at home (35–36);
- how a poor merchant at Baden (outside Vienna), through patient and applied hard work, made a small fortune for himself; followed by a long description of the unjust treatment of the peasantry in Wallachia, and a disquisition on the nature of patriotism and its absence at home (46–58);
- the neat clothing of the field labourers around Graz, compared to the ragged clothing at home (60);
- how at Vicenza even peasants go to the theatre to improve themselves, unlike in Bucharest, which, although a much bigger town, has only one theatre and the performances are in German. How an Englishman he met in Vienna found this situation ridiculous. His shame (70–71);

- the Romanians of the Banat of Temesvar. Like us but happier, because they are working in a better system (79–80);
- how good the baths at Mehadia are, built at the Empress's personal expense. 'We haven't yet become enlightened enough to make such things for the public good' (81);
- the idea of wealth: wealth of the community is the best kind, rather than the wealth which creates social inequality (82–85);
- how people dress; the equal terms on which different social classes greet each other (87–89);
- the domestic economy admired during a visit to a country cottage (97–98);
- how no buildings or institutions endure in Wallachia compared to Switzerland (100);
- how a peasant in Altsteten knows to distinguish Kronstadt in Transylvania from Kronstadt in Russia. Golescu compares this to a letter he received in 1824 from the logothete's Chancery in Bucharest addressed to Mehadia, Transylvania (inaccurately, for Mehadia is not in Transylvania but in the Banat of Temesvar) (103);
- the excellence of the inns in Europe (105–6);
- the University of Geneva, the superiority of their system of education to ours (108–11);
- the benefits of factories and the disadvantages of exporting raw materials (111–12);
- end: 'and from here, going back straight to Vienna, and having nothing more to write about the journey, I imagine that I ought to consider myself guilty for not finishing by praising a second time the agreeable and peaceable life of the Viennese, the beauty of the many walks around Vienna and the continuous lighting, from evening until day, in the whole of the park surrounding the fortress of Vienna.

And as hope remains with every man who finds himself still upon this earth, I too had hoped, and entertain the idea that the time will surely come when my Fatherland, I do not say in a few years, will exactly resemble the great cities that I have seen, but at least the first step will have been taken to bring all peoples towards happiness, which step is only Union for the common good, as I have said many times.' (116)

Cuvântări (from *cuvânt*, 'word') means discourses in the sense of speeches, and they have the quality of spoken harangues, a kind of orality influenced both by the almost universal fact of illiteracy in Wallachian society, and by the study of ancient rhetoric so integral to elite education in the period (Duțu 1971: 70–83; Diaconescu 1978; Anghelescu 1991 posits Xenophon and Fénelon as potential models).

Golescu also appeals a great deal to exclamation, to the authority of personal experience, to the testimony of emotion, and to general principles of behaviour or social harmony. He is aware that his habit of breaking off his description in order to speak about his home country may sometimes irritate the reader, or that his strictures may appear excessive: he excuses or justifies himself several times. But he insists on them: 'I have digressed greatly from my description of Vienna, but my soul was also greatly embittered on seeing the happiness of other nations' (21). The description itself thereby becomes somewhat demoted, a mechanical succession of observed facts, a kind of Russian roulette of annotations which may or may not trigger long moral disquisitions: if it doesn't, it descends into virtual meaninglessness. Barthes has written about the orientalist writing of Pierre Loti in terms of its approach to incident, as a technique for suggesting the languidity of the eventless East: 'what may *barely* be noted: a kind of degree zero of notation, no more than it takes to write merely *something*' (Barthes 1972: 173); Golescu's writing, in contrast, is full of *noted somethings*, but only some of them turn into incident and 'cause' discourses. His 'travels' from descriptive to discursive mode are remarkably abrupt:

> Returning from Geneva, I didn't follow the same road, but in order to see more things in Switzerland, as well as those famous Rhine Falls and to go further into the Duchy of Baden and the Kingdom of Würtemberg, I took a different route from the Morat station going through Aarberg, where the Aar river passes, and where the boundary runs between the Cantons of Bern and Solothurn, which latter has a population of 47,800 souls; Solothurn, a large town, through the middle of which the Aar River runs, with bridges for the communication of the townsfolk; Wiedlisbach, a fortified town; Der Mühle, a fort; Olten, a town on the side of the river Aar, which passes on a standing bridge [an aqueduct]; Aarau, a town in which cloth factories are up and running; Wildegg, where there is a factory for printed textiles.

Separate Discourse

> This multitude of factories can be found in all European provinces, for with these factories each government benefits its people, for that reason they give a variety of incentives to those who establish factories, rather than the reverse, for the princes to take their money because they have factories. (111)

And at the end of a 'discourse', he switches equally abruptly from sermonizing mode to the most minutious materialities of transportation:

> May the merciful Lord turn his eyes towards these people, turning wicked hearts into merciful ones, money-hungry ones into generous ones, and those overcome by bad habits into virtue.
>
> From Vienna to Trieste there are the following stops, which I couldn't take much notice of, for both when I went and when I returned I travelled by

Ailwagen, which runs without stopping day and night, pausing only at preestablished places for lunch and dinner. (58)

The word *'Ailwagen'* (German *'Eilwagen'*, express coach) is then glossed in very great detail in a footnote two pages long.

As for the idea of Europe, it is not in fact the principal object of Golescu's attention. He does not define it specifically. Nevertheless, it is worth reconstructing his usage of the term, if only to understand where travel books come from – for, as already noted, 'Europe is full, as of other things, so of such books' (4). What are those 'other things' Europe contains? The references are in fact rather incidental, for instance to 'a course of studies in enlightened Europe' (4); to 'the noble orders, distributed in all of Europe' (50); to the need 'to serve the fatherland, as it is served in all Europe [...] and then each and every one of us will attain true honour and happiness, and the people will in a few years not fail to reach the same level as the other nations of Europe' (52); 'Thiersch, that Professor famous in all Europe' (95).[7] One might be tempted to conclude that Golescu's Europe is not so much a place as a series of abstracted ideas: order, civilization, and particularly social harmony. It is clear, however, that he builds this idea on his conception of place. Despite his relatively positive assessment of Hungary and Transylvania – the social virtues he mentions are, apparently, already present in the Saxon villages around Kronstadt – he does not describe anything as 'European' until at least halfway through his description of Vienna.[8] I have already pointed out that Golescu's manner of composition involves placing all his data concerning a given town in a given section, irrespective of the order of travel in which he came by it (Fassel 2003 distinguishes between travel texts which describe routes in 'longitudinal sections' and those more particularly dedicated to describing places in 'cross sections'). And although he makes conscientious notes on his route, and the conditions of his journey, Golescu is principally concerned with cross-sections of towns, which form the basis of his chapter structures: they become objectified and distinct, like the reigns of kings in an old chronicle.

Compared to this, Golescu's Fatherland, the ostensible object of his love and the comparative referent for his accumulation of knowledge, has no concrete specificity: he refers to it in terms of its poor condition, not its topography. At one stage he even asks 'Where is that corner called the Fatherland?' (57) He attributes the question to 'that noted father Kone', whom Anghelescu (1990: xxiv) has identified with the German educationalist J.H. Campe, but who must surely be the patriotic poet Carl Theodor Körner, author of the very popular song 'Mein Vaterland' (1813), which begins, 'Wo ist des Sängers Vaterland?' But whereas Körner had given a rousing answer,[9] Golescu says that when he asked the citizens of Wallachia this question, then, 'the man of the people burst into tears; the boyar judge knitted his eyebrows and kept a dark silence; the soldier cursed me; the courtesan whistled at me; and the government tax farmer asked me "this word *patrie*, is it a kind of rent, or what?"' (57). It is as if another element of Wallachia's frequently attested inferiority were its failure to coagulate into a real place. For instance, Golescu gives a description of Kronstadt at the beginning of his book ostensibly as if it were the first city he arrived at, although he later reveals Kronstadt as having been his point of departure. He was describing the city for a Wallachian audience, but he had not come to it from Wallachia as part of his journey: it is describable because 'other' and exemplary, not because travelled to. The point of writing about abroad, then, becomes to create models for the Fatherland, which, Golescu hopes, 'I do not say in a few years, will exactly resemble the great cities that I have seen' (116). His problem, then, is not to topographize Wallachia – others in this period were engaged in that task, and Golescu would later continue their work[10] – but to create the terms on which it could exist.

It is a political question, more than an ontological one. For Golescu, the question asked of Montesquieu's imaginary Oriental travellers in France, 'How can one be Persian?' would not have been especially meaningful: he is not particularly prone to doubting the integrity of his own psychic identity. Golescu has been identified with the anonymous boyar mentioned by a French observer in 1821 as saying 'We are never ourselves', and 'Do we always have to be looked upon as not belonging at all to the great European family?' (Pippidi 1985: 1191). Although this is not impossible, the idea of personal inauthenticity or fragmented identity does not emerge clearly anywhere in Golescu's *Account*.[11] Now that scholars of Romanticism no longer consider the idea of profundity as obligatory when describing the Western self – 'the notion of internal depth served as only one of many models of subjectivity during the Romantic period' (Henderson 1996: 163) – then perhaps writers from marginal cultures could be let off from being described as 'fragmented' if the description doesn't fit the personality. In fact I am not sure we should speak about Golescu's personality so much as about his persona, for the represented self is 'always already oriented towards an audience' (Jürgen Habermas, in Chakrabarty 2000: 35; cf. Elliott 1982). He describes his 'great shame' on discussing the Bucharest theatre with an Englishman in Vienna, and admits to having personally committed 'a great error' in maltreating the peasantry, but these are precisely conditions which require an integral self to assume them. Rather than positing a 'split consciousness', then, perhaps it is better to compare Golescu's literary and political stratagems to the 'double consciousness' of Persian Occidentalist writers of the same period, 'whereby Persianate ethical standards were used to evaluate European cultural practices and European perspectives were deployed for the censuring of Indian and Iranian societies'.[12]

Golescu is considerably more veiled in his direct references to the present state of Wallachia. He has good words for the Prince: 'now that the Princedom has been entrusted to the hands of a native ruler, his Majesty Gregory Ghica Voevod, and the National Schools have been established [...] the time has come for us to awaken' (18). However, an apparently apolitical collection of proverbs which Golescu published at Buda at the same time contained very pointed criticisms which could easily be read as addressed to Ghica's government (Duțu 1971: 70–83). Golescu also may well have sponsored the translation of parts of the British traveller Thomas Thornton's *Present State of Turkey* (1807), which offered a damning critique of the system under which Wallachia was ruled: the anonymous author of the preface emphasized the shame of the Wallachians that their country appeared to European travellers to be so badly governed, but justified the publication of his work by arguing that the European evaluation was correct:

> [S]ome would reproach me and, I think rather would defame and curse me, saying: that I thought it was clever to bring to light and publish slanders against an entire nation. If I were to hear people saying this, or were they to ask me, I would reply that they have no reason to get upset or angry at me; for everybody reading it should realise that, that Englishman being a foreigner, and having no personal quarrel with any of the locals, wrote nothing false about the deeds and customs practised in Wallachia and Moldavia; nor did he pass over or ignore the excellent natural resources or the wretchedness of the poor inhabitants of those Principalities; but he wrote about the good things with sweetness and a humble heart; and like a member of a free nation, he wrote without shame and listed with his pen for ridicule those things worthy of defamation and jeering. When I read and saw these things, the quickness of shame overtook me, disgust at the wretchedness of my nation penetrated me, their shameful deeds, their slanderous things, idiocies, wretched habits, idlenesses, lazinesses, false expectations, sleepiness, deceit, blunder, theft, rape, punishment, torture and failure to attend to the beneficial, enlightening teachings and crafts. Seeing all these things told and written and printed in all the languages of Europe; and most of the libraries and most of the houses of the Europeans full of such books, and the people laughing while reading them and poking fun at us, just like we Romanians do for Gypsies [...] tell me, dear reader, without feigning and with a clean heart, whether I am guilty because I translated this rather short description into the language of the Fatherland? (*BRV* 3: 519–20)

In his *Account* Golescu makes exactly the same criticisms of Wallachia as the anonymous translator of Thornton's *Present State*:

[O]n account of this [luxury], we have been hit by poverty and the extinction of families, we have come to be ridiculed in the world's opinion, and foreign pens have painted us accordingly. But what good will it do us if we want to keep such things hidden amongst ourselves, and we make believe that they are not known, when all nations read them, as they are written by people who wish us ill? It is better for us to know them, to acknowledge them, and make a determined decision to rectify ourselves, protecting our Fatherland from these fires and conflagrations, for luxury and unlawful appropriation have wiped us off the face of the Earth, depriving everybody of any of the slightest honesty that might belong to a nation. (29)

These can be read in terms of a wider impatience with Ghica's rule which opposition boyars sought to contest by referring to a European model. For instance, Iordache Golescu used the idea of 'the Europeans' reproach' when chastising Ghica for not supporting education in the national language in 1823: 'Foreigners founded these schools and established their revenues, and, now that a native reigns over our nation, we are trying to keep the place in the ignorance, darkness and barbarism for which the Europeans rightly reproach us!' (cited in Hurmuzaki 10: 248). Dinicu's *Account* is full of such protests, directed less explicitly but still clearly enough against the status quo: 'The schools which, under the pretext of improvement, have been ruined in recent years, for which I would have taken up my pen against the foreigners, did I not know that they had plenty of assistance from the natives' (31). This is in fact a quite specific reference which would have been understood at the time to refer to the widespread scapegoating of foreigners, particularly Greeks, that the Ghica regime had more or less systematically undertaken. In a supplication presented in Turkish to the Grand Vizier in 1822, Ghica and his boyars promised to 'abolish and ruin' the 'Greek schools' in order to 'stop the disorder at its root' (Mehmet 1971: 76). The idea of expelling 'all the Greek boyars and the ones of Albanian and Bulgarian race' from 'Rumelia' 'since those of Greek race had occasioned so many betrayals, that it is not right that princes should be named again from among them' was proposed in a *telhis* (report) by the Grand Vizier and approved by the Sultan (ibid.: 66–7). The latter's *ferman* (edict), nominating Ghica, cast the exiles of Kronstadt as the 'Greek party' in contrast to the 'native boyars' (*Documente 1821* 5: 144–45), although in fact each group contained both Greeks and Wallachians. This official xenophobia was then echoed by a number of lesser writers in Wallachia in 1822 and 1823 (Naum Râmniceanu 1987; Zilot Românul 1987; Gheorghe Lazăr, speech on Ghica's arrival, in Bogdan-Duică and Popa-Lisseanu 1924: 29–45; memoranda in Vîrtosu 1932: 117–40, 158–61, 178–222; Mumuleanu 1825). Many of Golescu's critiques implicitly or explicitly unmask this cheap nationalist rhetoric and make it clear that the exploitation of the Principalities was the fault of 'both natives and foreigners' (20). Elsewhere he states that 'luxury and idleness', not 'foreigners', are the enemy of the fatherland (57).

Passages like the following also suggest a more urgent impatience with the present state of affairs, than a merely general interest in 'awakening' can explain. He asserts that, now that there is a native prince, 'there should be no more hanging around but an immediate embrace of enlightenment' (53), and later:

> Oh, most powerful father of all nations! Will this dark cloud, full of trials and wickedness, never lift from above the Romanian nation? Will we not be absolved once and for all of all our wants? Will we not be worthy to see a ray of light pointing us towards general happiness? But what am I saying? A ray? See, the whole light has shown itself, sent by the most merciful God, through the most powerful protector and defender of our Fatherland who awaits from us but a small and simple act – I mean union – for public happiness, for, with this, all satisfactions will come. (112)

In other words, he was not some unworldly middle-aged Oriental gentleman who suddenly took it upon himself to have a look at life in the West, but an astute and active political strategist pursuing a clear oppositional line to a hesitant and fragile regime. The idea of a travel text having political stakes was very widespread in European culture: Swift had satirized the crude functionalism of such a conception in *Gulliver's Travels*. In Germany and Russia, the genre of travel had been exploited by ambitious young men not only to convey models for 'correct' appreciation of sentimental and literary experience of the West but also as a stick with which to beat the present regime and advance one's own ambitions (Stewart 1978; Knopper 1995; on Russia, Roboli 1985; Jones 1984). It would soon spread further eastwards: in the same year as Golescu published his book, an Arab travelled from north Africa to France and subsequently composed an account which was considered to be 'a veritable repertoire of reforms' (at-Tahtâwî 1988: 16).

But did publication raise consciousness? As already noted, echoes of Golescu's *Account* in nineteenth-century Romanian culture are remarkable by their absence. Books and essays on 'Europe' appeared in Turkish, Arabic and even Georgian in the 1830s and 1840s, advocating reform and justifying travel accounts by reference to their utility for the fatherland.[13] But subsequent Romanian travel publications in book form are few before 1860, and do not particularly deal with western Europe: there is an account of a journey to Moscow on official business in the early 1830s (Asachi 1964), and another to Constantinople in 1844 (Codrescu 1844). Most of the travel sketches in Romanian periodicals in the 1830s and 1840s treat domestic scenes: they are busier constructing the fatherland than describing abroad.[14] Some private letters and diaries from the 1820s and 1830s described the West, but in nothing like the tones used by Golescu: although favourable overall, they were also sometimes quite critical, and also made full use of the relatively free intimacy of the epistolary mode, not always seeking to come to global judgments about 'Europe'.[15] This provides further evidence that Romanian encounters with the West at the beginning of the nineteenth century need not necessarily be interpreted in terms of a psychological crisis. Golescu's account is not representative: his publication of it might be, but rather in terms of political strategy than naive acceptance of European models.

Golescu, then, turned his experience into a public text – what Dipesh Chakrabarty, discussing the various modes and uses of patriotic Indian autobiographies, has called a 'transition narrative' (Chakrabarty 2000: 30–34). However, despite his fervently-proclaimed Europhilia and his clear proclamation of his 'shame' and 'error', there is no reason to see Golescu's writing self as 'colonized' by European imperialist frameworks. To give just one further example, although he proclaims the exemplarity of European travel accounts, he does not seem to have followed any particular European model. Just as scholars have begun to appreciate that not all non-Western forms of autobiography are derivative of Western types of self-expression (Reynolds 2001), so we can see Golescu as using a variety of both domestic and foreign rhetorical devices in the service both of cosmopolitan patriotism and of personal ambition. To conclude, his text tells us less than we might wish to know about Romanian identity at the beginning of the nineteenth century. We may or may not wish to read the literary criticism as symptomatic of twentieth-century dilemmas (as Kiossev 1995 has done for the interpretation of the Bulgarian fictional traveller figure Bai Ganyo). I have focused here instead on the way that rhetorical manoeuvres and the use of the particular persona of the traveller intertwined with publishing plans and political ambitions to produce a cultural construct even more complicated perhaps than that of the Romanian subject: I mean the travel book.

Notes

Florea Ioncioaia's insights, generosity with references, and observations on an earlier draft of this chapter helped me a lot. He also once sent me a book via Angela Jianu, whose acquaintance I thereby had the good fortune to make, and from whose criticism and scholarship I have benefitted here. Translations are my own unless otherwise attributed.

1. Critics have given little attention to these questions, some (e.g., Bucur 1989: 47) even affirming erroneously that Golescu's text was published posthumously.

2. Georgescu 1971: 40, called Callimachi the first Romanian to admire Europe as 'the source of culture and light'. Hitchins 1996: 140, attributes Georgescu's words to Callimachi (without acknowledgment to either) and backdates them to 1733. Both occlude the Russian context.

3. See the letter in Greek, August 1821 (*Documente 1821* 2: 327–31, with Romanian translation). As it is signed 'K.G.', Golescu himself may well be its author.

4. References to Golescu's *Account* are given in-text and are to Anghelescu's modern critical edition (D. Golescu 1990).

5. The Moldavian Ion Ionescu, a pioneer of Romanian ethnography, discusses the *Account* in a letter of 1849 to the Wallachian liberal C.A. Rosetti (Bodea 1982, 2: 1138); I am grateful to Angela Jianu for this reference, hitherto overlooked by analysts of Golescu's book. Still, what interests Ionescu is Golescu's analysis of the Romanian peasantry, not his account of Europe.

6. Thus Berindei 1980: 126 cites the historian Nicolae Iorga (an authoritative figure in Romanian culture) as saying Golescu's book had a 'necessary influence on the spirit of an age'. What Iorga actually said in 1910, in a review of the second edition, was that he hoped the book *would* influence the spirit of the (twentieth-century) age, not having been read by previous ones.

7. Thiersch, Friedrich Wilhelm (1784–1860), German classical scholar and philhellene, professor of ancient literature at the University of Munich.

8. Georgescu 1991: 108, citing page 65 of the 1915 edition, says Golescu speaks of 'that other Europe'. This cannot be traced.

9. 'Wo edler Geister Funken sprühten,/ Wo Kränzer für das Schöne blühten,/ Wo starke Herzen freundig glühten,/ Für alles Heilige entbrannt,/ Dar war mein Vaterland!' (Körner 1906: 16).

10. Notably the Greek-language works by Dimitris Philippidis, *Geographia tis Roumounias* (1816) and Konstantinos Karakas, *Topographia tis Vlahias* (1830).

11. The analogy with Montesquieu was made by M. Călinescu 1983, who argued that the fascination with the West causes a crisis in self-identity in modern Romanian culture; cf. idem 1996; Alexandrescu 2000; Roman 2003. A historian of Greece has referred to 'cultural schizophrenia' (Clogg 1981: 90); Ottomanists to 'cultural dualism' (Fortna 2001 discusses the fortunes of this concept). Bhabha (1984)'s popular term 'ambivalence' is, as Young (1990) has shown, really a rather static and indiscriminately applied concept.

12. See Tavakoli-Targhi 2001: xii. In a much older usage, the black social theorist W.E.B. Du Bois saw that the term need not imply fragmentation or loss: he wrote that 'the Negro longs to attain self-conscious manhood, to merge his double self into a better and truer self. In this merging he wishes neither of the older selves to be lost' (Du Bois 1905: 4). On the origin and destiny of this concept in African-American and Latin-American cultural theory see respectively Reed 1997: 97–125 and Mignolo 2000.

13. E.g., Sadik Rifat's 'Essay Concerning European Affairs' from 1837, the product of an embassy to Vienna; and Mustafa Sami's *Avrupa Risâlesi* (1840), both discussed by Berkes (1964: 128–32). An earlier Ottoman instance is Ebu Bekir Ratib's Vienna embassy narrative of 1790, discussed by Findley (1995).

14. Later Romanian travel acocunts are listed in *BAPR* 1: 1089–91 and 2, 1217–18; and in *BIR* 2, i: 62–70, 449–60. Mihai 2004 has published some hitherto unknown letters.

15. See e.g., Soutsos 1899, 45–46; Brăiloiu, in Hurmuzaki, 10: 628–29; Filipescu, in Eliade 1905, 265–83; Poteca, in Bianu 1888; and Poenaru, in Potra 1963, for a range of contemporary Wallachian approaches to the West in the 1820s.

References

Abramos, I., R. Golescu and I. Ştirbei. 1718. Memorandum addressed to Emperor Charles VI, in *Magasinu istoricu pentru Dacia* 4, 1847: 179–211. Extract in Hurmuzaki 6: 230–31.

Acte şi fragmente. Acte şi fragmente cu privire la istoria romînilor adunate din depozitele de manuscrise ale Apusului, ed. N. Iorga, 3 vols. Bucharest: Imprimeria Statului, 1895–1897.

Alexandrescu, S. 2000. *Identitate în ruptură: mentalităţi româneşti postbelice*. Bucharest: Univers.

Andronescu, Ş. and Gr. Andronescu. 1947. *Însemnările Androneştilor*, ed. I. Corfus. Bucharest: Institutul de Istorie Naţională.

Anghelescu, M. 1990. 'Dinicu Golescu în vremea sa', Introduction, notes, commentary, bibliography and glossary, in D. Golescu, *Scrieri*. Bucharest: Minerva.

———— 1991. 'Utopia as a journey: Dinicu Golescu's case', *Synthesis* 18, 25–31.

Antohi, S. 1985. 'Un modèle d'utopie à l'œuvre dans les Principautés Danubiennes', in *Culture and society*, ed. A. Zub. Iaşi: Editura Academiei.

Asachi, Gh. 1964. 'Jurnalul călătoriei la Petersburg', in *Reflector peste timp. Din istoria reportajului romînesc 1829–1866*, ed. G. Ivaşcu. Bucharest: Ed. pentru literatură.

at-Tahtâwî, R. 1988. *L'or de Paris: relation de voyage, 1826–1831*, trans. and ed. A. Louca. Paris: Sindbad.

BAPR. Bibliografia analitică a periodicelor româneşti, 1790–1850, ed. I. Lupu et al., 2 vols. Bucharest: Editura Academiei, 1966, 1972.

Barthes, R. 1972. *Le degré zero de l'écriture, suivi de Nouveaux essais critiques*. Paris: Seuil.

Bentham, J. 1971. *Correspondence, vol. 3 (1781–-1788)*, ed. I. Christie. London: Athlone Press.

Berindei, D. 1980. 'Die Reisen des rumänischen Bojaren Constantin (Dinicu) Golescu nach Mittel- und Westeuropa', in *Reisen und Reisebeschreibungen im 18. und 19. Jahrhundert als Quellen der Kulturbeziehungsforschung*, ed. B. Krasnobaev, G. Robel and H. Zeman. Berlin: Camen.

Berkes, N. 1964. *The Development of Secularism in Turkey.* Montreal: McGill University Press.

Bhabha, H. 1984. 'Of Mimicry and Man: The Ambivalence of Colonial Discourse', *October* 28, 125–33; repr. in idem, *The Location of Culture.* New York: Routledge, 1994.

Bianu, I. 1888. 'Întâii bursieri români în străinătate. Scrisori de ale lui Eufrosin Poteca, 1822–1825', *Revista nouă* 1:11, 421–31.

BIR. Bibliografia istorică a României, 10 vols to date. Bucharest: Editura Academiei, 1970–2004.

Blandiana, A. 1978. *Cea mai frumoasă din lumile posibile. Impresii de călătorie.* Bucharest: Cartea Românească.

Bodea, C., ed. 1982. *1848 la români. O istorie în date şi mărturii,* 2 vols. Bucharest: Ed. ştiinţifică şi enciclopedică.

Bogdan-Duică, G. and G. Popa-Lisseanu, eds. 1924. *Viaţa şi opera lui Gheorghe Lazăr.* Bucharest: Tip. «Jockey Club» Ion C. Văcărescu.

Bucur, M. 1971. Preface to D. Golescu, *Însemnare a călătoriii mele.* Bucharest: Eminescu.

———— 1989. 'La découverte de l'occident par les Roumains à travers Vienne (première moitié du XIXe siècle)', *Etudes danubiennes* 5:1, 39–50.

BRV. Bibliografia românească veche (1508–1830), ed. I. Bianu, N. Hodoş and D. Simonescu, 4 vols. Bucharest: SOCEC, 1903–1944.

Călinescu, G. 1988. *History of Romanian literature from its origins to the present day,* trans. L. Leviţchi. Milan: Nagard/ UNESCO. Originally published as *Istoria literaturii române de la origini până în zilele noastre.* Bucharest, 1941.

Călinescu, M. 1983. '"How can one be a Romanian?" Modern Romanian Culture and the West', *Southeastern Europe* 10:2, 25–36.

———— 1996. 'How can one be what one is?', in *Identitate / alteritate în spaţiul românesc,* ed. A. Zub. Iaşi: Editura Universităţii «A.I. Cuza».

Camariano-Cioran, A. 1974. *Les Académies princières de Bucarest et de Jassy et leur professeurs.* Thessaloniki: Institute for Balkan Studies.

Chakrabarty, D. 2000. *Provincializing Europe: Postcolonial Thought and Historical Difference.* Princeton, NJ: Princeton University Press.

Clogg, R., ed. 1976. *The Movement for Greek Independence, 1770–1821: A Collection of Documents.* London: Macmillan.

———— 1981. 'The Greek Mercantile Bourgeoisie: "Progressive" or "Reactionary"?', in *Balkan Society in the Age of Greek Independence,* ed. R. Clogg. London: SSEES / Macmillan.

Codrescu, T. 1844. *O călătorie la Constantinopol.* Iaşi: Cantora Foii Săteşti.

Constantin, I. 1973. *Vacanţa, o plecare. Articole şi jurnal de călătorie.* Bucharest: Albatros.

Cornea, P. 1972. *Originile romantismului românesc.* Bucharest: Minerva.

Cristea, M. 1967. 'Primul ziar românesc *Faima Lipscăi,* o valoroasă contribuţie la istoria presei române', *Muzeul Bruckenthal, Sibiu: Studii şi comunicări* 13: 273–84.

Diaconescu, M. 1978. 'L'œuvre littéraire de Dinicu Golescu et les traditions de la rhétorique roumaine', *Synthesis* 5: 163–70.

Djuvara, N. 1989. *Le pays roumain entre Orient et Occident. Les Principautés danubiennes au début du XIXe siècle*. Paris: Publications Orientalistes de France.

Documente 1821. Documente privind istoria României. Răscoala din 1821: Documente interne, 5 vols. Bucharest: Ed. Academiei, 1959–62.

Du Bois, W.E.B. 1905. *The Souls of Black Folk*. London: Archibald, Constable.

Duțu, A. 1967. 'National and European Consciousness in the Romanian Enlightenment', *Studies on Voltaire and the eighteenth century* 55: 463–79.

———— 1971. *Les livres de sagesse dans la culture roumaine*. Bucarest: AIESEE.

———— 1972. *Sinteză și originalitate în cultura română*. Bucharest: Ed. enciclopedică.

———— 1980. 'Europe's Image with Romanian Representatives of the Enlightenment', in *Enlightenment and Romanian society*, ed. P. Teodor. Cluj-Napoca: Dacia.

Eliade, P. 1905. *Histoire de l'esprit publique en Roumanie, t. 1: Les premiers princes indigènes (1821–1828)*. Paris: Ernest Leroux.

Elian, Al. 2003. *Bizanțul, Biserica și cultura românească*. Iași: Trinitas.

Elliott, R. 1982. *The Literary Persona*. Chicago: University of Chicago Press.

Fassel, H. 2003. 'Die enzyklopädische Donaubeschreibung: Eine Typus und seine Entwicklung', in *Beograd u delima evropskih putopisaca*, ed. Dj.S. Kostić. Belgrade: Institut des études balkaniques.

Findley, C.V. 1995. 'Ebu Bekir Ratib's Vienna Embassy Narrative: Discovering Austria or Propagandizing for Reform in Istanbul?', *Wiener Zeitschrift für die Kunde des Morgenlandes* 85, 41–80.

Fortna, B. 2001. 'Education and Autobiography at the End of the Ottoman Empire', *Die Welt des Islams* 41:1, 1–31.

Fussell, P. 1980. *Abroad: British Literary Traveling Between the Wars*. New York: Oxford University Press.

Georgescu, V., ed. 1962. *Din corespondența diplomatică a Țării Romînești, 1823–1828*. Bucharest: Muzeul Romîno-Rus.

———— 1971. *Political Ideas and the Enlightenment in the Romanian Principalities 1750–1831*, trans. M. Lăzărescu. Boulder, CO: East European Monographs.

———— 1991. *The Romanians: A History*, trans. A. Bley-Vroman. London: IB Tauris.

Giurescu, C.C. 1957. *Principatele Romîne la începutul secolului XIX. Constatări istorice, geografice, economice și statistice pe temeiul hărții ruse din 1835*. Bucharest: n.p.

Golescu, D. 1826. *Însemnare a călătoriii mele Constandin Radovici din Golești făcută în anul 1824, 1825, 1826*. Buda: Crăiasaca Tipografie a Universității Ungare. German: *Aufzeichnung meiner Reise*, trans. K. Haller. Bucharest: Kriterion, 1973; Hungarian: *Utazásaim leírása 1824, 1825, 1826*, trans. G. Beke. Bucharest: Kriterion, 1977.

———— 1990. *Scrieri*, ed. M. Anghelescu. Bucharest: Minerva.

———— 2006. 'Account of my Journey', trans. M. Kovacs, in *Discourses of Collective Identity in Central and Southeast Europe (1770–1945). Texts and Commentaries*, vol. 1: *Late Enlightenment – Emergence of the Modern*

'*National Idea*', ed. B. Trencsényi and M. Kopeček. Budapest: Central European University Press (extract introduced by M. Turda).

Golescu, I. 1990. *Scrieri alese*. Bucharest: Cartea Românească.

Grivel, C. 1994. 'Travel writing', in *Materialities of Communication*, ed. H.U. Gumbrecht and K.L. Pfeiffer. Stanford: Stanford University Press.

Hall, M. 1989. 'The Emergence of the Essay and the Idea of Discovery', in *Essays on the Essay: Redefining the Genre*, ed. A. Butrym. Athens, GA : University of Georgia Press.

Haneş, P. 1934. *Histoire de la littérature roumaine*. Paris: E. Leroux.

Hanţa, Al. 1985. *Idei şi forme literare pînă la Titu Maiorescu*. Bucharest: Minerva.

Henderson, A. 1996. *Romantic Identities: Varieties of Subjectivity, 1774–1830*. Cambridge University Press.

Hitchins, K. 1996. *The Romanians 1774–1866*. Oxford: Clarendon Press.

Hodoş, N. 1910. 'Întroducere' to D. Golescu, *Însemnare a călătoriii mele*. Bucharest: Minerva.

Hurmuzaki, *Documente privitoare la istoria românilor culese de Baron Eudoxiu de Hurmuzaki*, 22 vols. Bucharest: various publishers, 1876–1943. Supplement 1, 6 parts, Bucharest, 1886–95. Supplement 2, 3 parts, Bucharest, 1893–1900. New series, 4 vols. Bucharest, 1959–74.

IAkovenko, I. 1834. *Moldaviia i Valakhiia s' 1820 po 1829 god'*. St. Petersburg: V' tipografii N. Grecha. Romanian excerpts in *Călători ruşi în Moldova şi Muntenia*, ed. and trans. G. Bezviconi. Bucharest: Institutul de istorie naţională.

Ioncioaia, F. 1996. 'Viena, opt sute treizeci şi opt. Relatările de călătorie şi imaginarul politic european la mijlocul secolului XIX', in *Itinerarii istoriografice*, ed. G. Bădărău. Iaşi: Fundaţia Xenopol.

Iorgulescu, M. 1979. *Firescul ca excepţie*. Bucharest: Cartea Românească.

Jones, R. 1984. 'Opposition to War and Expansion in Late Eighteenth-Century Russia', *Jahrbücher für Geschichte Osteuropas* 32:1, 35–51.

Kiossev, A. 1995. 'The Debate About the Problematic Bulgarian', in *National Character and National Ideology in Interwar Eastern Europe*, ed. I. Banac and K. Verdery. New Haven, CT: Yale Center for International and Area Studies.

Knopper, F. 1995. *Le regard du voyageur en Allemagne du Sud et en Autriche dans les relations de voyageurs allemands (1775–1800)*. Nancy: Presses Universitaires.

Körner, C. Th. 1906. *Werke*. Leipzig: Inselverlag.

Kotsowilis, K. 1993. 'Die griechischen Studenten Münchens unter König Ludwig I von 1826 bis 1844', *Südostforschungen* 52: 119–237.

Lăsconi, E. 1998. Postface to D. Golescu, *Însemnare a călătoriii mele*. Bucharest: Gramar.

Macmichael, W. 1819. *Journey from Moscow to Constantinople in the years 1817, 1818*. London: John Murray.

Manolescu, N. 1990. *Istoria critică a literaturii române*. Bucharest: Minerva.

Marcu, A. 1930. 'Athènes ou Rome? A propos de l'influence italienne en Roumanie vers 1820', in *Mélanges d'histoire littéraire générale et comparée offerts à Fernand Baldensperger*, 2 vols, vol. 1. Paris: Honoré Champion.

Marino, A. 1976. *Carnete europene. Însemnare a călătoriei mele făcută în anii 1969–1975*. Cluj-Napoca: Dacia.

———— 1981. *Littérature roumaine – littératures occidentales. Rencontres*, trans. A. Bentoiu. Bucharest: Editura ştiinţifică şi enciclopedică.

———— 2001. 'Vechi complexe româneşti', *Observator cultural*, 6–13 August.

Martin, M. 2002. G. *Călinescu şi „complexele" literaturii române*, 2nd edn. Piteşti: Paralela 45.

Mehmet, M. 1971. 'Acţiuni diplomatice la Poartă în legătură cu mişcarea revoluţionară din 1821', *Studii* 24:1, 63–76.

Mignolo, W. 2000. *Local Histories/Global Designs: Coloniality, Subaltern Knowledges, and Border Thinking*. Princeton, NJ: Princeton University Press.

Mihai, N. 2004. 'Orizonturi spaţiale, orizonturi mentale. Corespondenţa unui student oltean la Paris (1842–1846)', in *Călători români în Occident*, ed. N. Bocşan and I. Bolovan. Cluj-Napoca: Presa universitară clujeană.

Mumuleanu, B. 1825. *Plângerea şi tânguirea Valahiei asupra nemulţumirii streinilor ce au dărăpănat-o*. Buda: Typariul Crăieştei Universitate.

Naum Râmniceanu. 1987. 'Izbucnirea şi urmările zaverei din Valahia', trans. N. Trandafirescu, in *Izvoare narative interne privind revoluţia din 1821 condusă de Tudor Vladimirescu*, ed. G. Iscru et al. Craiova: Scrisul Românesc.

Nemoianu, V. 1992. 'Displaced images: travel literature as conversational essay in the early nineteenth century', *Synthesis* 19: 3–11.

Pas, I. 1965. *Carte despre drumuri lungi*. Bucharest: Editura pentru literatură.

Pippidi, A. 1980. *Hommes et idées du sud-est européen à l'aube de l'âge moderne*. Paris: CNRS / Bucharest: Editions de l'Académie.

Pippidi, A. 1985. 'Identitate naţională şi culturală. Cîteva probleme de metodă în legătură cu locul românilor în istoria universală', *Revista de istorie* 38:12, 1178–98. Repr. in *Identitate / alteritate în spaţiul românesc*, ed. A. Zub. Iaşi: Editura Universităţii «A.I. Cuza», 1996.

Pleşu, A. 1996. *Chipuri şi măşti ale tranziţiei*. Bucharest: Humanitas.

Popovici, D. 1945. *La littérature roumaine à l'époque des Lumières*. Sibiu: Centre d'études sur la Transylvanie.

Potra, G. 1963. *Petrache Poenaru, ctitor al învăţămîntului în ţara noastră (1799–1875)*. Bucharest: Ed. ştiinţifică.

Reed, A.L. 1997. *W.E.B. Du Bois and American Political Thought*. New York: Oxford University Press.

Revoluţia 1821. Revoluţia din 1821 condusă de Tudor Vladimirescu: documente externe. Bucharest: Ed. Academiei Republicii Socialiste România, 1980.

Reynolds, D., ed. 2001. *Interpreting the Self: Autobiography in the Arabic Literary Tradition* (with K. Brustad et al.). Berkeley, CA: University of California Press.

Roboli, T. 1985. 'The Literature of Travel', in *Russian Prose*, ed. B. Eikhenbaum and IU. Tynyanov. Ann Arbor: Ardis.

Roman, D. 2003. *Fragmented Identities*. Lanham, MD: Lexington Books.

Salaberry, C.-M., comte de. 1799. *Voyage à Constantinople en Italie, et aux îles de l'Archipel, par l'Allemagne et la Hongrie*. Paris: Maradan, An VII.

Soutsos, Prince N. 1899. *Mémoires*. Vienna: Gerold & Cie.

Stan, A. 1977. 'Gîndirea şi activitatea social-politică a lui Dinicu Golescu', *Revistă de istorie* 30:6, 1071–86.

Stewart, W. 1978. *Die Reisebeschreibung und ihre Theorie im Deutschland des 18. Jahrhunderts.* Bonn: Bouvier.

Tavakoli-Targhi, M. 2001. *Refashioning Iran: Orientalism, Occidentalism and Historiography.* Basingstoke: Palgrave.

Văcărescu, I., A. Văcărescu and I. Văcărescu. 1982. Poeţii Văcăreşti, *Opere.* Bucharest: Minerva.

Vîrtosu, E. 1932. *1821: Date şi fapte noi.* Bucharest: Cartea Românească.

Warriner, D., ed. 1965. *Contrasts in Emerging Societies: Readings in the Social and Economic History of South-Eastern Europe in the Nineteenth Century.* London: Athlone Press.

Wolff, L. 1994. *Inventing Eastern Europe: The Map of Civilization on the Mind of the Enlightenment.* Stanford: Stanford University Press.

Young, R. 1990. *White Mythologies: Writing History and the West.* New York: Routledge.

Zilot Românul. 1987. 'Jalnica cîntare', in *Izvoare narative interne privind revoluţia din 1821 condusă de Tudor Vladimirescu,* ed. G. Iscru et al. Craiova: Scrisul Românesc.

Zub, A. 1986. *Cunoaştere de sine şi integrare.* Iaşi: Junimea.

CHAPTER 4

Writing Difference/Claiming General Validity: Jovan Dučić's *Cities and Chimaeras* and the West

Vladimir Gvozden

The travel texts of Jovan Dučić (1872–1943) merit analysis not only because he is generally regarded as a significant and influential modernist writer (his lyrics, refined in phrasing and form, show the influence of the Parnassians and the Symbolists), but also because he is a prominent figure in the modernization of Serbian culture. As early as 1936, Dučić's contemporary Nikola Mirković stressed the importance of the poet's role in the process of 'the modernization of Serbian literature and culture' (Mirković 1936: 335). By the same token, he is widely considered by both literary scholars and the public to have been obsessed with 'the great and wise West' (Deretić 1987: 205) – a writer who brought about a great synthesis of Serbian and Western literature, especially in his poetry from the first decades of the twentieth century. His letters from Switzerland, France, Greece, Italy, Spain, Palestine and Egypt appeared first in literary magazines and/or in the influential Belgrade newspaper *Politika*. The separate parts of his travelogue were then collected under the title *Gradovi i himere* ('Cities and Chimaeras'), and were published twice during the author's life, in 1930 and 1940. The book is both a text *about* culture (or cultures), as well as an indispensable text within Serbian national culture.

Critics usually stress that the most important change in Dučić's intellectual life happened when he moved from his native Herzegovina in 1899 to study in Geneva, where he finished his studies in 1906. More precisely, his journey started much earlier, when he left Herzegovina and went first to Sarajevo in Bosnia and then to Sombor, which was at that time part of Austria-Hungary, to complete his teacher training. Still, the second departure, to Geneva and Paris, made the poet aware of a higher education and 'higher culture', as he said. Europe as a cultural idea, as an 'image' which appeared in the humanist milieu in the West during the seventeenth century and developed further during the eighteenth century, replacing the medieval notion of the 'Christian world', had led Serbian travellers in the direction of European cultural and university centres, from the 'enlightened' and 'fortunate' Europe of the eighteenth-century writers and travellers Dositej Obradović (1961: 64) and Zaharije Orfelin (1768: 3) to the establishment of a modern Serbian state on a Western model in the nineteenth century. This ideal Europe led the poet Dučić in the same direction. After Geneva, he did not return to Herzegovina but went to Belgrade on a Serbian government stipend and soon began his career as a diplomat. He spent most of his life as a Yugoslav diplomat in several European capitals (Sofia, Bucharest, Athens, Geneva, Rome, Budapest, Madrid and Lisbon).

Jovan Dučić is a clear example of both horizontal and vertical social mobility. First as a student and then as a diplomat, he moved from one European country to another; but this was made possible by increasing vertical mobility in Serbian society at that time. The contradictions of this modernizing acceleration left its traces in his writings. For example, he did not develop a new poetry by abandoning the poetry of Romanticism, but by interiorizing its ideological and poetical presuppositions. An important transitional figure, Dučić produced work that is a synthesis and culmination of nineteenth-century thinking, yet at the same time it is a key precursor of new developments in Serbian literature and culture (of which the older Dučić sometimes disapproved).

While discussing *Cities and Chimaeras,* critics (e.g., Skerlić 1955; Pavlović 1964) usually emphasize its novelty and its crucial role in the development of the genre in Serbian. In a one-sided and slightly idealized argument in favour of modernization (considered as a set of certain potentialities and their possible expression), one could say that Dučić's travel writing incorporates particular horizons, not just geographical but also stylistic and ideological ones, that Serbian literature had lacked before. In a sense, *Cities and Chimaeras* simultaneously marks the 'youthfulness' and the 'oldness' of the genre of the literary travelogue in Serbian literature.

However, it is worth mentioning that Dučić had been acquainted with the key ideas of literary travel writing even before he went to Geneva to study in 1899. In his 1898 article on the Serbian travel writer Marko Car, Dučić insists on the possibility of a synthesis between the two types of travel writing dominant in the nineteenth century: the romantic travelogue, marked by one's own personality, and the scientific, positivist travelogue. He also underscores that in 'successful' travelogues the individuality of the author does not mean that he has absolute freedom – there are conventions that he or she must obey (Dučić 1969: 197–98).

Developing a particular economy of intellectual exchange in Serbian literature, Jovan Dučić devotes the final pages of his essay on the writer Isidora Sekulić to her literary travelogue *Letters from Norway* (1914). After his own experience of the genre, Dučić now gives a series of binary oppositions he considers important for every travel writer. His idea of the fusion of sensibility and intellect reappears here. According to Dučić, the literary travelogue should be a combination of knowledge and sensibility, emotions and intellect; as a didactic genre it has a cognitive function but at the same time it must contain the unique experience of the author. This opposition takes the form of the old alternative between 'classical' and 'romantic' tastes, as well as between intelligibility and sensibility as the highest measures of human understanding. Dučić addressed this issue very early in his letters from Switzerland (the first two chapters of *Cities and Chimaeras*), particularly in those pages dedicated to the binary opposition between Voltaire and Rousseau, Romanticism and Enlightenment, nature and culture.

In his essay on Sekulić, Dučić further argues that the literary travelogue should not be written by a 'literary tourist', but only by a writer focused on the 'essential quality' of a country: 'its racial genius, its artistic potential, the higher motives of its history, the soul and the spirit of its inhabitants, etc.' (Dučić 1969: 113; for a wider discussion of the usage of the term 'race' before the Second World War, see Todorov 1989). Besides the fact that a literary travelogue necessarily contains traces of the writer's personality, it should also be a scientific work in the sense that we can immediately 'spot the impostor'; it is 'always a novel about its author', so we can 'identify the prattler'; and, finally, 'the good travelogue' (the word 'good' here could safely be replaced with 'literary') 'requires great artistic and stylistic devices', enabling us to 'tell whether the author is a poet or not' (Dučić 1969: 113–14). In the last sentence of the essay Dučić deliberately summarizes this duality in the genre by saying that a literary travelogue is 'the autobiography of a heart and of an intellect' (Dučić 1969: 114).

To what extent are these ideas, and the book *Cities and Chimaeras* itself, related to the European tradition of travel writing? It must be noted that Dučić, like every other travel writer, describes the world through a familiar model, and reduces anything he does not know, or that is not compatible with his preestablished conceptions, to this model (Huenen 1990: 18). As a 'hybrid literary genre' (Kašanin 1968: 348), *Cities and Chimaeras* consists of different kinds of writing and areas of knowledge. In this travelogue, we can easily identify the presence of the autobiographical dimension, the horizon of cultural analysis, ethnogeographical remarks, and literary references. The travelogue is also the part of the process of 'essayization' of other genres which is typical of literary Modernism. In the first decades of the twentieth century, both the essay and the literary travelogue appeared to be an attempt to establish certain universal notions in the coming world of relativism, and both genres were the main examples of the 'humanist mythology' of the uniqueness and autonomy of the human self (Berger 1964: 203; Bogosavljević 1983: 6; Epštejn 1997: 57–58). In addition, both could still find a guarantee of meaning in 'authorship' – in the belief in the importance of the individual expression of general issues, problems, and subjects of humanity.

Dučić also inherited the ambiguous relationship between travelogue and reality: 'the travel writer's relationship to reality was never a question of objectivity vs. subjectivity but a question of the right to re-interpret reality through the medium of personal experience. Only when that right was fully affirmed did the travelogue acquire the potential to become literature' (Bogosavljević 1983: 7). Metaphorically, Dučić does always hover between 'cities' (as something 'real') and 'chimaeras' (as something legendary and fantastic, always in danger of flying away from the 'real'). As an important device which the writer could use in his approach to reality, the principle of selection is essential for understanding *Cities and Chimaeras*. One reviewer objected that Dučić made 'an arbitrary and tendentious selection. So he did not give his impressions from cities in which he had lived much longer – from Bucharest, Budapest, Constantinople or Sofia – which is a clear mark of his affinities' (Maksimović 1969: 257). Dučić's selection might be a matter of personal affinity but it could also be a question of belonging to certain political and cultural maps in the first half of the twentieth century. However, it seems this was more a matter of Dučić's relation to the European tradition of travel writing. Namely, the cities and lands described in *Cities and Chimaeras* had been privileged sites for educational and literary travels for centuries. Indeed, it could be said that Dučić's selection is 'tendentious' in the sense that he in fact privileges Southern cultures (in the best tradition of the 'Grand Tour') over 'Northern coldness' – a polarity which, whether the meaning is seen as positive or negative, stems from Tacitus' *Germania*, the Protestant/Catholic division of Europe, the ideology of the Napoleonic wars and Germaine de Stael's *De l'Allemagne*, a part of which Dučić translated in 1900. It is obvious that Dučić's conception of European identity is closely connected with his favourable evaluation of Mediterranean cultures, that is to say, Southern cultures, like ancient Greece and Rome, Renaissance Italy and contemporary France (which is, according to Dučić, both a Mediterranean and an Atlantic culture). Another of Dučić's principles in his mapping of Europe owes much to the idea of the 'Great Nations' – England, Spain and Germany. *Cities and Chimaeras* is mostly devoted to the 'civilized world', and Dučić's approach to the Balkans or eastern Europe, for example, could be described under the heading 'Internal and External Others'. This is apparent in his self-identification with an imagined European identity:

> There are only two Orients. One is Balkan and the other is Buddhist. The Balkan Orient: the cosmos has never yet seen such misery! Even today it lacks its own civilization, its own morality, its own nature. [...] The Balkans are even today a true Turkish desert. It will still take another hundred years before foreign tourists come to the Balkans. By that time the Turks will have strangled each other with their silken cords, the Greeks will have opened the world's largest gambling den in their capital Constantinople, the Romanians will have diverted the Danube into the Black Sea, the Bulgarians will have learnt Serbian, and we Serbs will have discovered America ... . (Dučić 1940: 117)

This kind of imagined European identity is further developed in 'Letter from Egypt', which clearly partakes of an 'orientalist' discourse. In short, the travel writer gives the image of Egypt as something unknown and unusual, and sees only contradictions:

> For Europeans, saturated with the numerous beauties of Greek and Christian identity, contemporary Egypt eventually becomes the land of mere paradoxes and the absurd, the richest soil and the poorest people! The oldest culture and the most impolite crowd! The best climate, and everybody is sick! The land with lots of water – since everybody lives next to the Nile – and the dirtiest creatures! The sun all around, and almost everybody catches cold and is rheumatic! Everybody is religious, and everybody is a tyrant! And, most of all, the desert everywhere, but solitude nowhere. (Dučić 1940: 299)

For Dučić the European, Egypt is a country of paradox and absurdity; this is apparently an unknown and unrationalized body of knowledge. But in fact it is an example of knowledge organized according to orientalist discourse (a familiar model), which sees only effects and which is interested only in history and past culture, and in the contemporary can grasp only internal clashes and discontent. However, Dučić's ideological image of Egypt is not, unlike the images of numerous 'real' colonizers, supported by his country's political power. Thus, it belongs to an 'empty' colonial discourse – a paper colonialism.

Significantly, Dučić was of the opinion that it is possible to represent a culture (scientifically) as a set of unchanging values, and simultaneously to embrace ethnic psychology (artistically) in a single metaphor. In an interview, he rejected the label *putopis* ('travelogue') for his account of countries in which he had 'lived' for a long period:

> I did not finish any of my 'travelogues', as you call them, in any country in which I had lived. In nearly all of my travelogues I spoke of travel in a different sense from that of spiritual travel. I always wanted to learn something about the past and the language of the people with whom I lived over many years. Only after that did I write those pieces, which were devoted very little to observations about the country itself, and which, on the contrary, were connected with something more important and deeper, that is to say, the genius of a race. For the same reason, I wrote about the genius of the Ancient Greeks, the French, the Spanish etc. [...] My purpose was to go far beyond the impressions of a travel writer. (Dučić 1932: 442)

He insists on such vague descriptors as 'true reflections of genius' or 'testimonies of history', and argues for an opposition between his deep insights and reflections, and the shallow impressions of travel writers. Dučić comfortably disdains the minutiae of everyday life in favour of a quest for 'eternal values' and 'national characters' (Dučić 1932: 442). Furthermore, in a letter from Bucharest dated 30 March 1938, Dučić argues that 'national characters' are important for 'a politician as well as for a historian or philosopher, but they are fundamental for the political life of a nation' (Dučić 1991: 259). We encounter here the idea of an ethics of literary production, which considers literary writing as a supplement to politics, as a gate to the realm of eternal relations and endeavours. Bogdan Popović, a Parisian student, Belgrade professor and a very erudite man, the editor of the best literary magazine of the time, *Srpski književni glasnik* ('Serbian Literary Herald') and the author of the influential *Antologija novije srpske lirike* ('Anthology of Modern Serbian Lyric Poetry'), set up a framework for Dučić and other Serbian literary modernists in a 1894 lecture on world literature: 'Literature can give us something which we cannot obtain from material achievement; it gives us knowledge about ourselves, our inner life, a source of worldly wisdom and a pledge of eternal pleasure' (Popović 2001: 6). As a good disciple of Popović, in a conversation with the Romanian man of letters Virgil Karianopol, Dučić later espoused a similar attitude:

> I think that true literature must be tied to great subjects, eternal ones, to subjects that interest us, as human beings, and that connect us to each other and that make us better, strengthening the mutual relationships that make it possible for society to live without turmoil. Human beings have the need to read, in books, about their own sufferings and joys, and they are happy if others suffer for them. That which we write, should go deep, even

to the darkest depths which are below the depth of an average person. I wish to add, as a kind of supplement, that anybody who writes must identify himself with everybody, that is to say, in his writings we must find all those factors independent of the settings and country of his origin. Namely, I would like to say that it depends on the writer himself whether he will survive or die. (Karianopol 1987: 119)

It is well known that writers' travels can contribute to the richness of international topics in a national literature or in a literary work (for example, the most important figures of Serbian literature, Vuk Karadžić, Dositej Obradović, Matija and Ljubomir Nenadović, Laza Kostić and Miloš Crnjanski were great travellers [Deretić 1996]). Ever since Herodotus, the journey has been represented as a privileged means of gaining knowledge of the world. Or, in Dučić's words from *Cities and Chimaeras*: 'We can acquire a proper knowledge of human beings only if we travel' (Dučić 1940: 275). Nevertheless, it is obvious today that travel writing cannot be an example of absolute or universal knowledge or truth, but a kind of mapping – a necessary reduction of cultural diversity. So how are we to reconcile these two attitudes: the universal belief in a 'human spirit' and the reality of cultural differences?

Nineteenth-century Europe set the stage for the race of every single culture to acquire its own national identity, and the struggle for culture became more urgent than the struggle for the nation-state itself. The existence of culture was perceived as an essential condition for the process of nation-building, even more important than the mapping of its territory (During 1990: 138–39). Imperial nations considered themselves as 'world-historical' and other nations usually perceived them as such – Dučić's images of France from *Cities and Chimaeras* are a good example of this: 'No patriotism is more beautiful than the French one. [...] French patriotism is not an expression of racial egoism and xenophobia. [...] France never has been without a great man, who appeared to be the head of the human family, its guardian and defender, the hero of the world' (Dučić 1940: 68). Following Renan's so-called voluntaristic definition of nationhood, Dučić asserts in his 'Letter from Egypt': 'A nation – this does not mean a common territory, name or language, but the collective spirit or, better to say, the collective soul' (Dučić 1940: 307). And, if national identity refers to a 'collective spirit' or 'soul', then it is, according to Dučić, quite natural to attempt to understand and describe this spirit, which actually appears to be the common tradition of a group. In that case, it could be said that the solution of the principle of individuation for nations in *Cities and Chimaeras* is the idea of narrative continuity, that is to say, of the production and reproduction of narratives that are perceived as fundamental for a nation. In this travelogue the voluntaristic conception of the nation, which is the main constituent of the positive image of France, triumphed over the deterministic nationalism attributed to Germany as highly negative (for this opposition, highly popular among intellectuals at the turn of the nineteenth century, see Woolf 1996: 13–15).

One Serbian literary historian, speaking of Dučić as a poet, points to his 'transcendental lightness in composing poetry in little lyrical forms about the great questions of the human being and his or her relationship to the world' (Leovac 1985: 293). By the same token, in the case of *Cities and Chimaeras*, we could say the following: even if one might talk about a 'transcendental [or unbearable] lightness' in the writing of this literary travelogue, it is more convenient to designate the writing of 'nation' as the product of a kind of 'transcendental relief' that allowed Dučić and most of his contemporaries to live in the world of culture (or cultures). Dučić's characterizations of nations reflect the twofold nature of the nation itself: first, there is the belief that the nation is always already present; secondly, there is the nation constructed in narration, which unfolds itself *hic et nunc*, marked by the repetition and pulsation of national signs. Dučić sees nations in the terms of their 'essence', as an a priori set of moral and mental qualities that differentiate nations or 'races' perceived as homogenous wholes. Today, we are more inclined to see nations in terms of conventions. 'Character' is a matter of reputation rather than identity (Leerssen 1991: 169).

In his *Location of Culture*, Homi Bhabha claims that 'the conceptual ambivalence of modern society becomes the site of *writing the nation*' (Bhabha 1995: 146), and suggests that '[w]e need another time of *writing* that will be able to inscribe the ambivalent and chiasmatic intersections of time and place that constitute the problematic "modern" experience of the Western nation' (Bhabha 1995: 141). This means that when we look at the past we need, for a better understanding of images of other nations, more complex strategies of cultural identification and discursive convention, which function 'in the name of "the people" or "the nation" and make them the immanent subjects of a range of social and literary narratives' (Bhabha 1995: 140). As the German scholar Ulrich Bielefeld notes: 'It becomes clear that through the stranger we could see that the fictional and the real are not opposites' (Bielefeld 1998: 15). The narrative strategy of the writing of the nation 'as an apparatus of symbolic power [...] produces a continual slippage of categories, like sexuality, class affiliation, territorial paranoia, or "cultural difference"' (Bhabha 1995: 140). Social history (ideology) and personal history (utopia) mix in the literary image of the stranger, as a history of separation and restraint.[1]

Jovan Dučić, as a follower of the intellectual insights produced by the 'great nations', aspired to reconcile the universal values of

Enlightenment and humanism and the relative characters of particular national identities. For him, as for many other intellectuals of the time, culture was synonymous with 'validity' and 'value'. It was perceived as something universal, and in *Cities and Chimaeras* Dučić skilfully hides the fact that culture is necessarily historical. For this reason, an analysis of the imagological aspects of *Cities and Chimaeras* could lead us to a deeper understanding of Dučić's conception of literature and the nature of the literary travelogue at the turn of the century.

Jovan Dučić adopted a humanist conception of literature as a form of knowledge of a special kind, one that differs from philosophical or scientific knowledge but could be equally, if not more, important. Accordingly, the major function of literature is seen to be to preserve high culture as a bulwark against barbarism and the assault of materialism. As a world-view belonging to the particular class that privileged the site of reading, this conception was accused of being elitist and idealistic, for it ascribes to itself deeper political and social insights, which all other practices or disciplines lack.

If we add to this Dučić's rejection of a characterization of *Cities and Chimaeras* as a literary travelogue, then his absolutization of literature as a cognitive instrument becomes clearer. According to him, the contemporary world, 'the spirit of the age', is bad, but (alleged) universality is good. The great moments of culture belong to the past, while contemporary culture is irrelevant. As something more reliable, a universal 'national spirit' is contrasted in *Cities and Chimaeras* to the passing 'spirit of the age'. The dominant emotion in many passages of the travelogue is a profound nostalgia for past eras at the expense of the present, as in this example from his 'Letter from Italy' (1928):

> For the ancient Romans are still with us and inside us. We still follow their roads on all the old continents; and we still cross their bridges over our own rivers; and in our fields the Roman world still lies in the graveyards which we excavate; and we still admire their triumphal arches and drink water from their cisterns as though from their hands. That is why they are so familiar to us. Moreover, even when we are not in Rome with them, they are with us, in our own house. (Dučić 1940: 146)

It is clear this *passéisme* (pastism) of Dučić's, the cult of a distant, radically different past, belongs to a major strand in the ideological development of literary Modernism (Bell-Villada 1996: 204–5).

Dučić thought his aristocratism was the product of literature more than anything else, because the Serbian elite of the time was a product of education, not of descent. As Terry Eagleton points out in *The Idea of Culture*: 'To elevate culture over politics – to be men first and citizens later – means that politics must move within a deeper ethical dimension, drawing on the sources of *Bildung* and forming individuals into suitably well-tempered, responsible citizens. This is the rhetoric of the civics class' (Eagleton 2000: 7). In many parts of *Cities and Chimaeras* Dučić represents ideological positions typical of Serbian society's modernizing elite. Dučić never visited Europe as a totally alien or unknown area, but as the quite natural surroundings of a diplomat and a man of letters. The issue of knowledge of other countries is connected with his own identity-formation, and the narrator of *Cities and Chimaeras* is privileged in this sense: he was the student in Geneva and Paris; the traveller who followed the paths of the 'Frisian ships'; the Mediterranean who used to swim in the bays of Dubrovnik; and the traveller accompanied by attractive women, rich tourists and English archaeologists in Egypt.

Undoubtedly, Dučić belongs to the Western discourse of representation of the nation as something particular that should be addressed through the rhetoric of the universal. It is clear that a national identity and the image of a nation do not have an empirical, natural or singular character, but they always address the imagined 'everybody'. In Dučić's time (much more than today), literature itself as a form of high culture was considered able to establish a direct connection between the individual and the universal, eluding through that process all arbitrary singularities. For Dučić and his generation, the literary canon was a collection of singular and unique texts that actually confirmed the universal spirit of humanity through their uniqueness. In addition, parallel with this conception of literature, was the ethics of liberal humanism, according to which 'I' am most peculiarly myself when I rise above my prosaic particularity (Eagleton 2000: 55). As literature is the artistic correlative of the relationship between the universal and the individual, the political correlative of that unity is known as the nation-state. To save itself from contingency and elevate itself to the status of necessity, a nation does need its own culture and the universal medium of the state. Thus, according to the words of Terry Eagleton, the hyphen in the term 'nation-state' signifies a link between culture and politics: 'Cultures are now becoming the basis of the nation-state, but a nation-state which nevertheless transcends them' (Eagleton 2000: 57–58). In an ideology of national humanism, the universal is compatible with the national.

Therefore, the major strategies that guide the production of meaning in the travelogue *Cities and Chimaeras* are both the writing of difference and the claim to general validity. I have located Dučić in the rich tradition of writing difference among modern European nations, in order to gain an insight into the fundamental source of semantic tension in the travelogue. The ambivalence of writing about other cultures constitutes the limits of nation as narration, but differences are simultaneously admitted as a threshold that has to be transgressed, erased and translated in the process of a unified 'humanist', i.e., Western, cultural production. Thus we can conclude that the imagological aspects of *Cities and Chimaeras* are both the product and a part of humanist discourse, in which the understanding of national identity was founded in the possibility of literary expression. In this sense, the images of other cultures are placed at the centre of the literary travelogue, rather than being its remote, undefended and forgotten boundary.

Notes

1. 'Au fond, la distinction entre image idéologique et image utopique de l'étranger est celle des pronoms latins "alter" et "alius", masquée par la méta-catégorie d'altérité et par le mot français "autre". ALTER est l'autre d'un couple, pris dans une dimension étroitement relative où se définit une identité et dons se contraire. ALIUS est l'autre indéfini, l'autre de l'identité et de tout élément qui s'y rattache, mis à distance de toute association facile, l'autre utopique. ALTER est intégré dans une conception du monde dont le centre est le groupe; ALIUS est éloigné, excentrique, et atteint au prix d'une errance hors de ce groupe. ALTER est un reflet de la culture du groupe; ALIUS un refus radical' (Moura 1992: 285).

References

Bell-Villada, G. 1996. *Art for Art's Sake and Literary Life: How Politics and Markets Helped Shape the Ideology and Culture of Aestheticism, 1790–1990*. Lincoln, NE: University of Nebraska Press.

Berger, B. 1964. *Der Essay. Form und Geschichte*. Bern: Francke.

Bhabha, H. 1995. *The Location of Culture*. London: Routledge.

Bielefeld, U. 1998. *Stranci: prijatelji ili neprijatelji*, trans. D. Gojković. Belgrade: Bibl. XX vek.

Bogosavljević, S. 1983. *German Literary Travelogues Around the Turn of the Century, 1890–1914*. Ph.D. thesis, University of Illinois at Urbana-Champaign.

Deretić, J. 1987. *Kratka istorija srpske književnosti*. Belgrade: BIGZ.

——— 1996. *Put srpske književnosti*. Belgrade: Srpska književna zadruga.

Dučić, J. 1932. 'Jovan Dučić o svojim putopisima', *Pregled* 97, 442.

——— 1940. *Gradovi i himere*. Belgrade: Srpska književna zadruga.

——— 1969. *Moji saputnici. Prilozi (kritike, članci, beleške)*, in *Sabrana dela*, vol. 4, ed. Ž. Stojković. Sarajevo: Svjetlost.

——— 1991. *Diplomatski spisi*. Belgrade: Prosveta.

During, S. 1990. 'Nationalism: Literature's Other?', in *Nation and Narration*, ed. H. Bhabha. London: Routledge.

Eagleton, T. 2000. *The Idea of Culture*. Oxford: Blackwell.

Epštejn, M. 1997. *Esej*, trans. R. Mečanin. Belgrade: Alfa, Narodna knjiga.

Gvozden, V. 2001. 'Polazišta i ciljevi imagološkog proučavanja književnosti', *Zbornik Matice srpske za književnost i jezik* 49:1–2, 211–24.

Herodotus. *The History of Herodotus*, trans. G. Rawlinson. At <http://classics. mit.edu/ Herodotus/history.1.i.html>, retrieved 9 April 2004.

Huenen, R. le. 1990. 'Qu'est ce qu'un récit de voyage', in *Les modèles du récit de voyage*, ed. M.-C. Gomez-Géraud (*Littérales* 7). Paris: X-Nanterre.

Karianopol, V. 1987. 'Iz bukureštanskih dana Jovana Dučića', *Letopis Matice srpske* 439:1, 115–26.

Kašanin, M. 1968. 'Usamljenik (Jovan Dučić)', in *Sudbine i ljudi*. Belgrade: Prosveta.

Leerssen, J. 1991. 'Mimesis and Stereotype', in *National Identity: Symbol and Representation*, ed. J. Leerssen and M. Spiering (*Yearbook of European Studies* 4). Amsterdam: Rodopi.

Leovac, S. 1985. *Jovan Dučić, književno delo*. Sarajevo: Svjetlost.

Maksimović, V. 1969. 'Dučićevi odlasci u svijet', *Izraz* 13:8–9, 252–57.

Mirković, N. 1936. 'Jovan Dučić', *Srpski književni glasnik*, new series, 48:5, 334–44.

Moura, J.-M. 1992. 'L'imagologie littéraire: essai de mise au point historique et critique', *Revue de littérature comparée* 66:3, 285.

Obradović, D. 1961. 'Pismo Haralampiju', in *Sabrana dela*, vol. 1, ed. V. Durić. Belgrade: Prosveta.

Orfelin, Z. 1768. *Slaveno-serpski magazin* [Venice] 1:1, 1–96.

Popović, B. 2001. 'O književnosti (Pristupno predavanje iz istorije svetske književnosti, 12. februara 1894)', in *Književna teorija i estetika*. Belgrade: Zavod za udžbenike i nastavna sredstva.

Skerlić, J. 1955 [1901]. 'Jovan Dučić', in *Pisci i knjige*, vol. 3. Belgrade: Prosveta.

Todorov, T. 1989. *Nous et les autres*. Paris: Seuil.

Woolf, S. 1996. 'Introduction', in *Nationalism in Europe, 1815 to the Present*, ed. S. Woolf. London: Routledge.

CHAPTER 5

Towards a Modernist Travel Culture

Dean Duda

Any attempt to situate an account of the modernist travel culture of a plural European region within the framework of the crucial issue of practices of literary self-representation requires more than a mere statement of caution. I shall therefore first briefly outline the conceptual and terminological framework of travel culture informing my analysis of modernist self-representation within a small/marginal European literature such as Croatian. Summarizing its most relevant aspects, this article will endeavour to enquire into the premises, as well as the effects, of the articulation I have named modernist travel culture, with respect to the specific exchange between literature and a broadly conceived travel culture. The article will not deal with the socially dominant (in terms of national or regional literary production) or generally accepted form of textual performance of travel in the decades marked by modernism in literature, but rather with the type of discourse that produces travel experience within the modernist mental model. This discourse structures self-representation by means of a few typical figures, and forms a culturally visible body of texts that can, in terms of a shared poetics, be related to a series of similar interventions in the field of literature. I therefore prefer to speak of distinctive practices that come about within the specific articulation of travel writing and modernism. This article starts from three preliminary and interrelated issues: the status of travel writing as a literary genre and its development in the first half of the twentieth century; the social/textual figures that define tendencies in travel culture and its main protagonists (especially the dichotomy of traveller/tourist as a particular figure of the dichotomy of high/popular culture); and, finally, the concept of modernism that enables a sound integration of all the elements necessary for such an analysis. In order to facilitate understanding, examples from English literature and travel writing will occasionally be given.

The first problem concerns the status of travel writing within the field of literature and its development in the decades marked by literary modernism. Even though it might seem somewhat quaint, the issue of travel writing's 'literariness' and its place in the literary hierarchy bears directly on the field of travel culture, and nowhere more so than in its modernist articulation. For instance, Carr proposes dividing English travel writing of the broadly conceived modernist period (1880–1940) into three stages: before 1900, 'the long, "realist" – not of course synonymous with reliable – instructive tale of heroic adventure remained dominant'; in the period to the First World War 'the "realist" texts have not disappeared, but much travel writing becomes less didactic, more subjective, more literary'; and finally in the interwar period there occurs 'a surge in the popularity of travel and travel writing … the literary travel book had become the dominant form: many of the best known examples of the genre were written by writers equally or better known for their fiction or poetry'. Travel writing thus at the end of the modernist period becomes 'a more literary and autonomous genre than we understand it to be today', which means that it is at once 'a more subjective form, more memoir than manual, and often an alternative form of writing for novelists'. However, even though its features changed, 'many of its themes did not' (Carr 2002: 74–75).

According to what principles would such a modernist travelling subject be fashioned? In other words, who is the social/textual protagonist steering travel writing towards literariness and subjectivity, i.e., modernism? Some simple but helpful insights produced by the study of travel culture may assist us in answering this question.

Let us now turn to the problem of the difference between the high and the popular, which, in the shape of the frequently used traveller/tourist dichotomy (Fussell 1980; Buzard 1993; Rauch 2001; Urry 2002), forms the key social distinction of travel culture in the second half of the twentieth century, while also having played an active role in the broadly conceived period of modernism.[1] This dichotomy is active as a point of differentiation between the 'genuine and spurious cultural experience' (Buzard 1993: 80), even though the origin of the terms used is not free of ambiguity. Namely, 'the term tourist, as used by Stendhal in his *Memoirs of a Tourist* (1838), designates a traveller who travels in order to improve his own personal culture' (Rauch 1996: 96), his bewilderment in the face of the masterpieces of the Italian Renaissance notwithstanding. With the appearance of the tourist on the social stage, travel suffered a sort of Benjaminian loss of aura. In contrast to the times when travelling was an art (Brilli 1996), usually in the form of the Grand Tour, in the final decades of the nineteenth century the aura was irretrievably lost. The activity that had formerly been the prerogative, in the form of individual experience, of the privileged members of the social elite, could now be reproduced across the social strata. The process whereby capitalism provided the impetus for the development of the leisure industry, of which tourism is arguably the key branch, enabled the democratization of the travel experience, but also revealed the reproductive, ready-made nature of its practice. As a genre legitimizing social change, tourist guides 'introduce[d] a kind of travel as leisure' and 'spread a style, a way of using travel that would for a long time define sophisticated tourism' (Rauch 2001: 60).

The traveller/tourist dichotomy heralds or perhaps reflects the system of differentiation characteristic of the historical period usually referred to as modernism. This leads to the third preliminary problem, i.e. a conception of modernism that would enable a sound integration of the moments fundamental for this analysis. Urry notes that modernism includes 'structural differentiation', i.e. the 'separate development of a number of institutional and normative spheres, of economy, the family, the state, science, morality, and an aesthetic realm'. Each of these spheres 'develops its own conventions and mode of valuation', and value 'within the cultural spheres is dependent upon how well a cultural object measures up to the norms appropriate to that sphere'. He calls this process 'horizontal differentiation,' and in the field of literary theory it could probably be justified by the Russian formalists' fundamental demand for the autonomy of literature. However, each self-legislative sphere is also subject to 'vertical differentiation', which in the cultural sphere includes a 'number of distinctions: between culture and life, between high and low culture, between scholarly or auratic art and popular pleasures, and between elite and mass forms of consumption' (Urry 2002: 76).[2]

If we were to situate travel culture more systematically within the processes of modernist differentiation, the traveller/tourist opposition would probably figure as a point of departure in the formation of a modernist travel culture. With respect to mobility, this dichotomy could be made more complex by introducing the modernist exile as a figure in opposition to collective tourism, or, conversely, by following its eventual dissolution into the character of the post-tourist, postmodern nomad (Rojek 1993; Kaplan 1996; Blanton 1997; Urry 2002), or the transformation of the modern *pilgrim* into its (postmodern) successors, the *stroller* (flâneur), the *vagabond*, the *tourist* and the *player* (Bauman 1996).

Since literary modernism fits Urry's idea of horizontal and vertical differentiation perfectly, it is only logical to pose the question of travel practices in the field of literature, i.e., the question of how and to what extent travel writing produces and partakes of the value system of modernist poetics. According to today's temporal demarcations, modernism in literature begins some time between 1880 and 1890, and ends in the period 1930 to 1940 – this is the time-scheme we have already seen employed in the analysis of English travel writing (Carr 2002), and it is the one proposed by Bradbury and McFarlane in their treatment of the period (1991). We must also bear in mind that this image of modernism, although structurally highly complex, is nevertheless not historically homogeneous. Each historical period can in its heterogeneity be revealed as the synchrony of the asynchronous (*'Gleichzeitigkeit des Ungleichzeitigen'* [Koselleck 1979]); as the intersection of many diachronic trajectories and of phenomena of varying duration. The simultaneous existence of, as Williams (1980) would put it, dominant, residual and emergent (travel) cultural practice, and therefore of its texts as well, is the basic assumption of modernist travel culture conceived in this manner. It follows that not every travel account published during this period belongs to modernist travel culture, as far as literature, i.e., literary travel writing, is concerned, but only such travel writing practices as share the dominant features of modernism, appropriating, confirming or even creating them as recognizable and distinctive. Modernist travel writing must, therefore, in some way demonstrate its worth as regards the 'cultural seismology' which has registered change and the emergence of modernism, but in a double articulation – with respect to literature, on the one hand, and the practice of travel, on the other. In other words, I would like to know: how does literary travel writing produce modernism?[3]

In order to answer this question, or at least to attempt to delimit the field of a possible answer, some markers must be introduced:

1. Can we speak of a specifically modernist itinerary, of privileged cultural spaces or destinations, emblematic of a modernist travel culture?
2. Can the narrative techniques used in travel writing be compared to the dominant narrative practices in modernist fictional texts, with respect to the use of the narrative voice, as well as the ways in which the information about the space through which one travels is mediated?
3. Can we discern legitimizing practices of the subject that would indicate modernist mental figures – from modes of perception, through frames of reference activated by the text, to behaviour in general?
4. Who is the addressee postulated by such modernist travel writing, not only in the text itself (the implied reader), but also within the larger context of a given cultural community, to whom literary or everyday

travel narrative is presented as a consequence of exchange in the border zone?[4]

The examples used in the following analysis are taken from Croatian literature which, in the middle decades of the nineteenth century, produced an interesting body of travel writing, which might almost occupy the place Anderson (1991) assigns to the novel in the constitution of an imagined community. The publication of travel writing – as a public activity by means of which the nation formulates its own chronotope, draws its cultural borders, builds internal coherence, demarcates occupied territory and defines others – may have been a significant element in (Croatian) nation-imagining. However, it would seem that in the initial years of the formation of modernist culture, travel writing practice remains occluded. A.G. Matoš, for instance, as an important literary intermediary between late Romanticism and the modern tendencies, deliberately points to an absence in Croatian travel culture. Two of his texts are of interest from the point of view of travel culture – 'Ferije' ('Holidays') (1908) and 'Napuljske šetnje' ('Neapolitan Walks') (1911). The former might be classified as travel writing, while the latter is actually a review of Milorad Pavlović's travel book, *Napuljske šetnje* (published in Belgrade in 1911).

The text of *Holidays* (Matoš 1973a) is four-fifths an apologia for modern travel; the final fifth being a critical evaluation of Croatian travel culture. Matoš is particularly harsh on the hidebound character of the Croatian intelligentsia who – in contrast to the peasant, who (in the form of the economic emigrant) sets off for 'the Americas the way his grandfather went to the country fair' – are content with 'sitting by the fire, spinning and scheming like village grannies'. The peasants are therefore 'Europeans', while through the Croatian intelligentsia a 'marshland parochialism blows'. He invokes Croatia's neighbours in a less than complimentary comparison: 'Whereas the heralds and harbingers of modern Serbia are travellers such as the wise Dositej and that witty old man Lj[ubomir] Nenadović, our people travel not because of travel itself but only out of necessity'. This is why, according to Matoš, the Serbs have a rich travel literature, while in Croatian literature travel writers are 'white crows'. From this situation Matoš reaches a diagnostic of cultural xenophobia: the Croats do not travel, and therefore do not even know Croatia, and he who does not know himself cannot know the world. This is why the Croats are, according to Matoš, 'one of the most retarded peoples of Europe' and why 'young Serbs and Bulgarians flock to the centres of European culture, while we Croats, children of the South and the Adriatic, neighbours, students and defenders of classical culture, languish culturally and travel – by reading the travel writings of others' (1973b: 282).

Matoš's image of his nation is an exceptional Croatian contribution to
the self-imageology of southeastern Europe/the Balkans. Here travel has
not lost its aura, for it simply never had one. His critique results from the
contradiction presented by the two types of sensibility that are the
synchronous forms of diachronically different moments. On the one
hand, it relies on a group, on the community within which every
traveller is a valuable piece in the mosaic of national travel culture, as,
for example, in the period of Romanticism and of the imagining/forming
of 'nations'. On the other hand, Matoš is a modern individual, an exile,
a pilgrim and a traveller, who, however, cannot sever all bonds with the
imaginary community and wake up, like Stephen Dedalus, from the
hold of history/nation as from a nightmare. It is interesting to note that
this contradiction is also characteristic of his rather voluminous travel
writings. Torn between the European experience and the situation in
Croatia, Matoš functions in the discourse of an ethnocentric individual
sorely anxious about the state of his homeland. The question of whether
this is an objective assessment of the real situation, the discourse of a
cultural *comprador* or the textual production of one's own exceptional
position, often resulting in national bathos, remains unresolved.
Nevertheless, Matoš's diagnosis indicates the cultural climate and the
symbolic baggage, as regards its double articulation or economy, that
modernist travel writing discourse inherits.

The discourse of modernist travel writing appeared in Croatian
literature completely unaffected by Matoš's critique. Its first manifestation,
in line with the typical principles of avant-garde poetics, looks almost like
a manifesto. In 1926, Miroslav Krleža (1893–1981) published his *Izlet u
Rusiju* ('Excursion to Russia'), in which the legitimation of the writing
subject is unmistakably modernist. The book consists of texts dealing with
his trips to Berlin (June 1924), Vienna (December 1924) and Moscow
(February–May 1925), previously published in newspapers and magazines
(*Hrvat, Književna republika, Obzor*) in the period from September 1924 to
May 1926.[5] Krleža's *Excursion to Russia* brings him into the interesting
group of travellers, of more or less the same political persuasion, who
witnessed the condition of Russia at the time: Ernst Toller, for example,
visited Russia in the spring of 1926 on a ten-day trip and published his
Russische Reisebilder later that year; *Le Voyage à Moscou* by Georges Duhamel
and *Zaren, Popen, Bolschewiken* by Egon Erwin Kisch were both published in
1927; while Walter Benjamin stayed in Moscow from 6 December 1926
until the end of January 1927, due to Asja Lacis' nervous breakdown,
writing his *Moskauer Tagebuch*.

If it is accepted that the itinerary can serve as a signal of modernist
travel culture, then Russia in the 1920s is undoubtedly a prime example
of such a destination. The revolutionary social experiment certainly

constituted more than a neutral, exotic travel destination, acting almost as a utopian magnet for all those who believed in Communist ideology. However, Russia by itself cannot be a sign of modernism, it must be produced as such within the text through the actions and perceptions of the travel writer. This is why Krleža avails himself of a multiple antithesis formed, on the one hand, by the social rituals of the Croatian bourgeois community and its collective perceptions, and on the other, by the modernist behaviour of a traveller to Russia. This antithetical play is already present in the almost oxymoronic title, which joins, from the point of view of his community, two socially irreconcilable elements: 'excursion' and 'Russia'. For who would undertake an 'excursion' to 'Russia' in the mid 1920s, and why?

The usual dichotomy of traveller/tourist seems to be at work here, but in an inverted form. By going to Russia on an 'excursion', the traveller presents himself in the guise of a tourist, adopting the practice of the latter, which defines an excursion as 'a (usually) short journey made for pleasure'. What the native bourgeois culture, reading every day 'mendacious and tendentious reports on the situation in Russia' (Krleža 1926: 11), sees as a space of abjection and peril, incompatible with the idea of an excursion, the writing subject perceives as a place of pleasure. This is why he can define his trip to Russia as belonging to leisure – as an excursion. He forms his exceptional position as an antithesis to the usual tourist ritual of his community by performing this ritual in a space the community can hardly accept as a suitable destination for an excursion, i.e., as a place of leisure. Even his nonchalant attitude toward his preparations for the journey suggests he is going to a nearby resort: 'I took a bottle of cologne, the most recent edition of Vidrić's poems, with an Introduction by Mr. Vladimir Lunaček, and headed for the railway station to board the train to Moscow' (Krleža 1926: 11). So Krleža travels for pleasure, just as a tourist on an excursion should. He is not, however, a ready-made product of the tourist industry, nor a representative of the community, but a traveller who demonstrates his individuality by his choice of destination. This does not exhaust Krleža's antithetical play, though, for an 'excursion' can also mean 'a diversion or deviation from the main topic', which further confirms modernist exceptionality and conforms to the persona of the traveller. The title, then, already contains the semantic interplay of two points of view, producing the trip to Russia as a double deviation and a sign of modernism. Not only does it legitimize the travel writer, but the title even, in a certain sense, presupposes the recipient. According to the logic of modernist poetics, the addressees of the *Excursion to Russia* are, beyond doubt, also those whose reaction can only be one of shock and repugnance; those who find it inconceivable that anyone could undertake an excursion to Russia at the time. The choice of itinerary functions as a 'slap in the face of social taste' – a transgression.[6]

Another example of the antithesis is to be found in the legitimating practice of the writing subject with respect to the dominant travel practice, the received ways of structuring information about the space of travel and the expectations of the reader. Lest there should be occasion for misunderstanding, the travel writer states his preferences clearly at the beginning of the text. The antithesis occurs in the form of a narrative contract offered to the reader, and its function is yet again to establish the distinctive role of the modernist traveller:

> Anyone who is a devotee of false pathos won't find much to read in these travel memoirs of mine. I don't like travels with pathetic cultural-historical reminiscences! Inasmuch as the subject is a skein of flesh and blood and as such a completely ephemeral phenomenon on the earth's surface, so all those waters, cities and people which roll through the subject, originate in that subject alone, and then disappear with him; accordingly, these few lines of mine don't have any great cultural-historical or particularly informative pretensions. Above all when I travel, I don't visit churches much, and I go to museums very rarely. I should stress that I prefer demonstrations, street scuffles, strikes, steam engines, women, coffins or any other dirty, everyday occurrence to pictures in Academies, the Baroque, the Renaissance. (Krleža 1926: 4)[7]

The need to be different changes both the form and the content that mediate travel experience. Cultural and historical reminiscences, the usual formal elements of travel writing, are a token of traditional travel sophistication. If the tourist guide defined the sophisticated gaze, it was precisely by means of cultural and historical data. It is by virtue of them that 'travel in space doubles as travel in time' [*Le voyage dans l'espace se double d'un voyage dans le temps*] (Rauch 2001: 46). The past, however, is certainly not the temporal mode that a modernist would prefer. Krleža does not need a regressive, but a progressive doubling of time. His concept of time is based on the present, which holds the promise of the future as a (utopian) project. In a bourgeois society, the travel writer states, 'we cannot all look in parallel' (1926: 4). This is why he foregoes the Renaissance, the Baroque, churches and museums, as signs of past times and snobbery, for demonstrations, strikes, coffins and other dirty and everyday occurrences: a variation, almost, on the Joycean history-as-nightmare. Moreover, the city as a privileged site of modernist cultural cartography is the focal point. The discarding of the form of cultural and historical reminiscence is predicated upon the choice of a different gaze, a different concept of time: in short, upon a modernist mentality.

At the same time, this mentality presupposes conflict, and this is an important feature of the subject of Krleža's travel writing. He 'detests the Renaissance' because of having been imprisoned in a fort on some 'Renaissance island'; he picks a quarrel with some sailors in Genoa, trying to explain that it is stupid for their battleship to be called 'Dante Alighieri'; he provokes an incident on board a train through Lithuania; he despises the accepted tourist forms of sightseeing, and is constantly reducing his fellow travellers and the people he meets to grotesque caricatures. To Krleža, conflict, as another form of antithesis, means action. And his travelling to Russia is a mode of action:

> This is how the matter stands: we are all living in a provincial halt on Austria's southern railway line and our railway station is a one-storey building of red brick. A province! A black, muddy, sorry province! And all that has happened over the last fifty years is the following: some idiots walk through these brutalities and inside them the weak sound of a muted string chimes painfully, saying that there's no sense in dragging oneself wounded like this through muddy city peripheries, breathing with difficulty, swathing one's nerves in fat, feeling a yearning for far distances while lazily sinking ever deeper into the mire. Looking at the one-storey railway station of red brick, the poplars, the sawmills, the garrisons, listening to the accordion, sensing perspectives, and at the same time realising that we, with our petty-bourgeois pseudo-intellectual quasi-talents, which yawn and ring from emptiness like empty vessels, will never be able to build bridges to the Real and the Actual. To seize, to raise ourselves, to do something. All this listening to the accordions behind glass doors, this spinsterish brooding on dead blind men, on forgotten girls, on bygone bugle calls, nauseated me, and I spat on the ground and set off the next day. (1926: 5)

A further element is being added: the backwardness of his native culture. Action is a reaction to its sorry state. It is necessary, therefore, for us 'to raise ourselves', 'to do something' in order 'to build bridges to the Real and the Actual'. The tension becomes unbearable. The avant-garde gesture is a logical slap in the face of the present situation: Krleža has slapped its face and gone off to Russia. According to Gumbrecht's (1997) analysis of the codes informing the year in which the *Excursion to Russia* was published, action is a recognizable mental figure of the time. 'Action' is opposed to 'impotence'; it is a transgression directed into the future, a token of exceptionality:

> A direct Action, then, is an Action that does not necessarily follow from the circumstances in which it occurs. It is an Action that attracts attention through the tension it establishes with its environment. Whoever performs a direct Action seems to claim implicitly that it is absolutely the right thing

to do, apart from generally accepted reasons, expectations, or legislation. Once such an Action has been performed, its mere facticity as a transgressive event appears to sanction the subjective grounds out of which it emerged, thus encouraging repetition or continuation. [...] There is no Action, no *Tat*, without this tension coming from and pointing toward the future. (Gumbrecht 1997: 253–54)

Such a concept flouts the usual limits and underlying assumptions of homogeneous constructions of cultural space. This is why Krleža points out that it is hard to determine 'where Europe begins, and Asia ends' (1926: 55), affirming the idea of the synchrony of the asynchronous. In this view, Europe and Asia function as intertwined mental figures that can be found in Berlin, Zagreb or Moscow. Even should one think that in this articulation Europe is nothing but a cultural, historical and snobbish figure of an aesthetic aristocracy, it contains a social element linking it to Asia as a metaphor for backwardness, for the blind beggar women in Berlin cry 'with the very same voice that all our blind cry, to the sound of the accordion, down by the Ćulinec bridge' (1926: 55). The solution is, of course, Leninism as a project, as 'the light that has illuminated the tenebrous ken of Europe, shining on the horizon ever more clearly with each new day' (1926: 141). Projection into the future makes it possible for asynchronous, even conflicting, structures to be perceived within an existing synchrony, but also for a resolution of their contradictions to be offered. The future, in all probability, has the benefit of hindsight.

These brief remarks on Krleža's *Excursion to Russia* help us to establish a framework for answering not only questions about modernist travel culture, but also the question of the visibility of the authors of marginal European literatures/languages. Travel writing is, of course, not a genre literary historians have foregrounded when describing the modernist upheaval, at least as literary and cultural seismology has registered it. Krleža's text, however, is a rare example of a fully fledged flaunting of modernist strategies. The change in the preferences of travelling practice and their textual form demonstrate the value of the *Excursion to Russia* within the double economy. Radical gestures and the antithetical legitimation of the writing subject, the concept of time he has before him, as well as the choice of destination, are all comparable to the crucial elements of the modernist, even avant-garde, literary onslaught. At the same time, as regards his perception of the situation in the USSR and his textual construction of Soviet reality, Krleža is no ideological dupe. The metaphors of beacon, signpost and lighthouse applied to Lenin are frequent in the text precisely because the travel writer does not perceive Russia as some final and definite state of things, but as a project in the state of becoming. In Krleža's discourse, modernism can be discerned immediately, almost as an exemplary product of Urry's (2002) differentiation. Vehemence, however, is only one aspect of modernism's prehistory. Introversion and introspection are its other side.

This other side of modernist travel culture can be seen in the travel writing of Slavko Batušić (1902–1979). Close to Krleža in his formative years, as well as later in life, Batušić offered a different kind of modernist travel sensibility. His experience is not peripheral in Gumbrecht's (1997) sense. He is a privileged traveller of the European centre. He began his travel writing in the early 1920s, travelled all over Europe and published three travel books – *Kroz zapadne zemlje i gradove* ('Through Western Lands and Cities') in 1932, *Od Kandije do Hammerfesta* ('From Crete to Hammerfest') in 1937 and *Od Siene do Haarlema* ('From Siena to Haarlem') in January 1941. If Krleža can be taken as the avant-garde manifesto form of modernist travel culture, Batušić is characterized by modernist introversion and introspection.

In general, modernism prefers the individual, solitude, melancholy, experimentation with the strange and the unknown, and a world where the centre is in doubt, so that the artist/traveller is actually a subject in exile: an existential loner who has no place or home to call his own. Modernism is thus founded upon a specific logic of situation: its subjects are so located that they are perpetually dislocated. Hence Batušić, during his stay on Crete in 1935, can say: 'My flight aboard a black ship into the black night is the flight of a desperate banished man' (1959: 250). Such a position of necessity implies a different narrative economy. How can a solitary subject in exile possess a travel experience? If the modern novel is to a large extent based on the fact that the events are shifted from the world into the mind of the character, this principle can, it would seem, be applied to modernist travel writing as well, especially as practised by Batušić.

In the assumed triad of the acting subject, the perceiving subject and the narrating subject, the perceiving subject is obviously dominant (in travel writing), not only as a mere observer and recorder of things offered to the eye of the traveller, but as a solitary, anxious and socially sensitive modern mind that visualizes the fragmented nature of the world and translates it into a travel-writing discourse that often shapes its lexical material in accordance with the principles of painting. Economy of expression favours the monological fragment. The world in fragments of necessity implies a mind in fragments, and this is brought to bear on the composition of Batušić's travel writing. His travel writing could reasonably be likened to postcard texts: they are focused upon a few isolated motifs and authorized by the consciousness speaking through them, above all to itself.[8]

Another feature of Batušić's modernism is the participation of the subject in the creation of collective identities. Enclosed within himself, produced as an individual, the writing subject cannot share the places of identification existing in the collective imaginary. The lyrical prelude *Vožnja* ('Ride') of 1928, that Batušić placed at the beginning of his first book of travel writing, includes some paradigmatic lines in this respect:

All, all alone,
butchered by this life so plain,
locked up in myself with three locks,
to save my soul I board the first train.
[...]

And then away with the muzzle,
I abandon the oar on the galley of the nation
without any feigned commemoration. (1959: 9–10)

These few lines could almost be said to summarize the modernist ideology of travel: loneliness, the brutally wounding hostility of everyday life, life as a slaughterhouse, hyperbolic introversion ('locked up in myself with three locks') chosen as a survival technique, and finally, travel, i.e., exile, as the only means of saving one's soul. To travel is to do 'away with the muzzle', but also to abandon the national collectivity represented in the form of the galley, which to the Croatian collective imaginary suggests the instrument of Venetian domination. This abandonment 'without any feigned commemoration' is not dissimilar to Joyce's *non serviam*, i.e., Dedalus's artistic project in *A Portrait of the Artist as a Young Man*: the modernist subject cannot serve what he does not believe in, whether it be (his) home, (his) fatherland or (his) church, and the only weapons that he has at his disposal are silence, exile and cunning.

Travel is a logical metaphor for such a modernist attitude towards life.[9] This modernist privilege, i.e., the individual's dearly-won right to differ, usually manifests itself in sharp contrast to the behaviour of a group, mass or mob, while travelling. For instance, in his *Reminiscencije na postaji Mestre* ('Reminiscences at Mestre Station'), Batušić recalls an 1848 engraving entitled 'Croatian sergeants, encamped at the Venetian suburb of Mestre'. Stationed in the atrium of the palace, the soldiers have had hay strewn on the marble floor and their clothes hung onto the assorted classical and pseudoclassical statues. Batušić notes that his travel would be free of the 'atavistic instincts of the sergeants from Otočac and Korenica'. Nor would he efface himself and 'play the favourite game of our feuilleton writers: imagining that in my gloves and my trench-coat I am more of a citizen of the Grand Canal and Carcassonne than those who had been born there'. He is quite simply 'neither one, nor the other'

(1959: 117–18). When pressed to *interact* socially in some way or another, he resorts to practices that legitimate him as a cosmopolitan, a citizen of the world. Thus when asked, aboard the ship to Hammerfest, to sing or dance something from his national culture, he decides to perform a Japanese trick.

Such reluctance to identify with the collective complements the modernist variant of the traveller/tourist dichotomy quite logically. The introverted individual finds his opposition in the unreflective, ready-made tourist, who is naturally, in his interpretation, beneath contempt. The Americans in Europe are a favourite subject of Batušić's from as early as 1925, and appear in his text *O sretnim i nesretnim putnicima* ('Of Happy and Unhappy Travellers'):

> A certain party of United States citizens embarks somewhere in New York, disembarks somewhere in Le Havre or Genoa, and then what for them must be an awful month of terrible hustle and bustle through cities, churches, galleries and wonderful vistas ensues. Who knows what they must actually make of this Europe of ours in the end ... . They are crammed into a car, dragged for a hundred kilometres, thrown out of the car, crammed into huge blue buses that take fifty individuals, while up front there is a professional *cicerone*, yelling, explaining every detail, showing them everything and then some, and then they are dragged back to the station, crammed into the car again, and taken a further hundred kilometres to the next town [...]. And so on relentlessly, ceaselessly. [...] They are dragged into a church; they immediately sit down on the pews, since they are exhausted. (1959: 63)[10]

The Americans come 'to this poor Europe of ours as if it were a flea market, making an unpleasant and tasteless racket' (1959: 111). To Batušić, they are the unhappy travellers while he belongs to the privileged 'happy' few, because he is an individual, a traveller who does not take part in group rituals and is not taken in by collective tourist practices – he takes no photographs with pigeons, he does not allow himself be fooled by the phoney *ciceroni*, nor tortured in the blue buses. He says much the same thing of the American tourists in Munich, or when looking at American newlyweds on the ship to Hammerfest: 'A sad, sorry and doleful industry. But it is their own fault: they have too much money' (1959: 63). However, the Americans are not the only or privileged figures of Batušić's contrastive legitimation. The motifs of everyday life are also made use of – the armaments of Italy in the early years of Fascism, the dirty beach at the Lido where the sea is a 'waste-paper basket' (1959: 43), Fascist architecture, or the stock market in Paris. All that belongs to the tourist industry, especially the markers of cultural attraction, is despicable. In Helsingør, he would not 'succumb to the suggestion of the legend' and pay a visit to 'a mound' supposed to be

Hamlet's grave: 'No, I did not go there; I would have been ashamed of myself' (1959: 169), and in Verona, he does not want to see the sarcophagus 'that bears the hi-falutin name of *"tomba di Giulietta"*, in front of which professional tourist spinsters from Ipswich and Southampton sigh and moan' (1959: 312). One's own sensibility is therefore also produced by the continuous exposing of one's travelling Other, as well as of received collective identifications. In this fashion, an almost archetypal dramatic tension develops between the solitary, sensitive individual on the one hand, and any form of collectivity on the other. This is not Krleža's disrespectful conflict – an outright confrontation – but the work of perception and its filtering through modernist monological discourse.

In Batušić's conception, the individual itinerary or a certain destination can hardly be a self-sufficient, distinctive sign of modernism. His modernist experience is predicated upon the constant accumulation of further parts travelled through and the frequency of travel. Since his substantial body of travel writing falls into a relatively short and coherent period between the two world wars, we can see in his case an early example of the situation that would, after the Second World War, enable English authors of travel writing to embark upon literary careers (Hulme 2002). His paths are more or less well trodden and, even when they are completely new from the point of view of Croatian travel culture – like Hammerfest, the northernmost town of Europe – his writing is far from journalistic discourse.

Finally, the last point in this discussion of the problem of modernist travel culture is represented by the writings of Marijan Matković (1915–1985). This does not mean that modernist tendencies cannot be detected in other authors, but Matković, another member of Krleža's circle, represents in his travel writing of the 1960s almost the last discernible variant of modernism. This refers in particular to the dialogical concept of consciousness, which first appears in a rudimentary form in his diaries as a narrative in the second person singular, i.e., some form of self-communication, and is then also used in *Američki triptih* ('American Triptych'), written in late winter and spring of 1964, published separately as a book in 1974. Although Matković's other travel writing dates from both before and after this work, his American texts are interesting precisely because they expose the travelling experience as effected by the work of at least two minds. The *I* and *you* of Matković's discourse are mutually complementary voices forming a complex narrative in dramatic form:

> No, you'll never get to the bridge like this: you long for the desolate Washington squares on Sundays. You have decided: I shall cross this road, then that lawn, I must get to the banks of the Potomac, and then upstream,

I am sure to find a crossing. And a taxi. Enough of this wandering. – Where
the heck am I anyway? – You stopped short. You can't really say how, after
that maze of roads, you wound up in a park all of a sudden. (2001: 145)

It is only logical that this kind of travel-writing discourse should be
situated at the border between the relaying of travel experience and self-
analysis. For Matković, all travel is disillusionment, which is why he
structures it as a dialogue between the expected, the experienced and an
eventual reflection on the difference between the two. The experience of
America is distributed among several narrative instances and mostly
either combined into narrated monologues or separated in a dramatic
dialogue. Anxiety, fear, indecisiveness and curiosity, on the one hand,
get enmeshed with weariness and sickness, on the other. He finds his
Other not only in the space he is visiting but in the very structure of his
mind. His travel is thus focalized from a variety of positions, which brings
about a more complex concept of time.

Matković's American experience is no longer an experience of the
periphery, as it might have been had he travelled to the United States
several decades earlier. His America is a Cold War country far removed
from childish delusions, at the same time fascinating and violent – 'an
unpleasant hotchpotch of colours, forms and sounds' (2001: 194). In its
textual form, it is conveyed by the narrative devices characteristic of the
modern novel. In this world, New York holds a special place: 'The
embrace in this ant-hill, the nations, the races, the continents, the
dreams of hope – and yet no one has found out and explained whether
this is an embrace or a strangulation to death' (2001: 196). A more
thorough analysis would have to take into account the fact that the
image and perception of 'native space' had changed significantly since
the Second World War. At the time, the Federal Republic of Yugoslavia
was a political fact between the two blocs, which leads us towards a new
articulation in which Croatian travel writers partake of a specific
(socialist) travel culture and of the new field of exchange between
literature and travel culture. The repertory of modernist devices and the
experience of modernist travel writers enters into the articulation of this
changed political situation, and this probably causes some shifts that
would be of interest to cultural seismology.

Notes

1. Fussell (1980: 39) reaches the dichotomy starting from a tripartite model of
    explorer–traveller–tourist.
2. It should be noted that Urry's analysis of modernism does not start from the
    period that might have preceded it, but is brought about through a

comparison with postmodernism, which by contrast involves 'de-differentiation', i.e. 'a breakdown in the distinctiveness of each sphere of social activities, especially the cultural' (2002: 76), and 'implosion'. The postdisciplinary field of travel culture is perhaps also a consequence of this implosion.

3. The analysis of modernist features of travel writing, mostly using examples from English literature (e.g., Fussell 1980; Cocker 1992; Blanton 1997) often singles out the feeling of dissatisfaction and anxiety that, together with the modern tendency towards self-exploration, makes travel the dominant literary metaphor of the time. Historians of modernist travel writing claim that the years immediately after the Second World War definitely mark the end of the original modernist culture of travel, an end signalled by the emergence of mass tourism and the disappearance of independent travel.

4. I draw here on my previous work on the elements of literary-historical rhetoric of travel writing (expository frame, itinerary, the subject of the text, lexicon, thematic 'upgrade', story, addressee) that I tried to establish using Croatian travel writing (Duda 1998).

5. The structure of the book was considerably altered in subsequent editions. Changes include the addition of the year of the stay in Russia to the title, the removal of the introductory paragraphs (the itinerary to Berlin), the inclusion of articles on Russian political topics, and a series of authorial interventions on the level of both content and language. This has, to a significant degree, deprived *Excursion to Russia* of its modernist impact.

6. The lexeme 'excursion' has a different meaning in Krleža's writings of the 1950s and 1960s: *Excursion to Hungary in 1947*, *Excursion to Istria* and *Excursion to the Youth Railway Line Brčko-Banovići*. The latter belongs to the interesting group of 'socialist travel culture', a distant echo perhaps of the modernist preoccupation with technology and progress, but also pointing toward the articulation of travel and work. The purpose of travel is to mobilize, for literature also should contribute to the building of the homeland in ruins. Within this ideological framework, work (literary and engineering) is experienced as pleasure. English leftist intellectuals participated in such projects: E.P. Thompson, for example, was in 1947 the 'commandant of the British youth group assisting the People's Youth of Yugoslavia in building a 150-mile railroad from Samac in Slovenia to Sarajevo' (Dworkin 1997: 18). Without wishing to include Dworkin in the discourse of 'imperial stylistics', we must observe that 'Samac' (Šamac) is not, nor has it ever been, in Slovenia, but in Bosnia and Herezegovina.

7. I am grateful to Wendy Bracewell for her permission to use her translation of parts of Krleža's text.

8. To quote some examples from *Prvi pohod Italiji* ('The First Journey to Italy'), published in the book *Kroz zapadne zemlje i gradove* ('Through Western Lands and Cities') (1932) and included in Batušić 1959: 'A black mass of people spilled like ink over the geometrical figures of the square, shouting, pushing each other, giggling' (30); 'I fear for the clarity of my mind, and I flee to the nearest church as if it were a cold bath' (45); 'I love this silence, I love not meeting people, for I am instinctively afraid of the *cicerone*, of the postcard and souvenir seller, and most of all the photographer' (54); 'I have been

through eight cities, and the railway stations always looked like cemeteries to me. I have always been drunk with sorrow upon departure, and this drunkenness was more beautiful that that induced by wine. Much, much more beautiful' (63).

9. The importance of travel for Batušić, not only as a metaphor, but as a guarantee of true life, can be seen from the text *Travel-Writing Imagination*, written in early May 1945. The end of war means that 'The scoundrel Terror', which had turned the travel writer into a 'goldfinch blinded with a burning needle' and 'flapping against the bars of the cage' (1959: 422) has been abolished. The cage has been finally been 'replaced by the railway tracks' and the globe has once again become 'a single homeland, a single home, a single house of man' (423).

10. A brief treatment of Americans in Paris and in Europe, as well as of the European perception of American tourists, can be found in Gumbrecht (1997).

References

Anderson, B. 1991. *Imagined Communities: Reflections on the Origin and Spread of Nationalism*. London: Verso.

Batušić, S. 1959. *Pejzaži i vedute: sabrani putopisi 1923–1958*. Zagreb: Naprijed.

Bauman, Z. 1996. 'From Pilgrim to Tourist – or a Short History of Identity', in *Questions of Cultural Identity*, ed. S. Hall and P. du Gay. London: Sage.

Blanton, C. 1997. *Travel Writing: The Self and the World*. New York: Twayne.

Bradbury, M. and J. McFarlane. 1991. 'The Name and Nature of Modernism', in *Modernism 1890–1930*, ed. M. Bradbury and J. McFarlane. Harmondsworth: Penguin.

Brilli, A. 1996. *Quando viaggiare era un'arte*. Bologna: Mulino.

Buzard, J. 1993. *The Beaten Track: European Tourism, Literature, and the Ways to Culture, 1800–1918*. Oxford: Clarendon Press.

Carr, H. 2002. 'Modernism and Travel (1880–1940)', in *The Cambridge Companion to Travel Writing*, ed. P. Hulme and T. Youngs. Cambridge: Cambridge University Press.

Cocker, M. 1992. *Loneliness and Time: The Story of British Travel Writing*. New York: Pantheon.

Duda, D. 1998. *Priča i putovanje: hrvatski romantičarski putopis kao pripovjedni žanr.* Zagreb: Matica hrvatska.

Dworkin, D. 1997. *Cultural Marxism in Postwar Britain: History, the New Left, and the Origins of Cultural Studies*. Durham, NC: Duke University Press.

Fussell, P. 1980. *Abroad: British Literary Traveling Between the Wars*. New York: Oxford University Press.

Gumbrecht, H.U. 1997. *In 1926: Living at the Edge of Time*. Cambridge, MA: Harvard University Press.

Hulme, P. 2002. 'Travelling to Write (1940–2000)', in *The Cambridge Companion to Travel Writing*, ed. P. Hulme and T. Youngs. Cambridge: Cambridge University Press.

Hulme, P. and T. Youngs, eds. 2002. *The Cambridge Companion to Travel Writing.* Cambridge: Cambridge University Press.

Kaplan, C. 1996. *Questions of Travel: Postmodern Discourses of Displacement.* Durham, NC: Duke University Press.

Koselleck, R. 1979. *Vergangene Zukunft: zur Semantik geschichtlicher Zeiten.* Frankfurt am Main: Suhrkamp.

Krleža, M. 1926. *Izlet u Rusiju.* Zagreb: Izdanje 'Narodne knjižnice'.

Matković, M. 2001. *Stope na stazi I. Izabrana djela 7.* Zagreb: HAZU – MH – NZMH.

Matoš, A.G. 1973a. 'Ferije', in *Sabrana djela 11 (O likovnim umjetnostima, Putopisi),* ed. S. Batušić and D. Jelčić. Zagreb: JAZU.

———— 1973b. 'Napuljske šetnje', in Matoš, A.G., *Sabrana djela 8 (O srpskoj književnosti),* ed. N. Mihanović. Zagreb: JAZU.

Rauch, A. 1996. 'Le vacanze e la rivisitazione della natura (1830–1939)', in *Invenzione del tempo libero,* ed. A. Corbin. Rome: Laterza.

———— 2001. *Vacances en France de 1830 à nos jours.* Paris: Hachette.

Rojek, C. 1993. *Ways of Escape: Modern Transformations in Leisure and Travel.* London: Macmillan.

Urry, J. 2002. *The Tourist Gaze.* London: Sage.

Williams, R. 1980. 'Base and Superstructure in Marxist Cultural Theory', in *Problems in Materialism and Culture.* London: Verso.

CHAPTER 6

Getting to Know the Big Bad West? Images of Western Europe in Bulgarian Travel Writing of the Communist Era (1945–1985)

Ludmilla Kostova

Commentators on the consequences of the collapse of communism in central and eastern Europe have repeatedly drawn attention to the crisis in (self-) representation which that major sociopolitical shift has occasioned.[1] The crisis in question has been attributed to a variety of factors, ranging from the novelty of the postcommunist experience for which few precedents could be found in other contexts, to the highly subjective character of postcommunist interpretations of the recent past. Admittedly, coming to terms with that past is still difficult. Underneath a facade of deceptive simplicity, life under communism was marked by complexities and ambiguities that Western 'observers' often failed to perceive, either because they were influenced by a deeply entrenched Cold War mythology presenting day-to-day existence in the so-called Eastern bloc solely in terms of indoctrination and victimization, or because 'native' resistance to the system usually expressed itself through semiotic codes based on camouflage and dense allusion that left outsiders puzzled and confused. On the other hand, central and east European 'participants' in the totalitarian scene still have to live with some of the ambiguities of the past as they continue to impact upon the present and to evade resolution.

As part of an attempt to counter simplistic approaches to life within the former communist bloc, a number of eastern European intellectuals have drawn attention to certain social and cultural practices that provided alternatives to official totalitarian policies. Thus Andrei Pleşu has highlighted the elaboration of strategies of intellectual survival under the Ceauşescu regime, which were to a considerable degree made effective by a spirit of arbitrariness characteristic of the totalitarian system itself (Pleşu 1995). Working within the Bulgarian context, Alexander Shurbanov and Boyka Sokolova have identified sites of resistance to the communist establishment and its cultural norms within Bulgarian theatrical productions of Shakespeare's plays (Shurbanov and Sokolova 2001: 133–230) while Miglena Nikolchina has elucidated the role of the quasi-academic seminar in the 1980s in challenging the regime's claims to total discursive control (Nikolchina 2002: 96–127). It should be noted that those intellectual projects have distinct ethical implications insofar as their authors have portrayed and assessed aspects of their own *lived* experience.

This chapter focuses on a selection of Bulgarian travelogues published between 1945 and 1985, which present images of western Europe. The texts under discussion reflect conditions of intellectual production during different phases of the communist era in Bulgaria, which was anything but monolithic. The first travel narrative, *Skitsi iz London* ('Sketches from London'), came out in 1945 during a brief interlude of relative pluralism and democracy, superseded two years later by the imposition of a completely repressive Stalinist regime. I conclude with three travelogues produced during the last and most controversial stage of the totalitarian system. With the exception of the first text, which, among other things, has a symbolic significance insofar as it embodies ideological choices that later Bulgarian travel writers were not in a position to make, all travel narratives under discussion appear to conform to the party line. At this point, it is hard to tell whether this conformity was the outcome of sincere conviction, willed self-deception or the consequence of a special pact with 'the Muse of Censorship'.[2] On the other hand, given the system's total control over the print media, the texts in question would not have been published had they in any way been openly critical of official communist policies. My project is thus different from the postcommunist projects briefly outlined above. Whereas Pleşu, Shurbanov, Sokolova and Nikolchina uncover elements of resistance to totalitarianism in the cultural practices they study, I fully acknowledge the politically conformist character of most of my material.

Despite the texts' conformism, they are worthy of study insofar as they provide insights into the development of Bulgarian travel writing in the post-Second World War period, contribute to our general knowledge of the narrative and ideological parameters of the travelogue as a genre, and shed light on the officially sanctioned process of othering characteristic of the communist establishment and upon its implications for individual writers. Moreover, writing about them is part of the multifaceted process of *remembering the past*, which should keep the debate about it alive rather than conveniently consign it to closure and oblivion.[3]

The travel writing produced under communism exhibits a degree of continuity with earlier stages of the genre's development and with the evolution of the dialectic of self and other through which travel narratives are generally structured. The first part of the chapter is therefore concerned with the development of Bulgarian travel writing between the 1840s and 1940s as well as with the dialectic of self and other that was central to it.

Bulgarian Travel Writing and the Dialectic of Self and Other (1840s to 1940s)

Travel writing emerged relatively late in the Bulgarian context and, from its very inception in the late 1840s, came to play a major role in the related processes of constructing a national identity and defining the shifting borderline between that identity and acceptable and unacceptable others. Mid nineteenth-century Bulgarian travel narratives are fairly close to a number of western European and Anglo-American travelogues produced in the same period, which tend to combine accounts of personal experience with demographic and ethnographic observations. Significantly, Bulgarian writer Lyuben Karavelov (1835–1879) exhibits some awareness of this proximity by explicitly engaging in corrective competition with 'superficial' foreign accounts of the Bulgarians in his *Zapiski za Bŭlgariia i bŭlgarite* ('Notes on Bulgaria and the Bulgarians') (1928: 9).[4]

Most mid nineteenth-century travel narratives are concerned with the Ottoman provinces in which the Bulgarian ethnic element predominated.[5] Defining the ethno-cultural boundaries of the prospective nation-state thus appears to have been of paramount importance for their authors. The process of national self-definition through travel accounts continued after the establishment of an autonomous Bulgarian state in 1878. Influential periodicals such as *Nauka* ('Science') (1881–1884), *Dennitsa* ('Morning Star') (1890–1891) and *Misŭl* ('Thought') (1892–1907) made a point of publishing travelogues focusing on Bulgaria alongside narratives detailing journeys into foreign lands. Travel writing eventually became a stable feature of Bulgarian periodical publications. As will be shown further on, this was to acquire special significance during the Communist era.

In the late nineteenth- and early twentieth-century Bulgarian context, the dialectic of self and other was part of a political-cultural scenario of *de-Orientalization*, a direct consequence of the country's long-term domination by the Ottoman Empire and an expression of strong anti-Ottoman feeling by the nation's educated elite. Central to the scenario was the absolute denigration of the period of Muslim-Oriental rule and its representation as a historical detour from Bulgaria's 'proper' road of development within European Christian civilization. Predictably, the scenario was intended to heal the trauma of the nation's separation from that civilization. The scenario was by no means unique to Bulgaria. Indeed, the country shared its distinctive features with its Christian neighbours in southeastern Europe.[6] What made Bulgaria's situation rather different, however, was the importation of some of the scenario's building blocks, including a species of Orientalism, in Said's sense of the word, from Russia.[7] As a result Russia acquired the role of 'a third voice' (Thompson 2000: 24) in Bulgarian political and cultural relations with Western and/or Eastern others. The viability of this role became the subject of a vehement debate throughout the period under consideration and after it. This debate resulted in a fracturing of the scenario into politically coloured Russophile and Russophobe versions. Significantly, the folkloric-mythical image of Russia as the Orthodox Christian protector *Diado Ivan* ('Grandpa Ivan'), which went back to the seventeenth century, was supplemented, in pro-Russian versions, by its representation as an important cultural factor in Bulgaria's attempts to 'catch up' with the 'civilized' world. Apart from being perceived as a source of inspiration and an example by virtue of its own cultural attainments, Russia was also a *mediator* insofar as it was via its culture and language that a number of Bulgarian intellectuals gained access to western European and North American systems of ideas and artistic achievements.

Ivan Vazov's 1891 travelogue 'Izvŭn Bŭlgariia' ('Out of Bulgaria') illustrates the ideological complexity of the turn of the century. It details a visit to Russia with a special emphasis on the Bulgarian writer's stay in St. Petersburg. Vazov, whose Russophilia was an important facet of his political and cultural makeup, represents Russia's modern history as a cautionary tale that Bulgarians should learn from. Thus he strongly disapproves of Russia's 'morbid ambition' to become part of 'Western civilization' which has impelled it to perform 'kangaroo jumps' (Vazov 1891: 209). On the other hand, his representation of the cosmopolitan atmosphere of St. Petersburg, traditionally perceived as the supreme product of Russian Occidentalization, is far from negative. Vazov emphasizes the status of the city as a 'contact zone'[8] in which representatives of different national and ethnic groups come together and establish various forms of political and cultural contact. For instance, the Bulgarian writer was able to attend Georg Brandes' lectures on the state of literary criticism in the nineteenth century (Vazov 1891: 212), which the Danish scholar delivered in French. He likewise tells a humorous story about a Bulgarian–Irish alliance against English oppression concluded by himself and his Irish landlady (Vazov 1891: 235–37).

Despite Vazov's sympathetic representation of a cosmopolitan St. Petersburg, a sense of the difference between Russia and 'Europe' was to play a dominant role in Bulgarian travelogues. Interestingly, nineteenth- and early twentieth-century writers on the subject rarely use the term 'the West' as a rhetorical and ideological device. Vazov is one of the few exceptions and his references to 'the West' in 'Out of Bulgaria' may be related to his interest in Russian Slavophile–Westerner debates, which, according to Christopher GoGwilt, were instrumental in 'transforming the idea of Europe [and] preparing for the reactionary formation of the term "the West" that emerg[ed] fully fledged in Oswald Spengler's *The Decline of the West* (1918–1922) and Arnold Toynbee's surveys of world history (1935–1954)' (GoGwilt 1995: 3).

The Bulgarian idea of 'Europe' underwent intensive development during the period under consideration. Thus while texts produced before 1878 and shortly after it tend to define 'Europe' almost exclusively through the simplistic opposition of Cross to Crescent,[9] more complex representations are in evidence in writing produced between the 1890s and Bulgaria's entry into the First World War in 1915. Predictably, the Bulgarian conception of Europe included 'core cultures' such as France and Great Britain as well as South and North European 'peripheries' such as Italy, Spain and the Scandinavian countries.[10] Despite a general recognition of the 'centrality' of French and British culture, there is a marked tendency, among late nineteenth- and early twentieth-century writers on the subject, to privilege Switzerland and central Europe and to locate the essence of 'Europeanness' in cities such as Geneva, Zurich, Vienna, Berlin, Leipzig, Dresden, and Prague.[11] Significantly, one of the key texts of the 1890s, Aleko Konstantinov's satire *Bai Ganyo* (1895), foregrounds a series of contrasts between prosperous, well-mannered Swiss and central Europeans, on the one hand, and the text's eponymous (anti-)hero, on the other. Konstantinov's itinerant Balkanite, who embodies the stereotype of the indestructible Oriental within, never gets to Paris or London. The stories of his dubious adventures are for the most part recounted by educated young Bulgarians, who claim to have experienced the 'civilizing' influence of 'Europe',[12] and tend to represent, in painstaking detail, their own humiliation at the sight of Bai Ganyo's uncouth antics.

The fictional narrators' stance was to be reduplicated repeatedly by 'real' travellers. A preoccupation with the behaviour of other Bulgarians abroad distinguishes a number of travelogues. Thus Stefan Minchev is filled with indignation at the sight of a bunch of irredeemably 'Oriental' Bulgarian students idling their time away at the *Café lyrique* in Geneva (Minchev 1908: 531). The text likewise expresses the narrator's sense of inferiority as, on his return journey, he experiences the provincialism and 'smallness' of Belgrade and Sofia after his intellectually stimulating contacts with 'European' culture (Minchev 1908: 532).

Minchev's attitude is in many ways representative of one of the national stances vis-à-vis 'Europe'. A considerable amount of Bulgarian writing produced in the late nineteenth and early twentieth centuries is informed by a nostalgic longing for a 'Europe' of the mind, perceived in terms of civilizational superiority. Conversely, Bulgaria and its Balkan neighbours are represented as sites of symbolic lack: for various reasons they are unable to efface the signs of their Oriental(ized) past and to adopt a genuine 'European' identity. The perception of this symbolic lack could also lead to strategies of self-aggrandisement and the corresponding downgrading of certain aspects of 'European' civilization. While strategies of this kind were psychologically compensatory in character, they could also be linked to political factors such as western European hostility to the Bulgarian national cause.

Great Britain is a case in point.[13] The pro-Ottoman stance of conservative British politicians at the time of the 1876 April Rising and the Russo-Turkish War of 1877–1878 came in for criticism and even ridicule.[14] Interestingly, a species of Anglophobe prejudice is in evidence in later contexts that at first glance appear to be far removed from politics. Thus, an essay on Alfred Tennyson by the Bulgarian poet and critic Pencho Slaveikov is frankly dismissive of the British laureate's life and achievements. In Slaveikov's opinion, both reflect the Philistine mentality of the English (1900: 13–27). Apart from bearing the mark of 'native' prejudice, Pencho Slaveikov's conception of 'Englishness' was strongly affected by Heinrich Heine's Bohemian disgust with 'the Phoenicians of the North Sea' (Heine 1948: 530), as he chose to call the English.[15] The Leipzig-educated Slaveikov followed the example of his German-Jewish mentor in representing them above all as a *Krämernation* that was incapable of appreciating even its own best poets, the romantic rebels Byron and Shelley.[16]

This negative image was further sustained by a Bulgarian cultural myth focusing on the despicable figure of the *esnaf*, a burgher preoccupied with the pursuit of private happiness and therefore radically opposed to the spiritually restless intellectual and/or revolutionary, who was represented as the chief motive force of social and political progress. The myth was intimately related to the position of the Bulgarian intelligentsia in the mid and later nineteenth century. Educated Bulgarians involved in the important task of forging a national consciousness and culture during the Ottoman period and after it were often confronted with the selfishness and incomprehension of a middle class that either rejected their grand projects out of hand or lent them a half-hearted, lukewarm support. *Esnaf*, a borrowing from Turkish, which initially meant an association of people practicing the same trade or a member of such an association, thus came to denote 'a person with limited interests and a narrow perspective upon the world' (Milev et al. 1964: 220).[17] Contempt for the ideological limitations of the 'native' middle class was extended to include 'bourgeois' tendencies within other cultures. This process was considerably facilitated by central and western European anti-bourgeois attitudes such as Heine's.

A similar tendency is apparent in the London letters of Bulgaria's leading modernist poet Geo Milev. The German-educated Milev visited the British capital shortly before Bulgaria's entry into the First World War with the intention of improving his English but his stay was too short for that. In his letters Milev claims that he stayed at cosmopolitan hotels where French and German were spoken. His knowledge of English therefore remained imperfect: he complains that people understood what he said to them, but he was unable to understand them because of their 'undisciplined pronunciation' (Milev 1976: 303). Not being able to penetrate into the culture's interior spaces through direct communication, Milev empowers himself by resorting to an updated version of the Heine-inspired stereotype of the English as a *Krämernation*. In a letter to his father he expresses his horror at London on account of the extremes of 'noise, greed, money, cold, coldness, and poverty' the like of which he never experienced in Germany (Milev 1976: 303). London, he avers, is thoroughly 'Americanized': it embodies the worst excesses of mercantile capitalism. In another letter Milev comments on the lack of 'true spirituality' and culture outside continental Europe. 'There is nothing', he says, 'outside the old world' (Milev 1976: 304), thus consigning Britain to the 'new' world. Moreover, the British have no taste for music, and, as far as he is in a position to judge, 'no modern poetry' (Milev 1976: 304).

Such views are indicative of a tendency within the Bulgarian cultural and political imaginary to problematize the idea of 'Europe' as a monolithic whole. In her analysis of the diversity of Eurasian ethno-geographical space, Milica Bakić-Hayden speaks of 'nesting Orientalisms' or a 'gradation of Orients' (Bakić-Hayden 1995: 918). Bulgarian intellectuals meditating upon the cultural and political destiny of their country in the late nineteenth and early twentieth centuries appear to have retroactively adopted a reversed version of her model. They approach Europe in terms of 'nesting Occidentalisms' or a 'gradation of Occidents'. From that perspective Switzerland and central Europe appear to embody an acceptable degree of 'Occidentalism' whereas Britain represents the 'old' continent's least appealing features: excessive materialism and a Philistine disregard for artistic and spiritual values.

Paris and, by implication, French culture, occupied a much more favourable position within the Bulgarian 'gradation of Occidents'. Predictably, Bulgarian narratives with a Parisian setting tend to be informed by a sense of their own belatedness: the city has been overdescribed by previous travellers to such an extent that Bulgarian writers make no secret of the fact that they cannot say anything new about it. Familiarity with the 'wonders' (*chudesii*) of Paris is usually taken for granted. Still, sightseeing is represented as culturally enriching and absolutely essential to a 'proper' understanding of the French. In Vazov's 1896 novel *Nova zemia* ('A New Land'), a French character called Mlle Debrollet urges the central character Stremski and his wife Nevyanka to visit Versailles, Fontainebleau and St. Cloud and thus experience some of 'the wonders and glories of France' (Vazov 1994: 388). She further instructs Count Bradlov, a devious Bulgarian masquerading as a Russian aristocrat, to 'overwhelm' the Bulgarian couple with 'French politeness', which, she claims, has been successfully 'transplanted into [his] Slavic soul' (Vazov 1994: 388). The idea that French culture is somehow 'congenial' to the 'Slavic' (and by implication, Bulgarian) temperament was to become a stable feature of the Bulgarian portrayal of 'Europe'.

The Bulgarian picture of 'Europe' is further complicated by representations of some of the 'peripheries' mentioned above. Spain appears to have attracted little attention before the 1930s. Italy emerges, on the one hand, as a treasure house of literary and artistic masterpieces, while, on the other, it presents a number of political and economic choices that Bulgaria should either make or refrain from making. Both aspects of the Italian image are well illustrated by Konstantin Velichkov's 'public' *Letters from Rome* and his private correspondence from Italy (1880s to1890s). While the *Letters from Rome* read like a textbook on Renaissance art, Velichkov's private correspondence expresses his disapproval of Italy's pro-Austrian policy and his apprehension that Bulgaria might choose to follow a similar course (Velichkov 2002: 310).

Representations of the Scandinavian countries are for the most part linked to Bulgarian interest in 'the giants of the North', as Ibsen, Strindberg, Hamsun and Bjørnson were called by their admirers. The cultural prominence of those writers at the turn of the century was part of the Scandinavian success story, which Bulgaria was expected to emulate. Apart from stressing literary success, Bulgarian accounts of the Scandinavian peninsula tend to focus on landscape as a setting for Nordic individualism and independence but also as decidedly conducive to 'Nordic gloom', the depression that was traditionally associated with that part of Europe (Andreichin 1900: 86–99).

Predictably, the major historical events and political movements of the post-First World War period affected Bulgarian views of 'Europe' and its constituent cultures. Most of the travel writing produced between 1918 and 1944 clearly testifies to the growing importance of political commitments in the representation of internal and external others. Thus there was a steady trickle of travelogues about 'Bolshevik Russia' and some of them made a point of denouncing the decadent West and emphasizing the advantages of life in the 'proletarian fatherland'.[18] Spain attracted considerable attention in the 1930s whereas Italy and Germany were drawn into the national debate about the 'New World Order' and Bulgaria's place in it. On the other hand, Paris largely retained its role as a cultural centre,[19] and accounts of the Scandinavian North continued to stress the grandeur of Nordic landscape and the deplorable continuance of 'Nordic gloom'. A systematic attempt was made to increase knowledge about Britain and thus improve its image in Bulgaria through the *Bŭlgaro-Britanski pregled* ('Bulgarian–British Review'), a publication with a relatively small circulation, which nevertheless managed to cover a wide range of topics from travel to joint economic ventures.

Admiration for the civilized ways of central Europeans never waned but attitudes to the region's cultures were increasingly affected by the debates mentioned above. A 1934 account of a visit to the Leipzig Trade Fair, a site that had attracted Bulgarians ever since the beginning of the nineteenth century, is full of admiration for German technological progress but also expresses uneasiness about its long-term effects. The narrator opposes the simplicity of Balkan tastes and ways to the sophistication of up-to-date technology, which threatens to destroy basic human pleasures such as the enjoyment of good food (Dobrev 1934: 121–24). Implicit in this representation is scepticism about totalitarian political projects aiming at radically changing human nature and the world.

As the Second World War started and Bulgaria drifted towards the Axis, there was a renewed concern with the legitimization of ethno-cultural boundaries. A number of travelogues produced between 1941 and 1944 recount trips to territories that were placed under Bulgarian control such as Macedonia, parts of Aegean Thrace and the island of Thassos. Curiously, apart from attempting to justify the Bulgarian presence on that island, some travelogues reproduce most of the features of what we have grown accustomed to perceive as *Western* exoticism, such as a distinction between a civilizationally superior centre and a backward periphery, spectacularization of cultural difference, and ethnic stereotyping.[20] Apparently, a culture that had traditionally been dominated by others could also don the rhetorical clothing of the dominator and thus join the power game – albeit on a part-time basis. Such examples illustrate the complexity of the dialectic of self and other and the need for a more nuanced approach to Western and non-Western types of hegemony (Simmons 2000: 113).

The travel narratives produced between the 1840s and the 1940s are structured by a *shifting* dialectic of self and other that registered changes in the political and cultural climate. The shifts were definitely not all for the better, and the last, quasi-colonialist phase in the development of the travel genre poses a number of ethical questions that Bulgarian scholarship urgently needs to address. It would therefore be naïve to celebrate pre-1945 travel writing for its lack of prejudice or to represent the next, highly politicized stage in the genre's development as a regrettable 'detour' from what might have been a straight road of unrestricted self-expression and continuous improvement.

Travel and its Uses under a Totalitarian Regime

During the communist era, perceptions of the West were characterized by the binarism noted by GoGwilt in the quotation above. Because of the politically sensitive character of travel writing, it is possible to establish analogies between individual narratives and the vagaries of the regime. My reading will try to combine the chronological and thematic approaches by foregrounding certain key themes within the travelogues under discussion and relating them to specific stages within the post-Second World War history of Bulgaria and eastern Europe. Continuities with pre-communist travel writing will be duly noted as I proceed.

The travelogues selected for analysis do not cover every single western European country. Most of them concentrate on Britain and Sweden, and this focus is to a considerable extent a consequence of the thematic approach I have chosen to adopt. It also reflects the sheer multitude of texts about travel produced between 1945 and 1985 (despite the regime's manifest control over individual mobility!) and a corresponding need for selectivity. The focus may further be related to the changed conditions in Europe and the world after the Second World War. Thus central Europe, which had previously occupied such an important place in the Bulgarian cultural imaginary, was split between the two political blocs, and this decidedly affected the Bulgarian gradation of 'Occidents'. Significantly, this gradation did not disappear completely during the totalitarian period. It reappeared in a *more* or *less* altered form and fulfilled different functions in different contexts: for instance, it could occasionally signify that the world's division into two polar opposites was not so absolute as it was made to appear by the two blocs' propagandist machines. However, it was likewise revamped in order to sustain that particular division, thus proving that continuity with pre-communist times did exist.

Assen Hristoforov's England: The Road That Could Not Be Taken

Skitsi iz London ('Sketches from London') is, significantly, a memoir. The book enjoyed a modest success during the brief interlude of fragile tolerance and democracy mentioned earlier. It went through two editions in 1945, and its author Assen Hristoforov was awarded the Aleko Konstantinov prize for travel literature by the Bulgarian Writers' Union.[21] He was a graduate of the London School of Economics and this was held against him after 1947 when a Stalinist regime was imposed in Bulgaria. However, the political climate was different in 1945. Bulgaria was ruled by the Allied Control Commission, which was dominated by the Soviet Union but also included representatives of the other allies. The Commission was not in a position to prevent the consolidation of communist power in the country but made it possible for an organized opposition to emerge and for certain standards of pluralism to be maintained. This would explain the book's success. Apparently, the Bulgarian Writers' Union, which was increasingly being infiltrated by communists and their sympathisers, had to demonstrate that a spirit of good will to the Western democracies was being fostered in the country by acknowledging in public the merits of a travelogue about Great Britain.

The Preface to the book's second edition indicates that Hristoforov was aware of the paucity of knowledge about Great Britain and the strong influence of negative stereotypes on Bulgarian perceptions of the British. His task therefore is 'to drive away the mist [...] concealing [their] *true* image [...] and the characteristics of [their] public life' (Hristoforov 1945: 8, my emphasis). Hristoforov's text thus carries on the post-Second World War tendency of increasing Bulgarian knowledge about Britain and dispelling prejudices about it. However, some of the narrator's comments also reproduce the discourse of ritual vilification of the capitalist system and 'bourgeois' values, which was rapidly gaining prominence at the time. For instance a brief encounter with a Bulgarian tobacco merchant, who seems to possess most of the embarrassing characteristics of a latter-day Bai Ganyo, makes him wonder if 'impudence is not the second major "virtue" in capitalist society' (Hristoforov 1945: 117), the first one presumably being greed. Hristoforov's text is noticeably the meeting ground of two tendencies: the earlier one of increasing knowledge and overcoming prejudice, and the penchant for finding a pretext to denounce 'capitalism' that was becoming an inalienable trait of travel writing produced after the Second World War. Luckily, the signs of the latter are still few and far between.

Sketches from London is primarily concerned with Hristoforov's experiences as a student in London in the early nineteen-thirties; its concluding chapter describes the narrator's return to Britain for a short visit on the eve of the Second World War. The travelogue's beginning illustrates the superficiality of the narrator's knowledge of Britain and the British and his tendency to turn even limited personal experience into a generalization about their 'national character'. A number of other early episodes recount what the narrator perceives as a series of blows to his pride. This perception mostly results from the clash between his self-image and the image that he projects within the context of the foreign culture.

Thus Hristoforov is mortified by the fact that he is practically denied the status of a 'white' man in Britain. Because of his 'Oriental' dark looks, the majority of Britons he has dealings with as well as some Indian students he meets take him for a 'non-white' person from the outskirts of the Empire (Hristoforov 1945: 17–19). The narrator is rather uneasy about this identity that two groups of 'unperceptive' others appear to have thrust upon him. At first he tries to explain their mistake by attributing his yellowish complexion to the lingering effects of the malaria from which he has not fully recovered. Somewhat later he resorts to a more complex strategy based on the age-old opposition between 'appearance' and 'essence'. Those who see him as a non-white visitor from some corner of the Orient go by the merely visible; they are totally unaware of the fact that deep down he is 'European'. To validate this assertion, Hristoforov establishes a standard of 'Europeanness', which the British cannot meet, insofar as it comprises 'good' knowledge of French and non-anglicized pronunciation of Latin words (Hristoforov 1945: 57–58). This helps him preserve his self-esteem in the context of the foreign culture and enables him to indulge in mild irony at the expense of the 'natives'.

Further on, Hristoforov is able to suppress his anxiety about his 'Oriental' appearance and even exploits Western associations of the Orient with magic and mystery by enacting the part of 'a Hindu fakir from the Northern Himalayas' and thus imposing on a bunch of credulous Englishmen and women (Hristoforov 1945: 138). This strategy points to an old and honourable tradition of ironic representation, that of the travelling *ingénu*, the naive but sharp-sighted barbarian visiting the West. A number of Hristoforov's witty comments on British political life, traditions, class prejudice, and puritanical moral standards are in full accord with this ironic persona. In additon, the non-partisan attitude to values and judgements inherent in it makes it possible for him to revise some of his own earlier attitudes.

Sketches from London ends on a rather sad note. On his return to the British capital in 1938, the narrator discovers that all of his close friends have either left London to go back to their own countries or that he can no longer relate meaningfully to the ones that are there. This sense of separation and loss is made more poignant by his awareness of the impending disaster of the war. His exploration of the other culture thus ends rather abruptly. Travellers writing about Britain or, for that matter, about other parts of western Europe, over the next forty years or so were not in a position to carry on the dialogue which Hristoforov had started. Timid attempts were occasionally made to go beyond ideological preconceptions and re-open it but the Muse of Censorship inevitably got in the way.

'The Great Battle Between the Two Worlds'

A lot of Bulgarian travel writing produced between 1947 and the collapse of communism in the late 1980s is informed by the idea of an insurmountable difference between two antagonistic worlds. In the late forties and early fifties the opposition between them is represented as a Manichean battle between good and evil. Thus an article published in 1949 alerts readers to the epochal significance of 'the great battle between [...] the world of truth and progress of the people's democracies, led by the great Soviet Union, and the world of darkness and poverty of Western Europe and the USA' (cited in Shurbanov and Sokolova 2001: 125). What is at stake in this historic conflict is 'peace, culture and well-being' (ibid.). Placing the United States after western Europe seems unusual as the predominant tendency was to rank the respective armies of good and evil behind the two colossi that were their leaders: 'the great Soviet Union' and 'the transatlantic aggressor'. Possibly because of the Marshall Plan, which Bulgaria rejected in 1947 together with the other Soviet satellites, the United States was represented as a demanding 'paymaster' trading reconstruction aid for obedience. In the late 1940s western European countries such as France and Great Britain were still seen as major imperialist powers desperately trying to keep their overseas colonies in subjection. On the other hand, the wave of decolonization in Asia, Africa and other parts of the world was presented as yet another victory for 'the world of truth and progress' whose advantages were assumed to be self-evident.

The negative image of the West was further sustained through the 'gradation of Occidents'. As far as western Europe was concerned, Britain still appeared least congenial to Bulgarians. For one thing, it was perceived as having a close affinity with the United States; for another, current interpretations of Bulgarian history and especially of the final years of Ottoman domination and the Russo-Turkish War of 1877–1878 tended to foreground Britain's anti-Russian and, by implication, anti-Bulgarian stance. In a context in which the Bulgarian ethnic identity was represented as predominantly 'Slavic' and therefore closely akin to the

Russian one, Anglo-Saxon coldness became the distinctive characteristic of Englishness/Britishness. Throughout the communist era, representations of ethnicity were frequently influenced by a re-hashed mythology of 'race' whose roots went back to the late eighteenth and early nineteenth centuries.[22] Despite the policy of internationalism, officially sanctioned by the communist establishment, this mythology played an important role in reducing the world's ethnic and cultural variety to a limited number of easily recognizable stereotypes such as peace-loving, hospitable Slavs; well-disciplined, unimaginative Germans; gloomy Scandinavians; oppressed (and 'uncivilized'!) Africans; and hard-working Asians.

Regardless of the manifest lack of congeniality which Bulgarian travellers made a point of imputing to the British, over fifty travelogues about visits to Great Britain were published in the literary journals *Septemvri* ('September') and *Plamŭk* ('Flame'), and the popular magazine *Zhenata dnes* ('Woman Today') between 1950 and 1989. The shorter pieces published in periodicals tended to attract a considerable number of readers. On the whole, they were more impressionistic in character than book-length travelogues, and, while not deviating from the party line, could convey something of the immediacy of the traveller's experience. Bulgarian readers of the communist era were likely to appreciate the latter quality as few of them were in a position to travel to the West and experience life there at first hand.

Some of the above points are illustrated by 'Shest dni v Anglia' ('Six Days in England'), a brief travelogue by leading Bulgarian poet Elisaveta Bagriana (1893–1991), published in the journal *Septemvri* in 1950. The text also exemplifies some of the formulas through which travel writing of the communist era was structured. Bagriana was a delegate to the Second World Congress of Peace, which was due to convene in Sheffield but was disrupted and eventually reconvened in Warsaw. An emphasis on the Bulgarian visitor's official and/or professional status was to become a standing characteristic of Bulgarian travelogues of the communist era. Travelling to western Europe as a private person was difficult, not to say impossible. Besides, a travelogue about a private visit was less likely to get published. As will be seen, only one of the narrators I discuss in this chapter claims to have travelled in a private capacity.

Bagriana's travelogue is in many ways a typical product of the Cold War era. The narrator begins her story by drawing attention to the difficulty of obtaining a British visa. As her plane takes off from Prague and makes for London, the increasingly gloomy weather functions as an 'objective correlative' preparing the reader for the hostility and general unpleasantness to be experienced in the capitalist West. The reader's expectations are not disappointed: upon landing the delegates are made to go through a series of very thorough checks, which is yet another sign of the antagonism of the two worlds. The composition of the delegation is apparently intended to illustrate the lack of social stratification in the new Bulgarian state: it includes Granny Saba, 'a partisan's mother', a shepherd, a miner and a textile worker as well as an eminent poet, a distinguished artist and a famous opera singer. The delegates are welcomed warmly by 'the comrades from the English Peace Committee'. The helpful intervention of a member, or members, of a 'progressive' organization of one kind or another is a recurrent feature of Bulgarian travel narratives of the communist era. Such gestures were meant to demonstrate the power of class solidarity, which transcended national boundaries, as well as to reassure the reading public at home that 'the world of darkness and poverty' was doomed since there were people who 'had seen the light' and strongly opposed the capitalist system (Bagriana 1950: 89).

Despite the good will of their 'English comrades', the delegates are accommodated in small, dark, unheated hotel rooms. The narrator claims that this 'brought back [to her] ..., with unprecedented vividness, the atmosphere of Dickens' *A Christmas Carol* and the character of the stingy capitalist Scrooge' (ibid.: 90). The imaginative leap back to Victorian times is also typical. During the communist era, the Bulgarian stereotype of Englishness/Britishness heavily relied on a reductive interpretation of nineteenth-century British history stressing the poverty and exploitation of the masses and the gross materialism of the capitalist middle class and implying that the 'spirit' of the Victorian age survived in the post-Second World War period.

Throughout the delegates' stay in London, the weather is said to have been 'terrible' except for one single day when the sun shone. On this day 'two or three' members of the Bulgarian delegation made their way to the British Museum and the National Gallery (ibid.: 90). This little detail spoke volumes to knowledgeable readers of the travelogue. For instance, it showed that only *some* delegates *knew* or *cared* about the cultural landmarks of the British capital and thus tacitly conveyed the idea of a latent stratification within Bulgarian society. Having alluded to a politically dangerous topic, the narrator moves on to safer ground by describing the crowd of children in 'the square in front of the National Gallery' (ibid.). Significantly, the place is not identified as *Trafalgar Square*. That would have involved mentioning Nelson's Column and reminding Bulgarian readers that Napoleon (an 'aggressor' frequently represented as Hitler's predecessor) had not been defeated by General Kutuzov and the Russian army only. Details that might appear minor and trivial at first glance were made part of the grand scheme of rewriting history from a 'communist' perspective. This involved downplaying the role of the West and attributing significant military victories in the recent or more remote past solely to the courage and endurance of the Russian (or Soviet) people.[23] Bulgarian writers were expected to toe the line and contribute – directly or indirectly – to the ritual glorification of Russian/Soviet fortitude.

The travelogue's narrator mentions going to the British Museum and the National Gallery but does not even attempt to describe any of the exhibits in them. Instead, she dwells on the amateur production of a play about racial discrimination in the United States. Having provided a summary of the play's contents, Bagriana speaks of the enthusiastic welcome that the Bulgarian delegation received from its author and audience. They remarked upon the great progress that '[Georgi] Dimitrov's motherland' had made along the road to socialism (ibid.: 91).

The account of the bus trip to Sheffield provides yet another example of transnational solidarity. One of the British peace activists is said to have used up his family's sugar rations to get boiled sweets for the Bulgarian visitors (ibid.). This representation, however, is not so much intended to relativize the familiar Bulgarian stereotype of English/British 'coldness' as to teach a lesson about the proletariat's exceptional moral strength and great potential for self-sacrifice. An emphasis on the virtues of the British working class figured prominently among the formulaic features through which Bulgarian travelogues of the communist era functioned.

For the travelogue's narrator Sheffield is 'a black city crowned with flames'. It thus embodies the worst aspects of Western industrialization but also boasts a politically active working-class population. However, despite this population's enthusiastic support and elaborate preparations for the congress (Bagriana mentions interpreters' booths), there were too many obstructions: ranging from hostile speeches by agents provocateurs, such as the pro-Yugoslav speaker Rogge (the travelogue was produced after Tito had broken up with the Soviet Union), to the significant absence of internationally renowned peace activists such as the left-wing French scientist Frédéric Joliot-Curie. The latter, it turns out, did not get a British visa because of the 'hypocrisy' of the British Labour government. The congress was nevertheless marked by a number of highlights: Bagriana and her fellow delegates had the pleasure of listening to Soviet writer Boris Polevoi and admired Picasso's skill in drawing a dove and then auctioning it off to obtain money for the International Peace Fund. The delegates eventually left for 'heroic Warsaw' where the congress reconvened a few days later (ibid.: 92).

The narrator claims that the journey back from Sheffield to London was more pleasant. The miner and the textile worker enlivened the atmosphere with their singing whereas the shepherd Petŭr Chemishanov managed to get a scattered herd of sheep together by whistling at them (ibid.). Bagriana remarks that 'the English sheep had no problem making sense of the Bulgarian shepherd's whistling' (ibid.). National boundaries are thus transcended once again by a representative of the people. Shurbanov and Sokolova (2001: 160–63) have repeatedly drawn attention to the veritable mythologization of 'the people' in a variety of communist discourses. The discourse of travel was no exception. The shrewd representative of the people was to become a stock character in travelogues of the communist era.

On the Bulgarian delegates' departure, their 'English comrades' are said to have expressed their anger at the hypocritical behaviour of their own Labour government. Further on that government is proclaimed to be in collusion with American imperialism, 'the worst enemy of world peace' (ibid.: 92). Textbooks of the communist era defined British Labour as 'a species of opportunism' and 'a right-wing deviation from Marxism-Leninism proper'. As will be seen, Bulgarian travel writers made a point of treating non-communist varieties of Western left-wing politics with suspicion.

Most of the narrative and ideological formulas that were identified so far were to resurface repeatedly throughout the 1950s. Thus writing some eight years after Bagriana, Brigita Yosifova explains to her readers how ill at ease she felt in the chic restaurants of Cardiff's shopping area as they were mostly patronized by 'owners of mines and steel plants and their affected wives' (Yosifova 1958: 91). The Bulgarian narrator sympathizes with the plight of Welsh miners and describes their poverty in moving detail. For her the strike of three thousand of those miners is 'the only bright, joyful spark of hope' in the present (ibid.: 92). She looks forward to the time when 'the whole people' will follow their example.

Writers of the Brezhnev era (1964–1979) seem less confident about the imminent fall of the capitalist system in western Europe. They nevertheless make some use of the formulaic repertoire of their predecessors. In her 1971 book *Okolo planetata Albion* ('Around the Planet Albion'), Penka Karadocheva recounts her experience of a Britain that is trying hard to cling to its imperial past but is increasingly forced to accept the inevitability of change (Karadocheva 1971: 9–19). The narrator examines the country's stock image as 'the land of tradition' and discovers that it is to a considerable extent justified. Thus she dwells on British attachment to the monarchy and provides a number of examples of excessive fondness for animals and gardening (ibid.: 14–17). Karadocheva bolsters up her arguments with quotes from articles by Western journalists and results from opinion polls. In this way she attempts to demonstrate that her narrative is based on solid research rather than on mere observation or sheer propaganda.

The Bulgarian traveller likewise presents what may be termed an *alternative* British tradition, which she associates with Karl Marx, Kropotkin, Lenin and other nineteenth- and early twentieth-century political émigrés (ibid.: 23–30). Predictably, she visits the sites 'sanctified' by this tradition in the company of a member of the British communist party. In the narrator's opinion, contemporary life in Britain is characterized by materialism and lack of spirituality. Mass culture as represented by Ian Fleming's James Bond novels is therefore her next target. 'What reading for young people!' she exclaims. 'Seductive ladies, practically in the nude ... in stories about sadists' (ibid.: 45). Because of the low quality of such mass-produced literature, young people cannot develop a proper appreciation for Art (with a capital 'A'!). The narrator agrees that the cultural life of the British capital is not restricted to the 'banal' and 'jejune' only (ibid.: 59). She mentions an experimental production of Brecht's *Mother Courage* at the Old Vic and a classical music performance at the Royal Festival Hall but apparently such examples of 'highbrow' culture have no appeal for British youth. Karadocheva next denounces the excesses of the 'hippie' counter-culture, which she views as a form of 'social schizophrenia' engendered by young people's inability to grasp the need for 'proper' opposition to 'capitalist society' and its debilitating morality (ibid.: 52–53).

Despite the fact that *Around the Planet Albion* differs from Bagriana's Cold War pamphlet in certain significant ways, it is organized through the same rhetorical opposition of 'us' versus 'them'. For the later narrator the fall of 'the world of darkness' may not be imminent but it is nevertheless inevitable – or must be made to appear so – in conformity with the dictates of what Shurbanov and Sokolova have aptly called 'the deeply hypocritical Brezhnevian settlement' (2001: 115).

Undesirable Allies

By and large, travel writers of the communist era approached the counter-cultures and political protest of the 1960s with great suspicion. The redefinition of 'classic' class conflicts, which played a central role in certain Western left-wing projects of that time, appeared unacceptable to the representatives of Soviet-style 'real socialism'. Nor could they be sympathetic to the politicization of culture and subjectivity implicit in the rising tide of feminism. Rethinking Marxism also appeared a dangerous exercise, incompatible with the Philistine spirit of the Brezhnev era. Bulgarian participation in the crushing of the Prague Spring produced a sense of guilt that could not be expressed openly in writing at the time. The outspoken criticism of the 'East European' political model by Western left-wingers acted as an irritant possibly because it resonated with Bulgarian intellectuals' own inner doubts. The deficiencies of that model became obvious when it was compared with Western welfare systems such as the Swedish one. Sweden came to play a limited but significant role in the cultural-political imaginary of Bulgarian travellers of the communist era. In this section I dwell on representations of *undesirable allies*: an assortment of groups and individuals whose rejection of Western capitalist practices, political doctrines, traditional standards of morality and cultural norms was not even remotely compatible with an idealization of Soviet-style socialism.

In Bulgaria, the 1960s marked the beginning of a fascination with Western music, youth fashions, and film which was to continue throughout the communist era. Indeed, some of the music was to inspire the marches and rallies of protesters against the totalitarian system in 1989 and 1990. The communist regime's reaction to young people's attempts to reproduce what was perceived as a Western dress code in the 1960s and 70s verged on the ridiculous: the police raided cafés and pubs that were known to be youth haunts and proceeded systematically to cut off long hair, rip off blue jeans, and stamp on the thighs of young women in miniskirts. Travel writers' reactions to the hippie counter-culture should be viewed against this background of anti-Western hysteria. Tzvetan Stoyanov (1930–1971), an erudite literary critic and translator, addressed the related subjects of the hippie movement and left-wing politics in two extended commentaries, which also conveyed his impressions of conference trips to Britain, France and Sweden. The first essay, 'Hipievskata "subkultura"' ('The Hippie "Subculture"'), was initially submitted for publication to the popular newspaper *Narodna mladezh* ('People's Youth') but was apparently deemed too subversive for the general public and came out in the exclusive *Bulletin of the Union of Bulgarian Writers* (1969). It was subsequently included in the posthumous edition of Stoyanov's work, which was issued in 1988 and was one of the signs of Bulgaria's tentative *perestroika*. From a present-day perspective, the essay appears anything but subversive of the communist establishment. In all probability, the authorities chose to restrict its circulation because of the commentator's elitist references to a wide variety of sources ranging from medieval mysticism to contemporary accounts of Beatlemania (Stoyanov 1988a).

The second essay is entitled '"Ultralevitsata" i revoliutsiiata' ('The "Extreme Left" and the Revolution') and initially came out in 1969. In it Stoyanov revives the myth of the middle-class *esnaf* and fits it into his analysis of late capitalism. He begins by arguing that rather than destroying the middle class with its characteristic *esnaf* mentality, late-capitalist society managed to integrate it within its structure. For him the latter-day *esnaf* is in principle torn between a desire for upward mobility and resentment of the people on top. These irreconcilable contradictions may occasionally lead to 'anarchistic' rebellion, which, according to the commentator, is purely subjective in character: 'it starts as a psychological reaction within the mind and ends in the same place – the mind'. Stoyanov claims that a recent visit to Sweden confirmed the truth of his reflections. In his opinion, Sweden, renowned for its 'legendary living standards' and 'affluent society', represents the 'middle ground' traditionally associated with the self-contradictory middle class (Stoyanov 1988b: 50–51).

The Bulgarian traveller presents the impact of left-wing politics on Swedish society in considerable detail:

> In bookshops you are likely to find books by Marx, Engels, Lenin, and, needless to say, Trotsky and Mao. [...] There is a growing interest in the Soviet Union, in Russia: thousands of young Swedes are studying Russian, the songs that the Red Army sang on its march to Berlin are very fashionable now. [...] The Stockholm Museum of Modern Art [recently organised] an exhibition on the impact of revolutionary art, more than half of which was dedicated to Soviet art in the 1920s. (Stoyanov 1988b: 51)

On the surface this is anything but 'dissident'. Yet it successfully conveyed a host of meanings to Bulgarian readers of the Brezhnev era and sharpened their awareness of the difference between Swedish permissiveness and the restrictions imposed by eastern European communist regimes. Thus the text's readers knew that books by Trotsky or Mao were not to be found in Bulgarian bookshops. Whereas Maoism was widely criticized in the press and the excesses of the Chinese 'Cultural Revolution' duly denounced, Trotsky literally reduplicated the fate of the Orwellian Emmanuel Goldstein and was vaguely represented as a 'primal traitor, the earliest defiler of the Party's purity' (Orwell 2000: 14). While there was no scarcity of Soviet marching songs, the experimental art of the 1920s, which predated the establishment of socialist realism as a norm, was largely ignored. Whether the text's anti-authoritarian effect was sought intentionally or Stoyanov unconsciously cast himself in the role of another Orwellian character, Winston Smith's overzealous friend Syme, who lacked 'a sort of saving stupidity' and 'said things that would have been better unsaid' (Orwell 2000: 58), did not matter much. His text decidedly stimulated readers' critical thinking and that might explain the difficulties he had in publishing his work.

Defining Stoyanov's position vis-à-vis the Bulgarian communist establishment of the late 60s is a difficult task – made doubly so by the lack of up-to-date critical commentaries on his work.[24] As was demonstrated above, his highly politicized travelogues, which combined extensive commentaries on topical ideological issues with a sprinkling of impressions of the places he visited, lent themselves to what may be termed an antinomian reading unveiling contradictions in the regime's claims. Whether this was part of a special pact with 'the Muse of Censorship' or merely reflected the nature of the 'Syme syndrome' must remain an open question.

Vasil Tsonev's memoir *Iz Evropa* ('Around Europe') (1973) contrasts strongly with the travelogues considered so far and indicates that 'the

Muse of Censorship' permitted occasional variety in the shape of heavy-handed humour. Significantly, this is the only travelogue under discussion which recounts a *private* journey through Europe: Tsonev travelled with his wife and his brothers. The *private* character of the journey was a way of demonstrating the permissive nature of the Bulgarian political regime. Throughout their visit to the West the travellers are said to have encountered a number of Bulgarian émigrés who expressed amazement and (justified) disbelief when they were told the government imposed no restrictions on private travel.

The travelogue combines loud, 'politically correct' declarations of loyalty to communism and derogatory remarks on Western tastes and ideas with comments on select aspects of everyday life and encounters with migrant workers from Yugoslavia, Greece, Turkey and the Third World. Moreover, it comprises a series of positive representations of Slavic communities and Southern localities characterized by a taste for easy living and distaste for hard work. These are opposed to images of 'cold-blooded' northern and western Europeans.

Predictably, left-wing politics comes in for a considerable amount of ridicule in Tsonev's text. A chapter significantly entitled 'West Berliners Try to Teach Us Socialism' (Tsonev 1973: 29–31) presents the narrator's first encounter with the New Left. Sweden, which he visits shortly after Germany, is represented almost entirely in terms of 'Nordic gloom' and female sexual aggression. In an episode that frankly enacts a male sexual fantasy Tsonev's eldest brother is surrounded by a group of sex-starved blondes, who proceed to touch and finger him with an 'avidity' reminiscent of cinematic representations of 'white missionaries' encounters with [black?] cannibals' (ibid.: 65). This combination of sexism and unashamed racism has numerous analogues in what has been identified as 'the classical imperialist mode' (Thompson 2000: 149) of Western literatures. Its significant presence in a Bulgarian travelogue of the communist era proves my earlier point about the continuing importance of a re-hashed mythology of 'race' throughout that period. As with nineteenth-century British and French writers, the narrator's objective apparently is to reassert the claims of a white androcentric 'normality'. The only difference is that he resorts to 'the classical imperialist mode' in order to disparage permissive sexual mores in post-Second World War Swedish society.

The narrator briefly sketches his visit to Britain which he chiefly diagnoses as having changed for the worse since the days of Shakespeare and that 'jolly old girl' (*mŭzhko momiche*) 'good Queen Bess' (Tsonev 1973: 68). He further decries the British for their narrow-mindedness and lack of imagination and proclaims in closing that he is 'happy to be Bulgarian' (ibid.: 71). The largely negative representation of Britain is followed by an updated version of the traditional, favourable portrayal of

France complete with an emphasis on the wonders of Paris and the congeniality of the French temperament to the 'Slavic soul'. A new element is added to this as France is proclaimed a haven of egalitarianism: 'there is no difference between blacks, whites, yellows or greens here; [t]hey're all human, they're all equal' (ibid.: 75). The narrator further contends that in West Germany and Britain 'progressive people' constitute a relatively small percentage of the population whereas French workers and intellectuals are ever ready to 'rise' en masse and defend their rights (ibid.: 76). Significantly, he does not attempt to analyse French 'progressive' politics. His readers are to assume that the French left-wing context is free from the 'hypocrisy' and 'false' ideologies of the West German one.

The rest of the text is concerned with the Bulgarian travellers' return journey and the narrator's subsequent trips to Moscow, Georgia, and Kiev. Needless to say, his account of the Soviet Union is entirely favourable. In the final chapter Tsonev briefly reminisces about the 'misty mornings' of 'remote Sweden' where 'the first light of day became visible at 11 A.M. and dusk settled in at 1 P.M.' and concludes on a note of gratitude to 'the happy opportunity that made me a Bulgarian and a Slav' (ibid.: 107). So much undiluted devotion to the party line (probably) made even 'orthodox' readers approach the text with a fair amount of scepticism. On the other hand, the final reference to Sweden is significant: evidently, the ghost of the social-democratic 'paradise' and the fantasies of sexual permissiveness it inspired refused to be laid to rest and kept coming back.

New Pacts with the 'Muse Of Censorship': ### Exploring 'The Limits of the Expressible'

The travelogues to be considered next reflect some of the contradictions of the final stage of the communist era: a time marked by the spirit of Charter 77 and increasing tensions within the Eastern bloc. While Bulgaria's status as the Soviet Union's staunchest satellite did not change dramatically during the late 70s and the 80s, attitudes to the regime and its ideology inside the country were increasingly characterized by ambivalence and scepticism. There was a growing sense of the system's bankruptcy. Thus a number of Bulgarian writers, artists and film directors managed to modify the officially sanctioned aesthetics of socialist realism without seeking to achieve a clean break with the communist party or aspiring to the 'dissident' status favoured by the West. Some of those 'experiments' in fact predated the 1970s. The existence of such voices in a country that had not 'experienced "Prague Springs" or "Hungarian Autumns"' (Magris 1989: 347) might be attributed to the 'arbitrariness' of the totalitarian regime diagnosed by

Pleşu as well as to its occasional attempts to persuade the outside world that it accepted 'difference'.

The discourse of travel produced during the last phase is distinguished by ambiguity insofar as it diverges from what might be termed *hardcore* anti-Western propaganda but for various reasons evades direct confrontation with the system. In his analysis of internalized censorship in GDR experimental fiction, Michael G. Levine remarks that such texts 'respect … *the limits of the expressible*' and 'claim … not to revolt [against them]' (Levine 1997: 120, my emphasis). The travelogues to be considered next exemplify this paradoxical condition.

Malka severna saga ('A Little Northern Saga') (1980) by Yordan Radichkov (1929–2004) is characterized by a decidedly sceptical attitude to ideological clichés and mandatory slogans. The journey it recounts is presented through a series of impressions worked into a narrative that resists closure and remains open-ended. While propaganda is mostly avoided and few attempts are made to extol 'real socialism's' advantages at the expense of life in the West, the existing political system is represented as an essential aspect of Bulgaria's historical destiny and no alternative or change is envisioned. The overall ideological tendency is thus preservationist. The travelogue provides yet another perspective on Sweden and is the most consciously 'literary' of all texts under discussion. Radichkov ingeniously weaves together sophisticated reflection, myth and village folklore to produce an ironic representation of the world in which inside and outside, home and abroad, personal memory and universal history are inextricably mixed up. Thus he begins by deconstructing the most pervasive stereotype of Sweden and northern Europe: the fiction that 'the [...] North enviously eyes the South' and is jealous of the latter's 'privileged' position (Radichkov 1980: 14). The narrator maintains that the North is preoccupied with its own problems and has no time for the South. Contrary to readers' expectations, this ironic insight is not elaborated further. The (anti-) strategy of readerly disappointment recurs throughout the narrative and continually alerts us to the futility of generalization while at the same enhancing our awareness of the complexity and mystery of the world and the diversity and richness of human experience. In other words, with Radichkov we are – for better or for worse – in the ambiguous realm of postmodernism, despite the fact that most communist-era *littérateurs* would have winced at the term.

Radichkov's trip to Sweden was carried out under the auspices of the Swedish Institute. It was his hosts' idea that he should visit northern Sweden first. However, the narrative does not reproduce the logical sequence of his journey from North to South. As the narrator's consciousness moves backward and forward in time, notions of space become problematic and North and South are deliberately confused. His experience of the Swedish winter is filtered though memories of the Bulgarian winters of his childhood and later hunting expeditions in the Balkan Range. The impressionistic texture of the narrative thus manages to accommodate stories about children, ('real' and imagined) animals and even inanimate objects (a clothes peg is portrayed as sailing through the world ocean) together with fanciful accounts of famous public figures such as Artur Lunkvuist and Ilya Ehrenburg. Traditional hierarchies are disrupted and familiar stereotypes and images are defamiliarized in the process. The pervasive reference to 'Nordic gloom', for instance, is initially made part of a deliberately pointless story about a little girl who tells her mother that she is a crocodile and must eat her up. Despite the mother's attempts at persuasion, the child 'eats' her. The narrator claims that children experience a metamorphosis suggestive of their innocence: 'they go to bed as blue-eyed little angels and wake up in the dark [Swedish] mornings as blue-eyed little crocodiles' whereas adults – irrespective of whether they are Swedes or Bulgarians – are doomed to be 'gloomy crocodiles' throughout their sleeping and waking hours (Radichkov 1980: 25). The deliberate rejection of the boastful exaltation of the South in the manner of Tsonev is significant: it contributes to the overall relativizing effect of the narrative.

The story of the 'blue-eyed little crocodile' is followed by an account of a conversation with the Swedish poet Artur Lunkvuist, a type of leftist that earlier Bulgarian travellers would have readily placed in the 'progressive' camp. Lunkvuist's stance is decidedly anti-Western. He discourses at length about 'the nuclear threat', 'the danger presented by atomic power plants' and the West's 'quest for a new Hitler'. The latter, he claims, is the bourgeoisie's last resort: confronted with the 'progress' of the communist East, the moribund class is bound to opt for such a desperate remedy. The Bulgarian narrator welds the Swedish poet's dire prognosis into a fanciful account of the Soviet-dominated world peace movement. He maintains that during the Cold War years Lunkvuist was one of the movement's 'trumpeters' and, together with Joliot-Curie and Ilya Ehrenburg, enthusiastically blew 'the Jericho trumpets of peace'. While the trumpets are silent in the present, the message of hope they conveyed should not be abandoned or, as Radichkov puts it, 'the delicate flower of hope [should not be] cast onto the damp asphalt'. The narrator is not bothered much by the West's presumed 'quest for a new Hitler'. Unlike Lunkvuist, who avers that the world faces imminent destruction, he believes in humanity's resilience and ability to survive (Radichkov 1980: 26–28).

The obverse side of Radichkov's postmodernist relativism is illustrated by his scattered comments on dissidents and Western criticism of the infringement of human rights in the Eastern bloc. Thus the narrator reminisces about the 1973 P.E.N. congress in Stockholm at which Heinrich Böll warned his colleagues against turning the Solzhenitsyn case into an international issue. He remarks further that 'it was then that the West [first] noticed certain unidentified flying objects in the East's sky and proceeded to identify them as "dissidents"'. Radichkov continues his extended cosmic metaphor and defines dissidents as 'heavenly bodies that disagree with the rotary motion of the universe'. He claims that the Western interest in eastern European dissidents was part of a 'fashion' for human rights and individual freedom, which was at its height in 1973, the year when the first volume of *The Gulag Archipelago* appeared. To the Western 'fashion' the narrator opposes his own conviction that material wealth is unevenly distributed throughout the world and a redistribution is imperative (ibid.: 97). This is reminiscent of Brezhnev's query to his regime's Western critics about respect for 'the right to work' in the 'capitalist camp'. Both responses were tinged with hypocrisy insofar as the distribution of material wealth within the Eastern bloc itself was far from 'even' and a number of individuals were deprived of 'the right to work' on political grounds.

The narrator's conservative stance is further illustrated by an episode that involves a Sabbatarian protesting against restrictions on religious worship in Bulgaria in front of the Bulgarian Embassy in Stockholm (ibid.: 164). The narrator professes to be amazed by his persistence and broadly hints that his protest is a put-up act. He even waxes melodramatic and defines it as a 'carcinogenic remnant from the Cold War era', which interferes with his 'sincere' desire to 'make friends' with the Swedes (ibid.: 165). The narrator avers that 'building bridges' was his main objective in visiting the Scandinavian country but does not explain why criticism should be incompatible with good will and friendship. His apparent unwillingness to grant any validity to the Sabbatarian's protest contrasts strongly with his avowed respect for difference throughout the travelogue. It cannot be denied that certain forms of eastern European political dissent were largely constructed by the Western media. While this produces moral ambiguity, it does not reduce *all* resistance to the totalitarian system to irrelevance. It is disappointing, though, that a writer of Radichkov's calibre did not explicitly oppose that system. In some of his other texts he alerted readers to its absurdities but he did not go so far as to question its key myths or claims unequivocally.

A glance at other travelogues produced in the 1980s indicates that the manifestations of what was essentially an accommodationist attitude to the regime ranged from evasion of 'awkward' subjects to circumspect references to some of the flaws of 'real socialism'. Vera Gancheva's 'Etiudi v zhŭlto i sinio' ('Studies in Yellow and Blue') (1984) exemplifies the former tendency. Like Radichkov's *Little Northern Saga*, her travelogue disrupts traditional strategies of narrative representation and relativizes conventional distinctions between North and South, East and West. At the same time, however, it presents an interesting – and instructive – contrast to the earlier text. Gancheva, a well-known Scandinavianist, translator and literary critic, sets out to 'correct' some of the clichéd images of Stockholm and the Swedes. She starts by highlighting the deceptive character of facile identifications across Europe such as the portrayal of Stockholm as 'the Venice of the North' (Gancheva 1984: 45). The narrator stresses key differences between the 'Adriatic Danaë', i. e., Venice, which, in her opinion, is focused primarily upon the past, and the 'symbiosis' of tradition and modernity that characterizes Stockholm. In emphasizing such distinctions she adopts the stance of a *knowledgeable, seasoned traveller*, which readers of the communist era were likely to find disconcerting insofar as it produced a false impression of unrestricted mobility outside the country. Radichkov does mention travel to other parts of the world but he also indicates that he visited them in a professional capacity. Gancheva's trips may well have been professional as well but this is not in any way specified in the text under consideration. 'Studies in Yellow and Blue' employs a narrator that persistently withholds personal information. Moreover, she literally conveys her impressions of the *places* she has visited without associating them with specific individuals. Even when Gancheva attempts to deconstruct the myth of 'Nordic gloom' she prefers to speak of Swedes in general rather than providing examples of experiences or encounters with particular people.

On the whole, Gancheva's text is marked by greater respect for ideological difference but this is contained within 'the limits of the expressible'. Transgressing those limits is out of the question.

Stoyan T. Daskalov's 'Do Florentsiia i obratno' ('To Florence and Back') (1985) may at first glance appear radically different from the two texts discussed above. For instance, as behoves a travelogue by one of Bulgaria's 'village writers', it is not marked by formal experimentation. At the same time, it shares the earlier texts' suspicion of what was termed *hardcore* anti-Western propaganda. 'To Florence and Back' focuses on Teofil, a driver at the Bulgarian embassy in Rome. In the travelogue's symbolic-ideological scheme, he is apparently intended to represent the best that 'real socialism' has produced. The narrator recounts the story of his life, which should illustrate the opportunities that the system provides for ordinary village folk. Thus we are told of his poor village background and his consequent support of land collectivization. Unlike him, his fellow villagers were initially reluctant to join the local cooperative farm but came to appreciate its economic advantages later on. Teofil claims that they went so far as to *reproach him for not having put sufficient pressure upon them to join earlier* (Daskalov 1985: 113). It is not difficult to read between the lines and provide what has been excised from this part of the text out of respect for 'the limits of the expressible': the repressive measures that accompanied land collectivization in Bulgaria and the morally and politically dubious role that a party activist such as the driver must have played in the process.

In the context of the travelogue, Teofil further embodies the practical spirit and bluntness of village folk. Despite his exemplary record as a 'builder of socialism' in the agrarian sphere, he does not idealize the system and is frankly critical of its flaws. Thus he begins by extolling the virtues of the ultramodern highway connecting Rome and Florence while at the same time admitting that Bulgaria cannot boast such superior roads (ibid.: 113). He further alerts his fellow travellers to the benefits of Italian vine growing and deprecates the bureaucratic factor at home, which makes it difficult for Bulgarian farmers to be flexible and adopt new agricultural techniques (ibid.: 114). The highway and Italian viticulture are tangible signs of Italy's success in the modern world. By suggesting that Bulgaria should follow the Italian example in this respect Teofil partially recovers the country's pre-Second World War image, which was briefly considered above.

Throughout the journey, 'the man of the people' adopts the role of a self-appointed *cicerone* commenting on a wide variety of subjects from history and art to the ways of Italian prostitutes. For him Italy is 'a book of legends' (ibid.: 116) and he regales his fellow travellers with several of those, thus reminding readers of Italy's traditional image as a treasure house of artistic and literary masterpieces. The stories that Teofil tells are also meant to illustrate the broad range of his intellectual interests and to suggest that 'real socialism' does possess certain advantages after all. Teofil may be an ordinary driver but his native intelligence has not been blunted and he possesses insatiable curiosity about the foreign culture to which he has been exposed. Interestingly, in the context of the travelogue, Teofil emerges as a parodic double of the 'all-round personality', the communist version of the Renaissance *homo universalis* that the totalitarian establishment was supposed to mould through educational and political strategies. Whether the parody was intentional or unconscious must remain an open question. On the whole, despite its traditional narrative form and scarcity of relativizing devices, Daskalov's text appears more politically daring than the two earlier travelogues. Arguably, it came closest to straining 'the limits of the expressible'.

Conclusion

As was pointed out above, travelogues are structured through a dialectic of self and other. While claiming to be predominantly stories about the other, they inevitably provide insights into the self. Travelogues of the communist era are no exception to this 'rule'. They exhibit continuity with earlier Bulgarian writing about western Europe. Predictably, there is also a very major difference: thus the pre-1945 tendency of idealizing some kinds of 'Europeanness' and representing Bulgaria as a site of symbolic lack because of its inability to efface the signs of its Oriental(ized) past and become genuinely 'European' practically disappeared from the communist context and was replaced by a quasi-mythical account of the country's miraculous transformation from an underprivileged 'periphery' to a front runner in the race for 'progress'. Significantly, travelogues informed by this ideological construct tend to represent *the West* as a site of symbolic lack by portraying aspects of life in western Europe in exaggeratedly negative terms and thus purporting to convince domestic readers of the capitalist system's bankruptcy and imminent demise. The anti-authoritarian youth movements of the 1960s and non-communist left-wing politics are likewise interpreted as signs of capitalism's bankruptcy.

The process of denouncing the 'Big Bad West' involved the erasure of contradictions at home. This erasure often reversed the intended effect of travel narratives about western Europe and gave rise to scepticism among readers. Scepticism was also fuelled by the litigious, self-righteous tone of a considerable number of travelogues. This encouraged *reading between the lines*.

Travel writing of the communist era is decidedly not characterized by uniformity. The differences observed and commented upon above were partially conditioned by the vagaries of the regime over a period of forty-five years. Special attention was paid to travelogues produced during the era's final phase (1979–1989), which took into account readers' accumulated scepticism about mandatory hostility to western European capitalism and attempted to project more balanced images of the others that they were involved in representing. However, even such texts did not envision any change or alternative to Soviet-style socialism. Insofar as they proclaimed the latter an inalienable feature of Bulgaria's historical destiny, they embodied a conservative, preservationist tendency.

The study of travelogues of the communist era provides a relatively novel perspective upon Bulgaria's recent past and thus introduces an element of diversity into what might otherwise become a standardized and uniform narrative of the totalitarian system and its propagandist machines. It foregrounds the role that specific stories play in the (re)construction of the past and helps us make better sense of the factors that would determine the thematic patterns and narrative fabric of travel writing in the present and future.

Notes

1. For a relatively early commentary alerting us to the fact, see Greenblatt, Rev and Starn 1995. Political terms such as 'communist', 'socialist', 'totalitarian', 'post-communist', 'post-socialist', 'post-totalitarian' and their cognate nouns are often used in ambiguous and/or partisan ways. Throughout this chapter, 'communism' and 'communist' will be used to refer to the repressive political regimes of the former Eastern bloc. The term 'totalitarianism' has come in for a lot of criticism over the last ten or fifteen years. For an informed commentary on the emergence and subsequent history of the concept, see Delfini and Piccone (1998). Despite scepticism among Western scholars and social scientists, I will retain the use of 'totalitarianism' and will follow a well-established eastern and central European precedent in applying it to the pre-1989 repressive regimes in eastern and central Europe. During the Brezhnev era those regimes tended to use the phrase 'real socialism' to define their own economic and ideological practices. The phrase 'real socialism' will always be placed in quotes and will be used interchangeably with 'totalitarianism', 'communism' and 'Soviet-style socialism' throughout. 'Post-communist' and 'post-communism' will refer to developments in eastern and central Europe after 1989.

2. George Steiner originally coined the phrase. It is repeatedly used by Shurbanov and Sokolova in their book on Shakespeare (Shurbanov and Sokolova 2001).

3. See Adam 2000.

4. The text was initially published in Russian in *Russkii vestnik* ('Russian Review'), Vol. 60/1867. It subsequently came out in Bulgarian in *Nezavisimost* ('Independence'), issues 37–52/1874; and *Zname* ('Banner'), issues 3–5/1876. The present reference is to the 1928 edition of *Zapiski*. Unless otherwise indicated, the translation of all titles and quotations from Bulgarian is my own.

5. See the exhaustive list of travelogues provided by Giurova (1979: 182).

6. Apart from similarities arising from the Balkan Christian countries' political situation vis-à-vis the Ottoman Empire and the West, there were significant differences. For a commentary on the Greek case, which has predictably received the greatest attention, see Leask 1992 (esp. pages 15–24), Herzfeld 1997 (esp. 89–108), and Roessel 2002 (esp. 132–58).

7. Pundeff 1994.

8. On the modern city as a 'contact zone', see Carr 2002.

9. See Kostova 1997: 213–17.

10. I have borrowed the terms 'core' and 'periphery' from Moretti 1998, 171–74.

11. The geopolitical and cultural term 'central Europe' is notoriously ambiguous. For the purposes of the present essay it refers to Austria, Germany, Hungary, the Czech lands, Slovakia and Poland.

12. Significantly, one of Bai Ganyo's adventures takes place in Russia.

13. Bulgarian culture generally shares the continental synecdochic reduction of Britishness to Englishness. In the texts under discussion, the words 'Britain'

and 'British' and their cognates are used occasionally, but hardly ever designate entities or characteristics different from the ones denoted by 'England' and 'English'. My own discourse reflects the conventional distinction between 'English' and 'British'.

14. See Kostova 1997: 213–16.

15. In a prose sketch introducing his 1896 collection of poems *Epic Songs* Slaveikov adopts the quasi-Germanic identity of the poet Olaf Van Geldern and claims that when he was in Germany he received hospitality from three excellent hosts: a Hellene (Goethe), an Israelite (Heine) and a Teuton (Nietzsche). See Slaveikov 1958: 1:254.

16. Kostova 1997: 215–16.

17. Svetlana Boym has produced a perceptive analysis of a similar Russian cultural myth implying 'strong opposition to everyday routine' and privileging 'heroic spiritual homelessness and messianic nomadism' (1995: 133). Even though some aspects of nineteenth-century Russian culture may have impacted on the Bulgarian myth, it should not be written off as yet another 'import'. The myth was clearly part of the Bulgarian intelligentsia's response to the tensions characterizing its relationship with a middle class that opted for compromise rather for a consistent opposition to either the Ottoman authorities or their Bulgarian successors in the post-Independence period.

18. See P. Stoyanov 1921/1923; Karima 1928; Stoikov 1930; Marchevski 1934–1935; Dimitrov 1941.

19. See L. Stoyanov 1936.

20. See, for instance, Dimov 1942, and Kamenova 1942, esp. 174–88.

21. The first edition was published in January 1945 to be followed by the second one in May.

22. See Kostova 1997: 17–18.

23. On this tendency, see Thompson 2000, esp. 100–102.

24. While some of Stoyanov's articles were re-issued and he is occasionally mentioned in memoirs, no attempt has been made to put his texts in perspective and to subject them to a genuinely critical reading.

References

Adam, H. 2000. 'Divided Memories: Confronting the Crimes of Previous Regimes', *Telos* 118, 23–47.

Andreichin, I.S. 1900. 'B. Bjornson: Literaturen portret', *Misŭl* 10:2, 86–99.

Bagriana, E. 1950. 'Shest dni v Anglia', *Septemvri* 3, 89–92.

Bakić-Hayden, M. 1995. 'Nesting Orientalisms: The Case of Former Yugoslavia', *Slavic Review* 54:4, 910–35.

Boym, S. 1995. 'From the Russian Soul to Postcommunist Nostalgia', *Representations* 49, 133–66.

Carr, H. 2002. 'Modernism and Travel (1880–1940)', in *The Cambridge Companion to Travel Writing*, ed. P. Hulme and T. Youngs. Cambridge: Cambridge University Press.

Daskalov, S.T. 1985. 'Do Florentsiia i obratno', *Plamŭk* 29:8, 113–21.

Delfini, A. and P. Piccone. 1998. 'Modernity, Libertarianism and Critical Theory: Reply to Pellicani', *Telos* 112, 23–47.

Dimitrov, B. 1941. *Na Iztok – vsichko novo! SSSR: vpechatleniia i razmishleniia.* Sofia: Hristo G. Danov.

Dimov, D. 1942. 'Iz subtropichni bregove', *Mir* 126, 23–28; reprinted in *Sŭchineniia*, vol. 4. Sofia: Bŭlgarski pisatel, 1981.

Dobrev, K. 1934. *Panairat v Laiptsig.* Sofia: T. Chipev.

Fortunati, V., R. Monticelli and M. Ascari. 2001. 'Foreword', in *Travel Writing and the Female Imaginary.* Bologna: Patron Editore.

Gancheva, V. 1984. 'Etiudi v zhŭlto i sinio', in *Teleskop, pŭt i dve siamski kotki.* Sofia: Narodna Mladezh.

GoGwilt, C. 1995. *The Invention of the West: Joseph Conrad and the Double-Mapping of Europe and Empire.* Stanford: Stanford University Press.

Greenblatt, S., I. Rev and R. Starn. 1995. 'Introduction', *Representations* 49, 1–13.

Giurova, S. 1979. 'Bŭlgarskiiat patepis: zarazhdane i utvŭrzhdavane', in *Za literaturnite zhanrove prez Vŭzrazhdaneto*, ed. P. Dinekov and T. Undjieva. Sofia: BAN.

Heine, H. 1948. *Self-Portrait and Other Prose Writings*, trans. and ed. F. Ewan. Secacus, NJ: Citadel Press.

Herzfeld, M. 1997. *Cultural Intimacy: Social Poetics in the Nation State.* New York: Routledge.

Hristoforov, A. 1945. *Skitsi iz London.* Sofia: Hristo G. Danov.

Kamenova, A. 1942. *Nepovtorimoto.* Sofia: Hemus.

Karadocheva, P. 1971. *Okolo planetata Albion.* Sofia: Partizdat.

Karavelov, L. 1928. *Zapiski za Bŭlgariia i bŭlgarite.* Sofia: Ignatov.

Karima, A. 1928. *V dneshna Rusiia.* Sofia: Sŭglasie.

Kostova, L. 1997. *Tales of the Periphery: the Balkans in Nineteenth-Century British Writing.* Veliko Turnovo: St. Cyril and St. Methodius University Press.

Leask, N. 1992. *British Romantic Writers and the East: Anxieties of Empire.* Cambridge: Cambridge University Press.

Levine, M.G. 1997. 'Writing Anxiety: Christa Wolf's *Kindheitsmuster*', *Diacritics* 27:2, 112–32.

Magris, C. 1989. *Danube*, trans. P. Creagh. London: The Harvill Press.

Marchevski, M. 1934–35. *Osem godini v Sŭvetskiia sŭiuz.* Sofia: S. Vasilev.

Milev, G. 1976. *Izbrano.* Sofia: Bŭlgarski pisatel.

Milev, A., Bratkov, Y. and B. Nikolov, eds. 1964. *Rechnik na chuzhdite dumi.* Sofia: Nauka i izkustvo.

Minchev, S. 1908. 'V Shveitsariia', *Misŭl* 13:12, 524–32.

Moretti, F. 1998. *Atlas of the European Novel 1800–1900.* London: Verso.

Nikolchina, M. 2002. 'The Seminar: *Mode d'emploi.* Impure Spaces in the Light of Late Totalitarianism', *Differences* 13:1, 96–127.

Orwell, G. 2000 [1949]. *1984.* Harmondsworth: Penguin.

Pleşu, A. 1995. 'Intellectual Life Under Dictatorship', *Representations* 49, 61–71.

Pundeff, M. 1994. 'Bulgarian Nationalism', in *Nationalism in Eastern Europe*, ed. P. Sugar and I. Lederer. Seattle: University of Washington Press.

Radichkov, Y. 1980. *Malka severna saga.* Sofia: Bŭlgarski pisatel.

Roessel, D. 2002. *In Byron's Shadow: Modern Greece in the English and American Imagination*. Oxford: Oxford University Press.

Shurbanov, A. and B. Sokolova. 2001. *Painting Shakespeare Red: An East-European Appropriation*. Newark, NJ: University of Delaware Press.

Simmons, C. 2000. 'Baedeker Barbarism: Rebecca West's *Black Lamb and Grey Falcon* and Robert Kaplan's *Balkan Ghosts*', *Human Rights Review*, October–December, 109–16.

Slaveikov, P. 1900. 'Chestit poet', *Misŭl* 10:1, 13–27.

Slaveikov, P.P. 1958. *Sabrani sŭchineniia*, 2 vols. Sofia: Bŭlgarski pisatel.

Stoikov, K.M. 1930. *V Sŭvetska Rusiia*. Lovech: Dragol Mitev.

Stoyanov, L. 1936. *Sŭvremenna Evropa. Fashizam. Kultura. Antifashizam. Dnevnik na edno pŭtuvane do Parizh po sluchai Mezhdunarodniia kongres na pisatelite v zashtita na kulturata*. Sofia: Bratia Miladinovi.

Stoyanov, P. 1921. *Istinata za ruskiia bolshvizm. Fakti i nabliudeniia na ochevidets*. Sofia: Slovo; reprinted Sofia: Pravo, 1923.

Stoyanov, T. 1988. 'Hipievskata "subkultura"', in *Sŭchineniia*, 2 vols, vol. 2. Sofia: Bŭlgarski pisatel.

——— 1988. '"Ultralevitsata" i revolyutsiyata', in *Sŭchineniia*, 2 vols, vol. 2. Sofia: Bŭlgarski pisatel.

Thompson, E.M. 2000. *Imperial Knowledge: Russian Literature and Colonialism*. Westport, CT: Greenwood Press.

Tsonev, V. 1973. *Iz Evropa*. Sofia: Profizdat.

Vazov, I. 1891. 'Izvŭn Bŭlgariia', *Dennitsa*, 2: 1–7, 23–265.

——— 1994. *Nova zemia*. Sofia: Strelets.

Velichkov, K. 2002. *Tsarigradski soneti*, ed. P. Anchev. Sofia: Zaharii Stoyanov.

Yosifova, B. 1958. 'Iz iuzhen Uels', *Plamŭk*, 13:1, 89–97.

CHAPTER 7

New Men, Old Europe:
Being a Man in Balkan Travel Writing

Wendy Bracewell

Much modern Western travel writing presents eastern Europe, and especially the Balkans, as a sort of museum of masculinity: an area where men, whether revolutionaries, politicians or workers, are depicted as behaving in ways that are seen as almost exaggeratedly masculine according to the standards of the traveller. Physical toughness and violence, sexual conquest and the subordination of women, guns, strong drink and moustaches feature heavily. This is a region where men are men – and sometimes so are the women, whether 'sworn virgins' living their lives as honorary men, heroic female partisans or, in more derisive accounts, alarmingly muscular and hirsute athletes, stewardesses and waitresses. But the notion of a characteristically masculine Balkans is not limited to outsiders. It can appear in travel accounts from the region as well, ranging from Aleko Konstantinov's emblematic fictional Bulgarian traveller, Bai Ganyo Balkanski, with his boorish disregard of European norms of behaviour (Konstantinov 1966 [1895]), to more polished travel writers who nonetheless find it useful to contrast a 'Balkan' model to Western versions of manliness. The area has not invariably been gendered as male: early German writings pictured the Balkan Slavs under Ottoman rule as feminized, unwarlike and subservient; while in the nineteenth century Philhellenes and others conjured images of Greece or Bulgaria as a defenceless Christian maiden, violated by a brutal Muslim tyrant (Petkov 1997; Roessel 2002). But associations of masculinity with the Balkans are sufficiently persistent to provoke curiosity. What purposes can they serve and how can they help us to understand the Balkans' place in Europe? [1] One way of pursuing the question might be to search for the origins of such images, whether in popular culture or in literary tropes. Tracing the genealogies of patterns of perception, however, does not necessarily tell us much about their uses and meaning. Instead, I propose a more limited investigation, exploring a handful of late twentieth-century travel accounts by Englishmen and by Yugoslavs, asking why their characterizations of place and people are engendered in particular ways in specific contexts, and what functions their gendered discourses of difference serve.

Concepts of gender become entangled with accounts of travel in complex ways. Notions of masculinity or femininity play a part in positioning traveller-narrators in relation both to their implied readers and to the objects of their commentary. The sources of authority men and women can draw upon may differ; so may the myths they use to structure their travel tales (Ulysses voyages, Penelope waits at home). Gender expectations help constitute travellers' national or cultural stereotypes: the voluble effeminacy of the Frenchman; the seductive, feminine languor of southern Europe; the dishevelled violence of a masculinized Balkans. And gendered characterizations encode – and naturalize – *relationships* between peoples and places, particularly relationships of hierarchy and power. The relation of male to female has conventionally represented relations of domination : subordination in Western culture – thus the regularity with which we encounter a gendered geography that opposes a masculine, rational and active West to a feminized, passionate and passive East.

Edward Said started off this particular line of discussion, along with much else, by noting the unchanging 'feminine penetrability' of the Orient in Westerners' accounts (Said 1978: 206). Others have enlarged on the variety of gendered characterizations of East and West – less coherent and more contradictory than Said initially suggested – but have shown how the notion of gender as a relationship keeps them linked in a permanent opposition (e.g., Lowe 1991; Behdad 1994; Schick 1999). Analyses of colonial discourse have pointed out the ways an opposition between the male traveller–colonizer and feminized colony meant that women, conquered territories and non-Europeans were made to occupy the same symbolic space in the stories that defined their place in the Western imagination (Carr 1985; Kabbani 1994; Lewis 1996). What was at issue, we hear, was not just Western elite males' self-definition, but their assertion of control over all these interchangeable domestic and foreign 'Others'. These binaries have come to seem both ubiquitous and unvarying in Orientalist (and colonialist) discourse. This is so much the case that in her book *Imagining the Balkans* (1997), Maria Todorova supports her argument that Western 'Balkanism' should be differentiated from Orientalism with the claim that persistent depictions of the Balkans as masculine place the region in a distinctive relation to the West. Unlike 'the standard orientalist discourse, which resorts to metaphors of its objects of study as female, balkanist discourse is singularly male' (Todorova 1997: 15). This is because Orientalism is 'a discourse about an imputed opposition', while Balkanism is 'a discourse about an imputed ambiguity', treating differences within Europe (ibid.: 17).

But just how stable and predictable are the double mappings of gender and power? One suggestion that things might not be so simple comes from studies of women travel writers. The neatly linked binaries of male/female, dominant/subordinate, West/East and colonizer/colonized did not easily accommodate Western women travelling and writing in the age of imperialism. The solidarities or distinctions such women invoked could cut across categories of gender, class or race in a variety of ways: women travellers might either draw parallels between their own subordinate position and that of the colonial population, or they might assert privilege as white Westerners in compensation for their oppression as women (Mills 1991; Blunt 1994; McClintock et al. 1997). Women travel writers could and did choose to write as adventurer-heroes, or as authoritative aesthetic 'beholders', in the process subverting and exposing the assumptions of discourses conventionally coded as masculine (Lawrence 1994; Bohls 1995).

Still, is it so different for men? The consistency of masculine discourses is sometimes taken for granted, as is their stability over time, in order to set up a foil to the differences that emerge from other positions. But understandings of gender, race and class shift and change, altering the meanings of the rhetorical patterns they underpin. Men differ among themselves, by age or sexuality or nation, and so can take widely differing positions with relation to the intersection of gender and power. And male travel writers, even white middle-class ones, can deliberately satirize and challenge myths of masculinity and write across the grain of dominant understandings. Different ways of being a man in travel writing, and the implications for travel writers' gendered geographies, deserve more explicit attention.

In what follows, some of these issues are explored through two sets of travel accounts: the first by Englishmen describing their adventures in the Balkans (and eastern Europe more generally) after the events of 1989; and the second by Yugoslav writers travelling in the West in the 1970s and 1980s. I do not propose to compare their conceptions of the Balkans in any detail; still less to trace possible linkages between the images that they deploy. However, the texts are comparable in that both sets of writers use depictions of gender relations, and particularly issues around masculinity, as an important element in their representations of identity and place. For both the Englishmen and the writers from

Yugoslavia, ideas of manliness define and reinforce divisions between us and them, self and other, norm and deviation, domination and subordination, and West and East. At the same time, the writers link depictions of masculinity and of otherness for other purposes, suggesting personal or local interests that cannot be understood solely in terms of relations between East and West. Each set of texts raises related points about the ways gendered discourses of difference have been used in Western and Balkan travel accounts. And when they are considered together, each casts an unexpected light on the other.

Englishmen in the Balkans

The fall of the Berlin Wall was triggered by the raising of restrictions on travel to the West, but the events of 1989 were also the occasion for a less dramatic current of travel from West to East. As well as works by foreign correspondents and academic pundits bearing witness to the collapse of the socialist regimes, a host of accounts by travellers in the 'new Europe' began to appear from the early 1990s. In contrast to texts asserting the authority of long acquaintance or earnest study (e.g., Thompson 1992; Garton Ash 1993; Kaplan 1993), a cluster of books by Englishmen presented a deliberately inexpert and dilettante-ish perspective on the region.

These journeys are unconventional, if not downright eccentric – though seldom without more serious ambitions. Giles Whittell, in *Lambada Country* (1992), cycled to Istanbul, while Jason Goodwin (*On Foot to the Golden Horn*, 1994) and Nicholas Crane (*Clear Waters Rising*, 1996) headed for the same destination on foot, all in pursuit of a deeper understanding of Europe's divisions and of themselves. Rory MacLean, in *Stalin's Nose* (1992), drove a Trabant through eastern Europe accompanied by an aunt and a pig, seeking to grasp the tension between individual responsibility and collective evil in eastern Europe's past, while Tony Hawks (*Playing the Moldovans at Tennis*, 2000) demonstrated the power of a can-do attitude by pursuing a bet that he could defeat the entire Moldovan football team at tennis, with the loser of the bet to sing the Moldovan national anthem, naked, in Balham High Street. Robert Carver (*The Accursed Mountains*, 1998) went to Albania looking for 'somewhere right off the map, with no tourists or modern development', and returned to 'explain Albania to the West'.

In *Lambada Country*, Giles Whittell adopts a typically self-deprecating tone:

> It was 1990. Like thousands of others, I wanted to see Eastern Europe before it disappeared and became a mere annex of Western Europe. In

particular – and this was as close as I got to what you might call a line of enquiry – I wanted to go to those parts which other forms of transport might not reach. That is, down minor roads, up steep roads, along dirt roads. Once there, the idea was to ask whether the revolutions had made a difference – to the beer, the newspapers, the prospect of going to work on a Monday morning, the way policemen spoke to you, the availability of bicycle spares [...]. Then there were the grandchildren to think of. ('Yes, Tom, what your father says is true. Many years ago I rode a bicycle to Istanbul ...') This being a bicycle trip, there was also, for the first time in my life, the prospect of developing some real muscles. (1992: xiii–xiv)

While these writers laugh off any claims to authoritative knowledge, they offer not only entertainment but also the implicit promise that the reader will in fact gain an insight into the region that other, more conventional commentators cannot provide – precisely because of the authors' combination of amateurism (and thus a paradoxical authority derived from apparently innocent observation) and their predilection for the unbeaten track (and access to the ordinary and random, and therefore truly 'authentic'). Furthermore, they attribute an unknown quality to the region travelled to, not reducible to its postsocialist status. This lies at the heart of its attraction for these writers. As with Carver, these travellers' routes lie 'right off the map'; they see a 'chance of finding places up there'; that is, places that are not yet like the rest of Europe, places that are – in short – different. And that difference is expressed, in all these travel accounts, in terms of gender and, particularly, in terms of masculinity.

But even before these travellers address differences of place, they deploy a series of gendered differentiations to establish their own identities. The writers' sense of what it means to be a man emerges, first of all, in the ways they set themselves in contrast to traditional images of the male traveller. For most, this takes the form of the heroic adventurer and gentleman scholar of the British imperial past. Their texts are haunted by men like Patrick Leigh Fermor, who set out in 1933 from the Hook of Holland to travel to Constantinople on foot. Carver sits at Leigh Fermor's feet, seeking advice on where to escape tourism and modernity; Crane solicits his approbation for his plan to hike Europe's mountain ranges; Goodwin cites him as an inspiration. Whittell mentions him only in passing in his own journey to Constantinople, but his account in many ways can be read as a comic inversion of the older traveller's journal: Whittell paints himself as inept where Leigh Fermor was omni-competent, pursued by the Lambada rather than accompanied by folksong, tumbled by orange-fingernailed tarts in campsite *cabanas* rather than tumbling peasant girls in haystacks, and passed from one Hungarian household to the next – for arguments over apartment kitchen tables rather than repartee in aristocratic salons. But similar elements of parody and bathos also structure the other accounts. These travellers recall the heroic men who preceded them only to present themselves in comic contrast, as incompetent, clownish antiheroes, who have no idea what to pack (Goodwin's mountain of hiking equipment includes both silk and thermal underwear and five bars of Bendick's Sporting and Military chocolate, which he contrasts to the rucksack holding 'a toothbrush, an apple and a pair of socks' carried by 'our predecessors' (Goodwin 1994: 13); whose embarrassing physical incapacities are detailed (Whittell's cyclist's crotch-rot, Goodwin's diarrhoea, Crane's endless list of excruciating ailments); and who cannot do anything without help.

Yet, for all their self-ridicule in comparison to the heroes of the past, these writers make sure to present themselves as travellers – never as tourists. They may not live up to the standards of the men who built the Empire, but they follow the same tradition of enterprise and adventure, although somewhat diffidently, perhaps, when it comes to the notion of an Empire, whose passing they note by blaming their 'khaki empire garb' for incubating sweat rash (Whittell 1992: 104); by poking fun at the anachronistic language and pretensions of know-nothing British diplomats, summed up by the figure of 'Carruthers, Our Man in Tirana' who is reduced to an embassy of 'three small rented rooms in an office building' (Carver 1998: 151–54); and by lampooning an annoying sidekick's resemblance to all the 'maverick Foreign Office Arabists known through the bazaars from Alexandra [*sic*] to Lucknow simply as The Englishman' (Goodwin 1994: 8). These writers are more confident about being adventurer-travellers when it comes to comparisons with their own contemporaries, particularly in chance encounters with Western tourists, who are usually likeable and well intentioned, but basically consumers of guidebook experiences, whether passive and uncomprehending or earnest and overprepared. Domestic social distinctions are not foregrounded in this familiar traveller/tourist dichotomy – but the travellers' dogged egalitarianism is not allowed to obscure their own very evident social advantages. (Carver does highlight his own superior daring as a traveller by dismissing the travels of 'waffling old Etonians on bicycles' (Carver 1998: 331), but he also ensures we know about his own public-school background.) National differences are a more acceptable substitute for social difference. Germans and Americans are particularly apt as foils to our heroes: German fellow-tourers are equipped with 'Lennon specs, Goretex overgarments, hyper-rugged bikes loaded for total self-sufficiency' (Whittell 1992: 172), or at least 'a long, hard sausage' (Crane 1996: 85), while American volunteers and tourists are unremittingly groomed and hail-fellow-well-met, as well as loaded with camcorders, super-soft sneakers, and money (Hawks 2000: 43, 144–45; Carver 1998: 276–77;

Whittell 1992: 181). But what are all these advantages compared to their own gentlemanly English virtues of amateurishness, stoicism and whimsy? For all their self-deprecation, the young Englishmen are nostalgic for a vanished imperial masculinity that would give purpose and legitimacy to their anachronistic attempts at adventure. Crane sums it up for all of them, comparing his experiences to those of Leigh Fermor: 'I was too late' (Crane 1996: 328).[2]

A certain nostalgia is perceptible, too, in the way these writers establish their relations with Western women. Several of the accounts record the shadows of ex-girlfriends and wives left behind, who have no intention of waiting for the traveller to return and are more interested in getting on with their lives than in taking part in boy's games. Goodwin, unusually, is accompanied by his girlfriend and future wife: she thought his plan of 'bridging the gap between traveller and indigene' by 'grubbing about in mud and boots' was 'dim', but realized she would have to come along if only to ward off possible dangers (Goodwin 1994: 10). Other Western women met on the road are self-confident travellers, more frightening than attractive. Their emancipation seems to imply a corresponding emasculation on their menfolk's part. Carver is quite explicit about the equation:

> Over the last thirty years the gradual feminization of society in Britain, and most of the formerly macho northern European democracies such as Holland and Germany, had blanded men down to an acceptably low-testosterone product, suitable only for occasional use by the quasi-liberated women, as and when required. (Carver 1998: 184)

He goes on to contrast 'use-and-chuck, Kleenex-style, Euro-wimps' to 'real, old-fashioned Western males, authentic gas-guzzling pre-feminist models' – whom he sees as now largely extinct (Carver 1998: 184). Carver is particularly scathing, but anxieties about what it means to be a modern man in a society where women are understood as equals are shared by all these writers.

The part played by local women is superficially similar to that of Western women. The travellers are constantly being taken in hand by local women who rescue them and solve their many problems. On the one hand, their calm assurance, like the confidence of the Western women, gives substance to the travellers' claims to incompetence. But while Western women do not need the travellers, these women do. Skilled, dynamic and capable Balkan women are regularly described as deserving better than the limited opportunities available to them – and as needing to be rescued. These are not instances of Gayatri Spivak's classic colonial romance: 'a white man is rescuing a brown woman from a brown man' and in the process justifying colonial rule as the protection of victimized women (Spivak 1988: 297). These abortive romances never reach fruition: an Englishman is *failing* to rescue a Balkan woman. But the reason is always the same: the woman's material motives and the fear that the man represents nothing but 'an escape route from this country' (Carver 1998: 184; Hawks 2000: 159). These Englishmen hesitate at the thought that these relationships might depend on something other than their own individual qualities: they want to be loved for themselves alone, not because they might stand for Western political and economic might. This is a masculinity that still romanticizes masculine power and feminine dependence (placed in piquant contrast to the independence of the modern Western woman). Yet, also in line with older understandings of bourgeois respectability, the travellers insist on hiding any hint of a more calculated transaction behind an ideal of sentimental reciprocity.

Encounters with prostitutes follow the same principle, but are much more straightforward. Not only does the sentimental Englishman never pay for sex, the very prospect of such a transaction confuses his reactions entirely. Nicholas Crane is importuned by an attractive Bulgarian prostitute : 'You, me – sex!' (Crane 1996: 357–58). He feels that a woman is a fair reward for his travails: 'Didn't I deserve a dose of delicious coddling?' But all he can think, as things get out of hand, is: 'What about the transaction? Do you arrange a price before, or after? Would she take a traveller's cheque or demand dollars? Is it a flat fee or do they charge by the minute?' He comes to himself by remembering who he is: 'No, thank you. I'm English'. The woman is incredulous: 'English? Polish? What the difference?' She does not understand. For Crane, men are *not* all the same, and for him, as for other postimperial travellers, it is crucial that the Englishman maintains that difference by preserving the boundary between eros and commerce.

Crane makes the prostitute and his encounter with her stand for Bulgaria in general: she smells of roses, the symbol of Bulgaria, 'not a subtle hint of roses, but an over-powering pall which must have been applied as body-lacquer with a high-pressure hose', while her cleavage echoes the countryside itself: 'wasn't there a Valley of the Roses in the Stara Planina?' The abortive romances between local women and English travellers regularly serve as a metaphor for the encounter between the East and West: these travellers are obscurely disturbed when it turns into a commercial exchange. Expecting gratitude and even love as the reward for deliverance, they find that the East has more material interests and knows what she has to bargain with. It is not the relationship that their nostalgia seemed to promise. The new Englishman can find the new Europa rapaciously capitalist, even if deliciously feminine.

These versions of modern, postimperial English masculinity are thrown into higher relief by encounters with local men. The travellers are constantly comparing themselves to their hosts and, once again, failing to measure up according to standard virility indicators. A whole series of set pieces sees them outmatched in competitions over drinking to excess, shooting guns off recklessly, driving dangerously, pursuing women, sword fighting or moustache growing. These encounters define a stereotypical machismo, compulsively competitive and rooted in physical or sexual prowess. The English travellers treat this hypermasculinity as both familiar and exotic. It is an aspect of eastern Europe's backwardness, a marker of a phase that their own society has passed through, as corny and outdated as the Lambada; but at the same time different, engrossing, simultaneously repellent and attractive. These may be 'real' men, but theirs is a version of masculinity that the writers see as lagging behind their own society's gender norms. Such machismo makes the region somehow less modern and less 'European' – though local men are never compared to the Spanish or Italians, nor indeed to working-class British men.

The reaction ranges from fear, through a sort of aesthetic appreciation, to attempts at emulation – sometimes all in the same text – as the writers position themselves and their hosts on a spectrum of manliness. Carver, for example, weighs up the risks of 'failing a local test of machismo' when offered a pot-shot with the bus driver's automatic on an unscheduled Albanian rest stop; he turns his back and walks away from the gaggle of armed Gheg passengers, trusting the camera-bulge under his shirt to suggest his gun-carrying credentials, simultaneously terrified and proud of his grasp of the rituals of Albanian manhood (he reasons that they will not shoot him if there is a chance of hitting the boy standing in his path and thus causing a blood feud) (Carver 1996: 229, 233–36). For Carver, it is a violent, patriarchal and irresponsible masculinity that defines Albania (the 'Land of the Eagle' is summed up in terms of its 'Sons': 'hospitable rapists and elegant torturers, welcoming robbers and wife-beating family men' and so on (Carver 1998: 337)). Other encounters are less melodramatic but equally emblematic: Rory Maclean falls in with a local man, Kristan, in Romania, and finds himself being instructed in womanizing, ingenious methods of counterfeiting cigarette packets, and black-market transactions in a chapter entitled, ambiguously, 'Riding with the Best Man' (ostensibly referring to conductors who take bribes on the railway, but also summing up Maclean's experiences with Kristan) (Maclean 1992: 169–78). Whittell is floored by *slivova* in Bulgaria while his smuggler companion drinks until morning and stumbles in to bed, but still manages, 'incredibly, to swivel back to the door and open it before urinating and vomiting' (Whittell 1992: 185–86). Whatever the sphere of action, the Englishmen usually come off second best by local standards of manliness.

However, there are limits to self-deprecation. Their hosts may possess an old-fashioned machismo, but this only highlights the qualities that the Englishmen see as their own defining features. The first of these, touched on by most of the writers, has to do with money and work. While local men may be virile in physical and sexual terms, they are emasculated by being poor – especially when they cannot provide adequately for their families. The travellers are constantly irked by the assumption that they, in contrast, are rich. Several contrive to be perpetually short of cash as part of their adventures on the road, lessening the apparent distance between themselves and their hosts and allowing them to accept hospitality gratefully or to reward it at their own whim – but without noting that their temporary penury is entirely self-inflicted and conceals their ability to spend their time at their leisure. (None of these writers tells us how his journey is financed.) They hesitate to interpret economic power in itself as evidence of a fundamental difference between themselves and the locals. They attribute the poverty they see to the collapse of the economy and the welfare network resulting from large-scale political and economic change: the structured inequalities between East and West cannot easily be translated into evidence of personal qualities or codes of behaviour. But this analysis is constantly undermined by the way they comment on the local men's passive, fatalistic acceptance of their circumstances, or else their desire for easy money – for something for nothing. It is not money that differentiates these Westerners from their hosts, but the work ethic. Even Tony Hawks, who admits that his aim of beating Moldovan footballers at tennis is a frivolous waste of time and money, in dubious taste in such a poverty-stricken country, differentiates himself from his Moldovan acquaintances on the basis of his conviction that any difficulty can be overcome by effort. His greatest victory in Moldova is not trouncing the footballers, but getting the teenage son of his host family to laugh at his antics (Hawks 2000: 139–40) and finally, as his crowning achievement, to admit the power of his positive philosophy and to take Hawks as his model of manhood for the future (ibid.: 249). The notion that passivity or inertia is a characteristic of local men is underlined by the pointed contrast made with enterprising (if frighteningly rapacious) local women intent on achieving change for themselves and their own families by any means possible.

This suggests a second quality that differentiates the Englishmen. The travellers notice the ways in which local women are exploited by their menfolk and by society as a whole. For Whittell, the typical rural family 'seems to consist of a hospitable alcoholic husband and a haggard, sober, overworked wife. In taking advantage of the hospitality I am abusing the wife' (Whittell 1992: 93). These Englishmen see the inequalities that go along with a division of gender roles and deplore them, open-mouthed at women who are proud of being dominated by their husbands (Goodwin 1994: 153). They accept their ministrations self-consciously, not as a right but as an embarrassing throwback to a 'colonial childhood' (Carver 1998: 92), only allowing their 'impeccable credentials as a politically correct male' to slip briefly when pushed beyond endurance by a woman whose ability to annoy outweighs the evidence of her oppression (Crane 1996: 223). Local men are presented as taking the patriarchal gender regime for granted. The Englishmen can see themselves as feminists by contrast. Straightforward and unreflexive, local men provide a contrast to the Englishman's stance of self-awareness and self-doubt. Balkan men may be shown as struggling to adjust to economic and political transition, but they have not noticed that it is no longer so simple for modern men in other spheres either.

These travel accounts should be read in the context of the so-called 'crisis in masculinity' in 1980s and 1990s Britain, a state of affairs usually attributed to feminism, changes in the economy (the decline in traditionally male-dominated industrial sectors, the growing presence of women in the labour market) and an increased acceptance of alternative sexualities. Responses ranged from the long-standing feminist critique of patriarchy to popular attempts to define a 'new man' (Connell 1995). The travel writers under discussion, too, use their adventures abroad to play with a variety of notions of manliness and stake out a revised version for themselves: more enterprising than their stay-at-home peers; more daring than the Western tourist with his package holiday; nostalgic for the privileges and certainties of an imperial past, but at the same time more responsible, more emotionally literate, more feminist, more politically correct than the standard Balkan male. The eastern Europe depicted in these accounts serves largely as a backdrop, painted in such a way as to foreground the revised English male identities being developed through travels in the East. While being a 'Euro-wimp' might be a source of anxiety to the Englishman abroad, the new masculinity he is in the process of mapping out is at least superior to the outdated and superseded models he encounters on his travels.

The character of the depiction does not match the mappings of gender and power conventionally attributed to Orientalist or colonial discourses: Western supremacy is not asserted in terms of the general pattern of 'the demasculinization of colonized men and the hypermasculinity of European males' traced elsewhere (Stoler 1991: 56). But just as studies of Western women travellers have drawn attention to the diversity of their purposes and circumstances, so too an examination of these male travel writers shows a variety of factors at work. Looking at the images used by Englishmen in the context of the 1990s 'crisis in masculinity' helps show why the usual gender polarities of alteritist discourse might have been reversed in this way, at this particular juncture, and using this particular tone. Parody and inversion of conventional expectations, motivated by changes to Western middle-class gender norms, underpin the discourses of these travel accounts.

It is sometimes precisely this 'revised' masculinity that works the hardest to sustain a hierarchical relationship between East and West. This is not always overt: straightforward assertions of superiority have become suspect, in geopolitics as in gender and class. The writers' self-parody as hapless antiheroes, undercutting and deflating their own pretensions, serves as a self-defensive strategy. But their self-deprecating depictions still have consequences: their stories draw on and reinforce older notions of geocultural difference, and they evaluate their simplifications and generalizations in moral and hierarchical terms. The West is still the superior norm and eastern Europe and, even more, the Balkans represent the inferior deviation. These English travellers may be 'new men' in contrast to older models, but what they give us is definitely an old Europe.

Yugoslavs in the West

The line of analysis followed above fits comfortably within the Orientalist (and Balkanist) paradigm (Wolff 1994; Todorova 1997; Goldsworthy 1998). However, scholars have insisted on the distinctiveness of the relationship between the Balkans and Western power: the absence of direct colonial rule in particular has meant a corresponding stress on Western *cognitive* hegemony in the region (specifically in the Gramscian sense of hegemony as the consent of the dominated). Claims have even been advanced that the categories of self-identity have been colonized by Western modes of thought. Whereas beyond the borders of Europe, 'the logic of domination is imposed by colonial rule', in the Balkans it seems to be 'the immanent logic of self-constitution itself that generates the incapacity to conceive of oneself in other terms than from the point of view of the dominating other' (Močnik 2002: 95). Internalization of Western ideas of the Balkans, and the notion of being *in* Europe but not wholly *of* it, are blamed for inflicting a whole series of traumas associated with ambiguity, assessed in terms that range from 'self-colonization' (Kiossev 2002) to 'self-stigmatization' or 'geocultural bovarism' (Antohi 2002). In such analyses of the Balkan variant of Orientalism, the idea of 'the Balkans' becomes essentialized even as it is deconstructed: understood in abstract structural terms, as a dark destiny imposed on southeast Europeans by the inescapable logic of centre and periphery.

Such notions can appear in a slightly different light if we examine depictions of masculinity, 'Europe' and 'ourselves' in different contexts. It is to this end that a second set of travel accounts, published in Yugoslavia in the 1970s and 1980s, will now be explored. At that time, travel accounts of western Europe and the United States were a well established genre in Yugoslav publishing, accorded a degree of literary prestige and often published by authors with a reputation in other genres. Examined below are three such accounts, by a fairly cohesive group of established writers. Momo Kapor is a Serbian novelist and journalist; his travel account, *Skitam i pričam* ('I Wander and I Talk') (1979), consists of brief, anecdotal sketches, grouped by region (Dalmatia, Europe, the USA and Belgrade), which use his travel experiences to pass judgement on cultural difference. Moma Dimić, a poet and novelist from Serbia, had also previously published travel accounts; his *Monah čeka svoju smrt* ('The Monk Awaits his Death') (1983) recounts his travels in Greece, western Europe and the USA, mixing literary encounters with cultural critique. Ivan Kušan, a Croatian playwright, novelist and children's writer, presented travels through western Europe, Russia and the USA in *Prerušeni prosjak* ('Beggar in Disguise', 1986) as erotic picaresque (a genre that the cover blurb identifies as 'globetrotterotica').

Accounts of the West had their own legitimacy in post-Second World War Yugoslav literature: they were frequently set in parallel to travels in the socialist bloc, with the point being to highlight ideological contrasts between Western capitalism, Warsaw Pact socialism and Yugoslavia's own brand of socialism. However, such distinctions became less emphatic from the mid 1960s, with the easing of ideological strife and the spread of international détente. In these accounts, differences are defined less in political-ideological terms than in civilizational ones. The writers draw on and reshape ideas of East and West, the Balkans and Europe, and Europe and its US other. Yugoslavia is the primary framework for the authors' self-identification in these texts, with greater or lesser emphasis on a Serb or Croat national affiliation. But the authors regularly blur any more specific definition of identity (whether Serb/Croat, Yugoslav or Balkan) by the frequent use of 'us', 'ours' or *po naški* ('the way we do it'). Who this 'we' is needs to be deduced in each context from the defining others – Europeans, Americans or Westerners for instance, or Russians and socialist fraternal 'brothers', or other Yugoslav and southeast European nations – all located in gendered terms. Balkanness, masculinity and difference are linked in each of these texts, as analyses of Balkanist discourses might lead us to expect. But at the same time, the Yugoslav writers actively *use* these equations to make a variety of claims that are difficult to understand solely in terms of self-stigmatization or imaginative colonization.

In these Yugoslav texts, sex is used extensively as a topos for representing difference and fleshing out conceptions of 'us' and 'ours'. Especially for Kapor and Kušan, contact with the West (and the rest of the world) is presented primarily through erotic encounters between 'our' men and 'foreign' women. Western women pose a challenge to the traveller's virility and authority, as well as a means to cultural mastery. 'Having a woman' is, predictably, a way of becoming a part of an otherwise unattainable world. Kušan's Parisian Bernadette is thus different from his Yugoslav *petites amies*; he needs her (and Monique S. and Jeanne and Colette and so on) in order 'not to feel a tourist'. 'I had to have a native Bernadette like this one to give me the illusion that I had at least some lasting root connecting me to this quay, to which I had no right at all [...]. I'm no longer completely a foreigner here' (Kušan 1986: 93). But sexual success is presented not in terms of masculine 'possession', but rather as passing an examination. The West is thus feminized and eroticized, but it is by no means subordinate or inferior: these women are shown as independent, choosy and critical. They may appreciate the travellers' Balkan virility but they insist on their own standards in other spheres such as gastronomy, hygiene and fidelity.

Western men scarcely appear in these encounters. At most they appear as vague collectives, the generalized voices of Kapor's stereotyped conversations, or distantly observed 'solid citizens' or 'queers'. They are not even rivals. If the Englishman's failed Balkan romance can be compared to Spivak's colonial plot, the Yugoslav romances are not comparable to Frantz Fanon's reverse fantasy, in which the possession of white (read: Western) women by black (read: Balkan) men constitutes both revenge against white men and the appropriation of their civilization and dignity (Fanon 1967). Here, women are not just the terrain upon which an East/West struggle is enacted; they have their own interests. And Western men are already emasculated in advance. The same is not true of Third World men, or men of other Balkan nationalities, who regularly appear in these texts as potential rivals. Their presence further locates the sphere of difference the writers are constructing. Kušan, for instance, finds the most threatening masculine challenges to his mastery and self-esteem in Paris in the person of a well-endowed Moroccan who also has a big wallet and native French (shared non-alignment does not prevent them aligning in their rivalry over the Englishwoman Gill) (Kušan 1986: 100–102). In America there is Petru, a tall, dark and handsome Romanian with British-accented English as well as near-native French ('as though Romanian were anything more than French *à la* Dracula, a Latin language on the lips of Slav bats' – ibid.:

209). Russians ('Scythians') do not threaten so much as thwart: Kušan's whole Russian journey is a tale of incapacity, which gives substance to references to Soviets/Scythians elsewhere in his text.

Much more striking than encounters with Western men, and more fully developed, are the writers' relations with 'our' own men, whether travellers, émigrés, friends or companions. These men function as yardsticks against which our heroes measure their own European acculturation (or the ability to 'pass') and maleness. Kapor's 'Piter' and 'Džordž', with their successes with women and in business and, equally, their distinctive capacity for pleasure, disrespect for bourgeois behaviour and their nostalgia for home, seem to serve as surrogate selves, placed in the narrative to show an idealized version of Balkan manliness abroad in contrast to denationalized emigrés with their foreign wives and children. Kušan has a whole series of sidekicks: most exemplify the shamelessly inassimilable Balkan man who takes his culture with him wherever he goes, picking up European habits (swapping his *Drava* cigarettes for *Gauloises*) but never adjusting his own values or abandoning his capacity for gross physical pleasure; there to show just how far Kušan, in contrast, has been changed in his encounter with the West.

'Our' women also play a prominent role in these travel tales, not just as sexual partners, but as emblems – for good or ill – of the differences between home and abroad. They are markers of all that the traveller has left behind (or wants to shake off). Kušan's Vera is his companion on his earliest French travels but is outgrown and discarded (along with a taste for home cooking, and the need to shop for textiles to take back as gifts). Later, Branka's sexual attractions wax and wane in Kušan's eyes in inverse proportion to the availability of her German or American rivals, registered by approving or derisive assessments of her 'Balkan' qualities – her mentality, appetite and bottom (sometimes 'a peasant girl's [...] firm and compact', but at other times described as 'like the bald, fat, red cheeks of our village alcoholics' [Kušan 1986: 166, 180]). Kapor's Snežana has left the Balkans behind: after wasting three years with a drunken charmer at home, she has sought security with a thoroughly Helveticized anaesthesiologist ('everyone thinks he is a native Swiss, he's so punctual; the greatest compliment that a barbarian from this unhappy part of Europe can receive'). But how can she be happy? 'Don't you want to quarrel like a human being, to break all the dishes, to sing while you wash the windows, to borrow coffee or oil from your neighbours, to eat watermelon without a knife or fork, and wash your fingers in the river?' (Kapor 1979: 123–24).

These Yugoslav authors, like the Englishmen discussed earlier, draw gendered maps of the Balkans and the West, with contours that are sometimes strikingly similar. But while those Englishmen use the

Balkans as a point from which to reconsider modern masculinities, these Yugoslav writers are more interested in using the mantras of masculinity in order to comment on 'us' and 'them' – on the meanings of the Balkans, Yugoslavia and Europe. While they agree on the fact of difference, and even on some of its markers, they do not all come to the same conclusions. The Yugoslav writers produce a range of assessments of East/West differences and use these concepts to place themselves in different ways, for a variety of purposes.

Comparing accounts of prostitutes and sex shops, a recurring topic in these travel accounts, provides a convenient way of illustrating this point. A scandalized description of prostitution had been a standard set-piece in early socialist accounts of the West, serving to condemn the degradation of women under capitalism. By the 1970s Momo Kapor, in contrast, can poke fun at prudish socialist travel accounts from the 1950s describing a 'Parisian hell' where, 'just imagine, the girls in the Pigalle sell love for money!' Now the world is no longer so simply divided; 'the West hasn't been sunk in eternal darkness for a long time, and the sun doesn't invariably rise in the East'. Instead, Kapor identifies another pattern of exchange, with 'our' young men offering Paris 'their fresh Balkan blood and new ideas that they never dream have long since been being taught here in the primary schools', writing poetry and living off susceptible French women of a certain age who translate their verses. 'Older women in Paris are in luck, as long as our boys go there! Any one of them can find an Edith Piaf who remembers better days. And one day his French verses will be retranslated into Serbian and our grandsons will have to memorize them in school'. This allegorical relationship between French women and Balkan men turns on an established geocultural difference: 'our unrequited love for Paris is as old as our provincial yearning for world-wide fame' (Kapor 1979: 114–16).

Kapor hints at the way he sees the relationship between the Balkans and the rest of the world in his European travels, but he develops his vision of 'us' and 'them' most fully in the United States section of his account, entitled 'The Marquis de SAD' – SAD being the Serbo-Croat abbreviation for the USA. Here again, selling sex becomes emblematic. Kapor spends an entire day on New York's Broadway and 42nd Street, escaping 'the crowds of transvestites, homosexuals and whores', as well as a cold north wind, by visiting a peep-show. Though his description echoes the disapproving sociological investigations of earlier accounts, he also makes unfavourable comparisons with sexier European shows: 'Not a trace of the coquetry of the Parisian ladies in the Pigalle, none of the fleshy femininity of the Antwerp prostitutes in their red window displays … Nothing apart from the deadly boring parting and closing of legs, twisting of bodies and monotonous changes of position, like an anatomy lesson'. But the real point of his observations is elsewhere: 'I'm almost more interested by the faces belonging to the feverishly burning eyes peering through the little openings than I am by the tired movements of the two enslaved female bodies offering themselves listlessly to this painful curiosity' (Kapor 1979: 164–65). What sort of men are these Americans, to satisfy themselves in such a manner? The peep-show sets up a dichotomy between US perversion and *European* pleasure that persists throughout this section, with work- and money-obsessed US men contrasted, for example, to 'a whole naïve army of European lovers, who are still up for love. They haven't forgotten how to be tender, coarse when necessary; rogues hungry for love, just like their old continent, unpredictable and crazy. They aren't ashamed to buy yellow roses at six dollars a stem and to whisper tender words' (Kapor 1979: 194). They are doomed to disappointment, though: the US women only have time for this sort of thing at weekends. And there is always the danger of losing your true self in this alien land. Kapor lunches with 'one of our countrymen' in San Francisco, but he had become 'so refined and delicate that he had gone completely vegetarian. His great-grandfather had hoisted a live Turk in his teeth, his grandfather had eaten roast ox for dinner, his father had snacked on a half a lamb from the spit, his mother had raised him on fresh liver, but he says: "A vegetable cocktail, please, with extra carrots"!' (Kapor makes a point of ordering the beefsteak, very rare: *he* is not going to be a traitor to his sex or to his origins) (Kapor 1979: 158–59).

Kapor's scale of values sets appetite, abandon and the capacity for pleasure against reserve, control and an obsession with time and money, in what might be called an 'affirmative Balkanism'. But, strikingly, it's not always Balkan. In Kapor's US travels, 'ours' is equivalent to 'European'. Sometimes this is ironic: 'The Americans have a "European complex". And it's well known that we are part of Europe. That means they have a complex about us, too. Oh, what sweet consolation!' (Kapor 1979: 175). But elsewhere the distinction is between a 'European' sensibility and 'ours'. In his descriptions of Paris, in his 'Sentimental Journey' through southern and northern Europe and, even more, in his observations of domestic and foreign tourists in Dalmatia ('Summer') and in his celebrations of Belgrade, 'ours' is interpreted as Balkan, Yugoslav or Serbian, depending on the context. The pair of compasses measuring this symbolic geography have their pivot planted at the centre of a circle that can expand or contract, depending on the alliances or exclusions that are implied. But virtue lies at the centre for Kapor: 'Balkan' is beautiful. He sums up his position in considering the concepts of East and West in his 'Sentimental Journey': 'Since we happen to live in between the East and West, we believe that truth and the measure of man lie somewhere in the middle' (Kapor 1979: 92).

While Kapor is interested in evaluating the divisions between home and the world, Moma Dimić's preoccupations are more local. His account of Hamburg dwells on the Sankt Pauli district, but without much trace of moral condemnation. Prostitution is primarily an economic activity, one that has 'done its part in Germany's postwar "economic miracle"' by soliciting the financial contributions of 'our Gastarbeiters', among others (Dimić 1983: 117). The description of the possibilities on offer and the conventions governing the transaction is completed – and given animation – by a quizzical vignette of a pair of compatriots:

> Once, in nearly the same place [the Eros-Centre brothel], I saw two of my countrymen. The farther north you go, the easier it is to pick out our men. Lean, no longer quite so young, they wander indecisively through the voluptuous twilight, gape, and stare endlessly at the girls on display: the heart shapes formed by their unclad buttocks, the tender skin of their thighs, their uncovered shoulders. Anything above and beyond that would cost too many of their Gastarbeiters' marks – carefully hoarded but never enough. They will go round all the courtyards and the streets with girls on display several times. They will approach the doors of topless restaurants and variety shows featuring female mud-wrestling or boxing, timidly, but these too will be too expensive for them. They begin their free Saturday night with such excitement and such luxuriant nakedness, but they end it alone, in a cheap Oriental café, with a piece of *burek*. (Dimić 1983: 119)

Dimić's countrymen have little in common with him besides nationality. He takes for granted what they desire but cannot afford, whether sex or other Western consumer goods. These emasculated Gastarbeiters are doomed to remain mired in the Balkans wherever they may actually travel, work or live, subsisting on *burek*, that emblematic Balkan fast-food pastry. Dimić, with his experience, savoir faire and economic power, has access to other ways of life. In such texts, Dimić – like other writers – uses concepts of East and West to mark out (and perpetuate) the social distinctions that existed at home, as well as abroad, between an educated elite and a working class. Yugoslavia's Gastarbeiters had their own extensive experience of the West and made this evident at home (not least in the form of hard-currency savings accounts). But experience of the world counts for nothing in Dimić's account unless it translates into discernment and the power to choose. In spite of his use of the word 'ours', Dimić places himself on the other side of a cultural divide from his 'oriental' compatriots. He is aligned against the Balkans, alongside the cosmopolitan men of the world who know how to enjoy Hamburg's opportunities and have the means to do so, rather than with his working-class compatriots.

Ivan Kušan is much more ambivalent about being Balkan. Neither his attempts to master the Western world through his sexual adventures with its women nor his attempts to pass as a Westerner are presented as successful; each failure contributes to his sense of inferiority and lack of entitlement to the life he tastes in the West. Hence the title, with its inverted reference to Odysseus:

> I put on a pretence that I wasn't only here [in the West] by chance, but had been here from the beginning. The point of my mimicry wasn't to hide, but rather not to stick out as an undesirable, inassimilable intruder. Not disguised as a beggar, so that the suitors (the swine) wouldn't guess, but disguised as a man of means, a beggar in disguise. (Kušan 1986: 363)

Each failure serves to show where he really belongs: 'I had turned out to be what I really was: a little Balkan scribbler megalomaniacally trying not to fart, in the face of the world's iron indifference' (ibid.: 108). Kušan can never be a Western man of the world. He is constantly dragged back by cultural and geopolitical circumstance, his self-doubt reinforced by Yugoslav socialism's unattainable promises of a paradise of 'tempting fruit, hams, bottles and, above all, beautiful naked girls' (ibid.: 104) and the West's abandonment of his half of Europe 'to the favour and disfavour of the Scythians' (ibid.: 107). But neither is he the same as his Balkan compatriots who do not even worry about such differences and enjoy themselves without anxiety. He makes this clear in a text that, once again, focuses on prostitution. He cannot emulate a colleague who feels completely 'at ease' in Western brothels ('he didn't even bother to think in our language').

> Standing in front of those famous Amsterdam windows, I recalled how, when his eye fell on some modest 'housewife' in her display window, darning and reading her Bible on her immaculately clean bed, with gleaming sanitary ware in the background, he burst into the idyll without a second thought. The curtains closed, the light went out, the Bible thumped onto the nightstand – and my colleague ordered the complete programme, since it didn't have to be paid for in advance. Only afterwards did it occur to him that he was only carrying dinars. Since the girl's madam had never seen anything like them, she phoned the bank – and she clearly heard bad news. They carted my colleague off to the police, questioned him, expressed their disgust, and let him go. The whole time he was completely at ease, grinning childishly. He was still enjoying it the fifth time he told me this story, behind the bar of a luxury Frankfurt brothel, while we sipped *Sekt* from real champagne flutes, naked, with our numbers on a chain around our necks (the Germans love order, they immediately take your name and give you a number) and selected our partners (I was only careful that she shouldn't be one of 'ours'). I paid in advance, naturally, but that's why he's the one who is a business operator

on an international scale and is contributing – in his own Amsterdam way
– to the exchange value of the dinar. (Kušan 1986: 54–55)

It is not so much economic power as it is shamelessness and the inability
to see the difference between 'them' and 'us' that separates his colleague
from Kušan. But Kušan, like Dimić, asserts that he is different: he has
learnt to think in terms of shame and self-consciousness (he has scruples
about 'our girls'), and has acquired a Westernized sensibility that
distinguishes him from his countrymen, even though his sense of
inferiority prevents him from asserting equality with European 'men of
means'.

All three of these writers used their accounts of sex, masculinity and
their travel adventures in general to elaborate a slightly rebellious and
unconventional authorial persona. Their positions make more or less
political points. Kapor's raffish Bohemianism was deployed against
'bourgeois values' (though his rebelliousness had limits: his critique of
Western capitalist gender norms fit comfortably with Yugoslav socialist
ideals, though with successive editions of his book the balance would
shift to a celebration of values named as Serbian). Dimić and Kušan
stood more directly at odds with the existing system in their matter-of-
fact acceptance of prostitution and their frank appreciation of capitalist
consumerism (and their implied criticism of the Yugoslav failure to
match Western standards). Kušan, in particular, criticized Yugoslavia's
in-betweenness, 'non-aligned' alongside the Third World but not quite
free of 'Scythian' socialist fraternalism; just capitalist enough to
introduce time-clocks to control the workers but not capitalist enough to
care about satisfying consumer desire. This rebellious individuality was
marketable in the 1980s, as the Yugoslav political and social system
began to lose its legitimacy and new forms of criticism and dissent were
finding not just a voice but also an avid reading public.

But for all their subversiveness, these writers lay claims to a
masculinity recognizable in conventional terms – independent,
experienced and virile. Their air of mastery asserts a manliness not
always available or conceded to the intellectual in a society where the
man of letters is not necessarily quite a man (*v.* Džadžić 1987: 180–202).
Moreover, these accounts promote the intellectual as having enviable
masculine advantages: the resources to travel, the experience and the
taste to participate in the good life of the European elite, and aspirations
to equality with Westerners. This, in turn, reinforced domestic divisions:
the gap created in the text between the educated man of the world and
the emasculated and orientalized Gastarbeiter legitimated the Yugoslav
intellectual's claims to prestige and authority at home as well as abroad.

These discourses of difference, derived from depictions of masculinity
(and from other categories), trace a symbolic geography that divides up

the world in familiar ways. What these divisions are named, and how they are evaluated, however, varies. It is significant that the term 'Balkan' does not appear consistently in this second set of texts, and the writers' use of 'us' and 'ours' varies too. Who 'we' might be expands and contracts, ranging from Kapor's Belgrade or Kušan's Zagreb suburb, to a shared Yugoslav sense of belonging or a larger Balkan identity, to all of Europe, in contrast to the USA. (The English travel writers' maps, in contrast, locate 'them' on a sliding scale that differentiates the Balkans from the rest of eastern Europe only as a matter of degree.) Neither is the stigma attached to 'Balkanness' constant: Kapor's celebration of a positive Balkan Orientalism contrasts with Kušan's ambivalence and Dimić's disassociation from the label. 'The Balkans' would appear much more regularly – and in a much more consistently negative light – in accounts written in the 1990s by travellers from the former Yugoslavia, but by then the context had changed considerably. The ideas of masculinity helping to define the boundaries being erected between 'us' and 'them' need to be understood in context, too. Exaggerated masculine egos and physical appetites paired with a lack of shame or constraint might recur in representations of the Balkans from inside and from without (see also, for example, travel accounts of Greece by Henry Miller and Patricia Storace [Miller 1958; Storace 1996]), but this is neither the only available local model for manliness, nor is it limited to the Balkans.[3]

What *is* constant in both the Yugoslav and English accounts discussed there is the 'technology of place': the way that the shifting categories of us and them, the Balkans and Europe, are defined in opposition to one another, insisting on the fact of difference regardless of the content. These differences often have much less to do with great geopolitical dichotomies than with specific local divisions and agendas: 'Europe' and 'the Balkans' become weapons to be used in contests that lie much closer to home. Others have analysed the ways Orientalist stereotypes have been used in the Balkans in a process of 'nesting orientalism', intended to consign neighbouring nations to Eastern darkness while advancing one's own claims to European legitimacy (Bakić-Hayden 1995; Kiossev 2002). But representations of East and West can also trace lines of division *within* a society. Yugoslav political and ideological changes, as well as its persistent social tensions, can be seen reflected in the ways the writers in the second group chose to align themselves through their evaluations of Europe and of masculinity. The politics of gender and the unravelling of class privilege in a postimperial Britain also shaped the ways the English travel writers engendered difference.

Thinking about the choices made by these travel writers and the uses to which they put notions of East and West, us and them, and machismo and emasculation, opens up new perspectives on 'the Balkans'. It begins to seem less a matter of a Western projection imposed upon the region or a traumatic geocultural destiny (however such claims might suit Kušan's defensive self-inculpations, for example) than a strategy – available to be used for particular purposes in particular contexts, and varying in salience and in character according to when and how it is applied. Neither the Yugoslav nor the English writers discussed here are free to invent their own identities – they are constrained by the social and ideological resources they draw upon – but they are *makers* and *users* of difference as well as its victims. Thinking about the ways these writers used notions of masculinity and gender also helps move us beyond generalizations about the 'feminized other' and 'Western hegemony' based on monolithic and ahistorical concepts of both gender and power to an appreciation of the varied and changing ways in which systems of difference can interact, and at the same time to a more complex understanding of the character of East/West divisions within Europe.

Notes

This research was supported by an AHRC Research Leave Award, and was carried out in the framework of the AHRC Research Project 'East Looks West'. I have benefited a great deal from comments by Bob Shoemaker, who knows a thing or two about gender, power and history.

1. This was neither a new mode of writing travel, nor one limited to writing on the Balkans: Holland and Huggan (2000: 27–37) discuss imperialist nostalgia and the 'English gentleman traveller' with particular reference to Eric Newby and Redmond O'Hanlon.
2. For further discussion of gender models in the Balkans in historical perspective, see Jovanović and Naumović (2004).

References

Antohi, S. 2002. 'Romania and the Balkans: From Geocultural Bovarism to Ethnic Ontology', *Tr@nsit-Virtuelles Forum* 21, http://www.iwm.at/t-21txt8.htm. Accessed June 2007.

Bakić-Hayden, M. 1995. 'Nesting Orientalisms: The Case of Former Yugoslavia', *Slavic Review* 54:4, 917–31.

Behdad, A. 1994. *Belated Travelers: Orientalism in the Age of Colonial Dissolution.* Durham, NC: Duke University Press.

Bjelić, D. and O. Savić, eds. 2002. *Balkan as Metaphor: Between Globalization and Fragmentation.* Cambridge, MA: MIT Press.

Blunt, A. 1994. *Travel, Gender and Imperialism: Mary Kingsley and West Africa.* London: Guilford Press.

Bohls, E.A. 1995. *Women Travel Writers and the Language of Aesthetics, 1716–1818.* Cambridge: Cambridge University Press.

Carr, H. 1985. 'Woman/Indian: "The American and his Others"', in *Europe and its Others: Proceedings of the Essex Conference on the Sociology of Literature,* ed. F. Barker et al. Colchester: University of Essex.

Carver, R. 1998. *The Accursed Mountains: Journeys in Albania.* London: John Murray.

Connell, R.W. 1995. *Masculinities.*Cambridge: Polity Press.

Crane, N. 1996. *Clear Waters Rising.* London: Viking.

Dimić, M. 1983. *Monah čeka svoju smrt: proza, zapisi, epifanije.* Priština: Jedinstvo.

Džadžić, P. 1987. *Homo Balcanicus, Homo Heroicus.* Belgrade: BIGZ.

Fanon, F. 1967. *Black Skin, White Masks.* New York: Grove.

Garton Ash, T. 1993. *The Magic Lantern: The Revolution of '89 Witnessed in Warsaw, Budapest, Berlin, and Prague.* New York: Vintage.

Goldsworthy, V. 1998. *Inventing Ruritania: The Imperialism of the Imagination.* New Haven: Yale University Press.

Goodwin, J. 1994. *On Foot to the Golden Horn: A Walk to Istanbul.* London: Vintage.

Hawks, T. 2000. *Playing the Moldovans at Tennis.* London: Ebury.

Holland, P. and G. Huggan. 2000. *Tourists with Typewriters: Critical Reflections on Contemporary Travel Writing.* Ann Arbor: University of Michigan Press.

Jovanović, M. and S. Naumović, eds. 2004. *Gender relations in South Eastern Europe: Historical Perspectives on Womanhood and Manhood in 19th and 20th Century.* Münster: Lit.

Kabbani, R. 1994. *Imperial Fictions: Europe's Myths of Orient.* London: Pandora.

Kaplan, R. 1993. *Balkan Ghosts: A Journey Through History.* New York: St. Martin's.

Kapor, M. 1979. *Skitam i pričam: putopisni dnevnik.* Belgrade: Prosveta.

Kiossev, A. 2002. 'The Dark Intimacy: Maps, Identities, Acts of Identification', in *Balkan as Metaphor: Between Globalization and Fragmentation,* ed. D. Bjelić and O. Savić. Cambridge, MA: MIT Press.

Konstantinov, A. 1966 [1895]. *Bai Ganio.* Sofiia: Bŭlgarski pisatel.

Kušan, I. 1986. *Prerušeni prosjak.* Zagreb: Znanje.

Lawrence, K. 1994. *Penelope Voyages: Women and Travel in the British Literary Tradition.* Ithaca: Cornell University Press.

Leigh Fermor, P. 1986. *Between the Woods and the Water.* London: John Murray.

Lewis, R. 1996. *Gendering Orientalism: Race, Femininity and Representation.* London: Routledge.

Lowe, L. 1991. *Critical Terrains: French and British Orientalisms.* Ithaca, NY: Cornell University Press.

MacLean, R. 1992. *Stalin's Nose: Across the Face of Europe.* London: HarperCollins.

McClintock, A., A. Mufti and E. Shohat, eds. 1997. *Dangerous Liaisons: Gender, Nation, and Postcolonial Perspectives.* Minneapolis: University of Minnesota Press.

Miller, H. 1958. *The Colossus of Maroussi.* New York: New Directions.

Mills, S. 1991. *Discourses of Difference: An Analysis of Women's Travel Writing and Colonialism.* London: Routledge.

Močnik, R. 2002. 'The Balkans as an Element in Ideological Mechanisms', in *Balkan as Metaphor: Between Globalization and Fragmentation*, ed. D. Bjelić and O. Savić. Cambridge: MIT Press.

Petkov, K. 1997. *Infidels, Turks, and Women: The South Slavs in the German Mind, ca. 1400–1600*. Frankfurt am Main: Peter Lang.

Roessel, D. 2002. *In Byron's Shadow: Modern Greece in the English and American Imagination*. Oxford: Oxford University Press.

Said, E. 1978. *Orientalism*. London: Routledge and Kegan Paul.

Schick, I. 1999. *The Erotic Margin: Sexuality and Spatiality in Alteristist Discourse*. London: Verso.

Spivak, G. 1988. 'Can the Subaltern Speak?', in *Marxism and the Interpretation of Culture*, ed. C. Nelson and L. Grossberg. Urbana: University of Illinois Press.

Stoler, A.L. 1991. 'Carnal Knowledge and Imperial Power: Gender, Race and Morality in Colonial Asia', in *Gender at the Crossroads of Knowledge*, ed. M. di Leonardo. Berkeley: University of California Press.

Storace, P. 1996. *Dinner with Persephone*. New York: Pantheon.

Thompson, M. 1992. *A Paper House: The Ending of Yugoslavia*. London: Hutchinson Radius.

Todorova, M. 1997. *Imagining the Balkans*. New York: Oxford University Press.

Whittell, G. 1992. *Lambada Country: A Ride Across Eastern Europe*. London: Chapmans.

Wolff, L. 1994. *Inventing Eastern Europe: The Map of Civilization on the Mind of the Enlightenment*. Stanford: Stanford University Press.

Notes on Contributors

Wendy Bracewell is Deputy Director of the School of Slavonic and East European Studies, University College London. As well as publishing on subjects in Balkan history ranging from sixteenth-century frontiers to issues of gender and nationalism in the former Yugoslavia, she has directed an AHRC-funded project on East European travel writing. With Alex Drace-Francis, she edited *Under Eastern Eyes: A Comparative Introduction to East European Travel Writing* (Budapest: CEU Press, 2008) and *A Bibliography of East European Travel Writing on Europe, 1550–2000* (Budapest: CEU Press, 2008).

Alex Drace-Francis is Lecturer in Modern European History, University of Liverpool. He has published *The Making of Modern Romanian Culture* (2006), and numerous articles on Romanian and Balkan history, literature, travel, identity and historiography.

Dean Duda is Associate Professor of Comparative Literature at the University of Zagreb; he has written primarily about literary theory, travel culture and the culture industry in post-socialist circumstances. He is the author of *Priča i putovanje: hrvatski romantičarski putopis kao pripovjedni žanr* ('Tale and Travel: The Croatian Romantic Travel Text as a Narrative Genre') (2002).

Vladimir Gvozden teaches at the Department of Comparative Literature, University of Novi Sad. He has conducted research on Serbian modernist travel writing and wrote *Jovan Dučić putopisac: ogled iz imagologije* ('Jovan Dučić as Travel Writer: An Essay in Literary Image Studies') (2003) and *Činovi prisvajanja: od teorije ka pragmatici teksta* ('Acts of Appropriation: From Theory to Pragmatics of Text') (2005).

Maria Kostaridou works for the Benaki Museum in Athens. Formerly a research fellow at University College London, with a doctorate from the University of York, she is a researcher specializing in European travel and is currently preparing an on-line descriptive catalogue of the Museum's extensive travel book collection. She is also a tutor in European Literature for the Hellenic Open University.

Ludmilla K. Kostova is Associate Professor of British Literature and Cultural Studies at St. Cyril and St. Methodius University of Veliko Tŭrnovo. She has published on eighteenth-century, romantic and modern British literature as well as on travel writing and representations of cultural encounters. Her book *Tales of the Periphery: The Balkans in Nineteenth-Century British Writing* (1997) has been frequently cited by specialists in the field. Together with Corinne Fowler, she edited a special issue of *Journeys – The International Journal of Travel and Travel Writing*, Vol. 4:1 (2003), on ethics and travel.

Index

English alphabetical order has been adopted, without distinct treatment being given to accented or transliterated letters. Names of Eastern Orthodox monks are recorded Christian name first. Place names are recorded according to the most frequent usage in the texts or periods discussed; if this is different from the main contemporary English name, the latter is given a heading with a cross-reference. Valuable additions and rectifications were made by Anna Turnbull, whom it is a pleasure to thank here. (AD-F)